ONE WEEK LOAN

Mergers & Acquisitions

MERGERS & ACQUISITIONS

A Condensed Practitioner's Guide

STEVEN M. BRAGG

WILEY

John Wiley & Sons, Inc.

For general information on our other products and services, or technical support, please contact our Customer Care Department within the United States at 800-762-2974, outside the United States at 317-572-3993 or fax 317-572-4002.

Wiley also publishes its books in a variety of electronic formats. Some content that appears in print may not be available in electronic books.

For more information about Wiley products, visit our Web site at http://www.wiley.com.

Library of Congress Cataloging-in-Publication Data

Bragg, Steven M.
    Mergers & acquisitions : a condensed practitioner's guide / Steven M. Bragg.
        p.   cm.
    Includes index.
    ISBN 978-0-470-39894-4 (cloth)
    1. Consolidation and merger of corporations.   I. Title.   II.   Title: Mergers and acquisitions.
    HG4028.M4B69 2009
    658.1'62–dc22

                                                                                2008023252

Printed in the United States of America

10 9 8 7 6 5 4 3 2 1

To my extremely tolerant wife, Melissa. Thanks for handling everything while I hide behind my computer.

Contents

Preface

Thousands of companies are bought and sold every year. Many of these transactions leave the buyers and sellers frustrated, because either they don't know how the process works, or because the results are below their expectations. Here are some common problems:

- The seller does not know how to maximize its value before being acquired
- The seller does not know how to conduct an auction, or the issues related to doing so
- Both parties are unaware of the various methods used to value the transaction
- The buyer misses key issues during due diligence that adversely impact the value of the deal
- Both parties are unaware of the key points in the purchase agreement to be negotiated
- The seller discovers too late that the transaction is not structured to be tax-deferred
- The buyer has difficulty accounting for the acquisition
- The buyer does not realize that it has run afoul of government anti-trust regulations
- The buyer does not know how to integrate the acquired company into its operations

Mergers & Acquisitions: A Condensed Practitioner's Guide provides answers to all of these problems, and many more. It is designed for the business manager who must be fully aware of all key steps in the acquisition process, and is organized to approximate the flow of an acquisition.

Chapter 1 addresses the overall acquisition process. It also notes why companies are interested in buying and selling businesses, the risks of doing so, how to locate and qualify acquisition targets, and how to both initiate and fend off a hostile acquisition attempt.

Chapter 2 describes the roles of the multitude of participants in the acquisition process, including the acquisition team, attorneys, board of directors, brokers, investment bankers, investor relations officer, lenders, line managers, and consultants.

Chapter 3 addresses the key area of valuation. The chapter reveals a broad range of valuation methodologies, with particular attention to the discounted cash flow method. It also notes the impact on valuation of the control premium, synergies, earnouts, and qualitative factors, as well as the strategic use of various types of payment.

Chapter 4 describes the use and contents of a term sheet, and gives examples of its primary components.

Chapter 5 delves into the due diligence process in considerable detail. Supplemented by the due diligence list in Appendix A, it describes the due diligence team and how it functions, and offers pointers on many due diligence topics, including such key areas as marketing, culture, intellectual property, risk management, capacity planning, customers, and many financial issues. It also highlights red flags, complexity analysis, and how to handle missing information.

Chapter 6 describes all main components of the purchase agreement and related exhibits and disclosure schedules. It includes sample text, and also notes which areas are the most important from the perspective of the buyer and seller. It also provides commentary on post-closing activities, and how to negotiate the purchase agreement.

Chapter 7 covers the acquisition integration process. This is a massive chapter, given the exceptional importance of the topic. It covers the timing, planning, and implementation of an acquisition's integration, and also delves into the identification and realization of synergies, communications processes, cultural issues, employee management, and numerous additional topics.

Chapter 8 is designed for the accountant who must consolidate the results of an acquisition into the financial statements of the buyer, including the use of purchase accounting, goodwill impairment testing, and push-down accounting.

Chapter 9 addresses the various legal forms of acquisitions, including their tax implications to both the buyer and seller.

Chapter 10 covers anti-trust regulations, who they affect, and the related reporting requirements of the buyer. It also covers key environmental regulations that the buyer should be particularly aware of.

In short, the book comprehensively addresses the entire acquisition process, and so should make <u>Mergers & Acquisitions: A Condensed Practitioner's Guide</u> a well-thumbed addition to any manager's library.

Steven M. Bragg
Centennial, Colorado
May 2008

About the Author

Steven Bragg, CPA, CMA, CIA, CPIM, has been the chief financial officer or controller of four companies, as well as a consulting manager at Ernst & Young and auditor at Deloitte & Touche. He received a master's degree in finance from Bentley College, an MBA from Babson College, and a bachelor's degree in Economics from the University of Maine. He has been the two-time president of the Colorado Mountain Club, and is an avid alpine skier, mountain biker, and certified master diver. Mr. Bragg resides in Centennial, Colorado. He has written the following books through John Wiley & Sons:

Accounting and Finance for Your Small Business

Accounting Best Practices

Accounting Control Best Practices

Accounting Reference Desktop

Billing and Collections Best Practices

Business Ratios and Formulas

Controller's Guide to Costing

Controller's Guide to Planning and Controlling Operations

Controller's Guide: Roles and Responsibilities for the New Controller

Controllership

Cost Accounting

Design and Maintenance of Accounting Manuals

Essentials of Payroll

Fast Close

Financial Analysis

GAAP Guide

GAAP Implementation Guide

Inventory Accounting

Inventory Best Practices

Just-in-Time Accounting

Management Accounting Best Practices

Managing Explosive Corporate Growth

Mergers and Acquisitions

Outsourcing

Payroll Accounting

Payroll Best Practices

Revenue Recognition

Sales and Operations for Your Small Business

The Controller's Function

The New CFO Financial Leadership Manual

The Ultimate Accountants' Reference

Throughput Accounting

Also:

Advanced Accounting Systems (Institute of Internal Auditors)

Investor Relations (Accounting Tools)

Run the Rockies (CMC Press)

Free On-Line Resources by Steven Bragg

Steve offers a broad array of free accounting resources at www. accountingtools.com. The site includes dozens of *Accounting Best Practices* podcast episodes, as well as hundreds of best practices articles. It also contains control charts, process flows, costing methodologies, job descriptions, metrics, and much more.

Mergers & Acquisitions

Chapter 1

The Acquisition Process

An *acquisition* occurs when a buyer acquires all or part of the assets or business of a selling entity, and where both parties are actively assisting in the purchase transaction. If the buyer is doing so despite the active resistance of the other party, this is known as a *hostile takeover*. A *merger* occurs when two companies combine into one entity. The vast majority of all business combinations are handled as an acquisition, where one entity clearly takes over the operations of the other.

In this chapter, we will address the basics of the acquisition process—why buyers acquire, why sellers have an interest in selling, and the process flow for both a basic acquisition and one conducted through an auction process. The chapter also addresses a variety of other issues, including acquisition strategy, risks, target criteria, and hostile takeovers.

WHY WE ACQUIRE

Why do companies feel compelled to acquire other businesses? After all, the typical buyer knows its own market niche quite well, and can safely increase its revenues over time by continual, careful attention to internal organic growth. Nonetheless, thousands of acquisitions occur every year. Here are some reasons for doing so:

- *Business model.* The target's business model may be different from that of the buyer, and so generates more profits. For example, a target may operate without labor unions, or have a substantially less burdensome benefits plan. The buyer may not be able to re-create this business model in-house without suffering significant unrest, but can readily buy into it through an acquisition.

- *Cyclicality reduction.* A buyer may be trapped in a cyclical or seasonal industry, where profitability fluctuates on a recurring basis. It may deliberately acquire a company outside this industry with the goal of offsetting the business cycle to yield more consistent financial results.

- *Defensive.* Some acquisitions take place because the buyer is itself the target of another company, and simply wants to make itself less attractive through an acquisition. This is particularly effective when the buyer already has a large market share, and buying another entity in the same market gives it such a large share that it cannot be bought by anyone else within the industry without anti-trust charges being brought.

- *Executive compensation.* A buyer's management team may be in favor of an acquisition for the simple reason that a larger company generally pays higher salaries. The greater heft of the resulting organization is frequently viewed as being valid grounds for a significant pay boost among the surviving management team. This is not a good reason for an acquisition, but it is a common one.

- *Intellectual property.* This is a defensible knowledge base that gives a company a competitive advantage, and is one of the best reasons to acquire a company. Intellectual property can include patents, trademarks, production processes, databases that are difficult to re-create, and research and development labs with a history of successful product development.

- *Internal development alternative.* A company may have an extremely difficult time creating new products, and so looks elsewhere to find replacement products. This issue is especially likely to trigger an acquisition if a company has just decided to cancel an in-house development project, and needs a replacement immediately.

- *Local market expertise.* In some industries, effective entry into a local market requires the gradual accumulation of reputation through a long process of building contacts and correct business practices. A company can follow this path through internal expansion, and gain success over a long period of time—or do it at once through an acquisition. Local market expertise is especially valuable in international situations, where a buyer has minimal knowledge of local customs, not to mention the inevitable obstacles posed by a different language.

- *Market growth.* No matter how hard a buyer may push itself, it simply cannot grow revenues very fast in a slow-growth market, because there are so few sales to be made. Conversely, a target company may be situated in a market that is growing much faster than that of the buyer, so the buyer sees an avenue to more rapid growth.

- *Market share.* Companies generally strive toward a high market share, because this generally allows them to enjoy a cost advantage over their competitors, who must spread their overhead costs over smaller production volumes. The acquisition of a large competitor is a reasonable way to quickly attain significant market share.

- *Production capacity.* Though not a common acquisition justification, the buyer may have excess production capacity available, from which it can readily manufacture the target's products. Usually, tooling differences between the companies make this a difficult endeavor.

- *Products.* The target may have an excellent product that the buyer can use to fill a hole in its own product line. This is an especially important reason when the market is expanding rapidly, and the buyer does not have sufficient time to develop the product internally before other competing products take over the market. Also, acquired products tend to have fewer bugs than ones just emerging from in-house development, since they have been through more field testing, and possibly through several build cycles. However, considerable additional effort may be needed to integrate the acquired products into the buyer's product line, so factor this issue into the purchase decision.

- *Regulatory environment.* The buyer may be burdened by a suffocating regulatory environment, such as is imposed on utilities, airlines, and government contractors. If a target operates in an area subject to less regulation, the buyer may be more inclined to buy into that environment.

- *Sales channels.* A target may have an unusually effective sales channel that the buyer thinks it can use to distribute its own products. Examples of such sales channels are as varied as door-to-door sales, electronic downloads, telemarketing, or a well-trained in-house sales staff. Also, the target's sales staff might be especially effective—in some industries, the sales department is considered the bottleneck operation, and so may be the prime reason for an acquisition offer.

- *Vertical integration.* To use a military term, a company may want to "secure its supply lines" by acquiring selected suppliers. This is especially important if there is considerable demand for key supplies, and a supplier has control over a large proportion of them. This is especially important when other suppliers are located in politically volatile areas, leaving few reliable suppliers. In addition to this "backward integration," a company can also engage in "forward integration" by acquiring a distributor or customer. This most commonly occurs with distributors, especially if they have unusually excellent relationships with the ultimate set of customers. A company can also use its ownership of a distributor from a defensive perspective, so that competitors must shift their sales to other distributors.

No matter which of the reasons previously mentioned are central to a buyer's acquisition decision, it ultimately involves enhancing the price per share of the buyer's stock. This may not be immediately apparent, especially for smaller acquisitions where resulting share price changes are trifling, but a long-term acquisition strategy should gradually build a company's price per share.

WHY A TARGET SELLS

The general assumption is that a target's shareholders are willing to sell strictly so that they can be paid the maximum price. This is not necessarily the case. A target may have a strong preference for remaining independent, but a variety of factors may require it to search for a new owner. The buyer should be aware of the principal reason for a sale, so that it can tailor its bid accordingly. Here are some reasons why a target may be interested in selling:

- *Anemic profits.* If a target has minimal or no profits, it cannot sustain itself. In this scenario, a buyer may complete an acquisition for a low price, but also find itself having to restructure the acquiree in order to dredge up a profit.
- *Competitive environment.* The number and aggressiveness of a target's competitors may have increased substantially, resulting in a current or impending revenue and profit decline. While a buyer can certainly obtain such a business for a small price, it must also question whether it wants to enter into such a difficult environment.
- *Estate taxes.* The owner of a target may have died, and his estate must sell the business in order to pay estate taxes. The deceased owner's relatives may not have a clear idea of the value of the business, so a prospective buyer may have a relatively easy time negotiating with an inexperienced counterpart.
- *Patent expiration.* A target may be selling in a protected environment, using a key patent that keeps competitors at bay. However,

that patent is now close to expiration, and the target is not sure if it will be able to compete effectively. Due to the increased competitive environment, the target may lose a great deal of value, and the buyer can acquire it for a low price.

- *Rapid growth.* A target may be growing so fast that it cannot obtain sufficient working capital to support the growth. This scenario is a good one for the target, since it has proof of strong growth, and so may be able to negotiate a high price.

- *Retirement.* The target's owner wants to retire, and needs to cash out in order to do so. If the owner has established a long timeline for the sale, he can sort through a variety of offers and negotiate at length, resulting in a higher price. Conversely, a rushed retirement timeline can force down the price.

- *Shareholder pressure.* If the target is privately held, then its shareholders will have a difficult time selling their stock. A buyer can provide complete liquidity to these shareholders, either through an all-cash offer, or by issuing shares that can be registered for sale to other investors. This is an especially common reason when the management team does not hold majority ownership of the target's shares, and so cannot control its direction.

- *Stalled growth.* A target may find that its growth has stalled, for any number of reasons. Maximized revenue is a logical point at which to sell, so the target puts itself up for sale, on the assumption that a buyer can re-invigorate growth.

- *Technological obsolescence.* The target may have based its core business on a technology that is now becoming obsolete, and it cannot afford the massive overhaul required for replacement. If the buyer is already operating under newer technology, it may be able to snap up such a target for a low price, and quickly convert it to the new systems.

All of the points above make it appear that sellers want to do a deal because of external forces that are not under their control, and which result in decreased value to them. However, a canny seller will have the sale transaction in mind for a number of years in advance of the actual event, and will position his company for sale at the time when its value is properly maximized, and he has stripped out as many risks as possible. For example, the seller should settle lawsuits and any government regulatory actions in advance, shorten the terms of any asset leases, and avoid launching any major, capital-intensive activities. These actions yield a clean, profitable enterprise for which a buyer would willingly pay top dollar.

Knowing why a target wants to sell is not just an input into the pricing process—it is also a very good question for the acquisition team to ponder. If the target's management is essentially giving up, and they are the ones most knowledgeable about their company, then why should the buyer want to acquire it? In many cases, examining the issue from the perspective of the seller may cause the buyer to back out of a prospective deal.

ACQUISITION STRATEGY

A surprising number of buyers do not consider the total corporate strategy within which they conduct acquisition activities, if indeed they use any formal strategy at all. Instead, they simply look for modest extensions of their current core business. Given the large investment of funds and management time needed to buy and acquire another company, a buyer should instead spend a great deal of time formally pondering why it wants to make acquisitions in a particular market niche, and of an identified target in particular. The details of this analysis will vary considerably by company; several of the more common strategic issues are noted in this section.

The single most important strategic consideration is the size of an acquisition. It is much better to complete a series of small acquisitions than one or two large ones. By doing so, a buyer learns a great deal from each successive acquisition, so that it develops a significant experience base. If it buys a number of these smaller firms, a buyer can hone its acquisition skills remarkably. Conversely, if it only acquires large companies, it will not have such a skill set, and will therefore have a higher risk of failure. Also, a buyer can impose its own systems more readily on a small acquisition, whereas it may have a substantial tussle on its hands with a larger one. Finally, some acquisition efforts will fail, so it is better to have one or two small deals fail than one large one.

The buyer should always acquire a business that supplements its strongest business segment, and ignore acquisitions that would bolster its weakest segment. By doing so, it is concentrating its management efforts on that part of its business that generates the highest revenue or profit growth, and so builds the most long-term value. The buyer would be better off divesting a weak segment than adding to it.

A *bolt-on acquisition* is a direct add-on to the buyer's existing business; it is very similar to the operations the buyer already has. In this case, the buyer should have an excellent idea of what synergies can be obtained, so the acquisition is more of a mundane, tactical nature than a strategic one. However, the buyer must give a great deal more thought to strategy if it is contemplating an acquisition located in an entirely new business area. Since the level of uncertainty over a bolt-on acquisition is greatly increased, the buyer must be prepared for a broad range of outcomes, from serious losses to outsized gains. The buyer should also factor into its planning a proper retention plan for the target's management team, since it cannot reasonably expect to manage a business itself in an entirely new business arena.

One of the more likely strategic issues faced by a buyer is the reactions of its competitors to an acquisition. They may buy a company themselves, or jump into a bidding war for the buyer's current acquisition foray, or file an anti-trust lawsuit, or enter into a protective alliance with other competitors—the list of possible reactions is substantial. This does not mean that the buyer should back away from an acquisition because of its fears of competitor reactions, but simply that it must be aware of how the deal will lead to a restructuring of the competitive environment in its industry. There may even be cases where the buyer deliberately backs away from an acquisition, leaving it to a competitor to acquire. This can be an excellent ploy when the target has several known flaws, and there is a strong possibility that the competitor may stumble in its integration of the target.

Another strategic concern is the avoidance of competitors. If a buyer has thus far subsisted in areas away from ferocious competitors, then it would do well to continue down the same path, and find unexploited niches that those competitors have not addressed. The worst possible strategy in a great many cases is to make an acquisition that places the buyer squarely in the path of large, well-run competitor; the result is usually an acquisition whose results rapidly head downhill.

If a buyer is publicly held, it may report in its quarterly and annual financial statements the key metrics upon which it relies (such as changes in revenue or backlog). If these metrics are properly communicated, the investment community also will focus on them, which means that changes in the buyer's stock price will be tied to those specific metrics. Thus, the buyer should focus on acquisitions that can help it improve those key metrics. For example, if the investment community focuses on increases in a company's revenue growth, then it should focus more on target companies with the same characteristic, rather than entities that perform better under other metrics.

If a buyer intends to pay for an acquisition with stock, then it should be mindful of the impact that a group of new shareholders may have on its ability to conduct business in the future. For example, this new voting block could interfere with the buyer's intent to sell off pieces of the newly acquired company. It could also contest director elections and oppose a variety of actions requiring shareholder approval, such as the creation of a new class of stock. Thus, a buyer may prefer to pay cash for an acquisition, strictly to avoid activist shareholders.

The strategic issues noted here include the size of the target, business segments to support, industry niches to invest in, and the reactions of both competitors and the investment community. None of them directly involve the purchase of a specific company, but rather the framework within which the buyer competes. A buyer should constantly test acquisition targets against this framework, and also test the veracity of the framework itself on a regular basis.

THE BASIC ACQUISITION PROCESS FLOW

The buyer usually initiates contact with the target company. The best method for doing so is a direct call between the presidents of the two companies. This allows for a brief expression of interest, which can be discreetly broken off if the target's president is not interested. If there is some interest, then the presidents should meet for an informal discussion, after which their management teams can become involved in more detailed negotiations. If the buyer's president has difficulty obtaining access to his counterpart, then it is best to only leave a message regarding a "strategic transaction" or "strategic alliance," and wait for a response. Offering to buy someone's company through a lengthy voice mail may not be considered a serious offer, and will be discarded. A formal letter containing a purchase offer can be misconstrued as notice of a hostile acquisition, and so is to be avoided.

If the buyer wishes to contact a target but does not want to reveal its identity, it can use an intermediary to make the initial contact. This can be an investment banker, consultant, attorney, or some similar individual who can discreetly represent the buyer. The intent behind using an intermediary is to see if the target has any interest in a potential buyout. If not, the buyer can quietly depart the scene, with no one learning of its acquisitive desires. This is a useful ploy when the buyer is scouting out an industry for possible acquisitions.

If there is an agreement to exchange information, then both companies must sign a non-disclosure agreement (NDA). Under the agreement, they are obligated to treat all exchanged information as confidential, not distribute it to the public, and to return it upon request. Otherwise, even if the acquisition does not occur, the buyer will retain all information about the target, and could use it for a variety of purposes in the future. In a worst-case scenario for the target, its confidential information could be spread around the industry, with adverse consequences. There are occasional cases of one-way NDAs, where the buyer signs it but the target does not. This is to be avoided, since there is an increased chance that the target is simply trying to publicize the deal, in hopes of attracting other bidders.

The target may hire a professional negotiator, or proxy, to represent it in any discussions with the buyer. Though expensive, the proxy allows the target to create a buffer between itself and any of the more strident negotiation disputes. This allows relations between the buyer and target to remain cordial, with any ire being deflected onto the proxy.

A reasonable way to begin discussions between the parties is to avoid any mention of the target's financial or operational condition. This information will shortly become almost the sole topic of conversation, in order to see if the target meets the buyer's purchasing criteria. However, buyer's initial objective is to foster a sense of trust among the target's executives. Not only does this sometimes result in more willingness by the target to divulge information, but it may also mean that the target will be more likely to sell to the buyer, rather than some other bidder who has taken less time to build relations. Consequently, a good first step is complete avoidance of numbers, in favor of "softer" discussions about the needs, concerns, and operating styles of both companies.

In general, the target has more negotiating power at the beginning of the acquisition process, while the buyer has more control at the end. This is because the buyer has inadequate information about the target until it has completed the due diligence process, after which it will use that information to attempt to lower the proposed purchase price. Thus, a common scenario is for the buyer to initially agree to a high proposed price by the target, and then gradually whittle that number down through a variety of adjustments. The target is more likely to agree to these changes near the end of the negotiations, when it has become more firmly committed to concluding the sale.

If the buyer makes an offer, the target may be tempted to shop that offer among other potential bidders in hopes of attracting a better offer. Though common, this practice represents a considerable breach of good faith with the original buyer. Thus, the target should first consider the adverse impact of losing the original bid from a now-irate buyer before engaging in bid shopping.

Irrespective of how the two parties position themselves in regard to pricing, the ultimate price paid will be founded upon a detailed valuation analysis that is conducted by the buyer. As a baseline, this valuation uses a five-year discounted cash flow analysis, as well as an estimated termination value for the selling entity at the end of that period. However, it is best to supplement the analysis with a low-end breakup valuation, as well as a valuation that is based on prices recently paid for comparable companies. The later valuation works best for a high-growth target that has minimal cash flows. By creating and comparing a range of these valuations, a buyer can derive a reasonable price range within which it can negotiate with the target. This topic is covered in more depth in the Valuing an Acquisition Target chapter.

Under no circumstances should the buyer allow the target access to its valuation models. If it were to do so, the target would likely alter its figures for the numerous variables and assumptions in the models, resulting in a significantly higher price. Instead, the buyer should consider this to be a closely guarded secret, and only offer the target a final price, with no supporting documentation.

As an interesting sidelight, the buyer can estimate in advance the selling president's reaction to a purchase price by estimating its impact on the president's outstanding stock options. If the president's options will not be exercisable at the offered price, then a certain amount of indifference can be anticipated. However, if the exercise price is greatly below the offer price, the buyer may find itself with an inordinately cooperative counterparty.

Alternatively, there are situations where the buyer is not likely to meet with a favorable reception. For example, if the target has just obtained significant funding or brought in a new president, it may have major growth expectations, and would prefer to wait until a later date, when it will presumably have a higher valuation.

The target may insist on an excessively high purchase price, or else it will not proceed with the acquisition. The buyer can work around this problem in two ways. One is through an earnout provision, where the target has the opportunity to be paid substantially more if it can generate significant revenue or profit increases in the near future. Alternatively, the buyer can offer to pay at least a portion of the price with a long-term, low-interest note. The face value of the note makes it appear that the buyer is paying full price, but the low-interest nature of the instrument actually results in a substantial discount over its term.

The buyer can depress the purchase price by making it clear that it is evaluating several alternatives to the target company. By doing so, the negotiating power shifts to the buyer, who is now in a better position to obtain a more reasonable price. Also, many negotiations fall through, for any number of reasons. Because of these pricing and closing problems, it is extremely important for a buyer to constantly be searching the industry for targets, and to always have a number of potential deals in various stages of completion.

After the parties have discussed the acquisition and arrived at the general terms of a deal, the buyer issues a *term sheet* (also known as a *letter of intent*), which is a non-binding summary of the primary terms of what will eventually become a purchase agreement. The term sheet is discussed later in the Term Sheet chapter.

Many buyers do not have access to sufficient funds to complete an acquisition, but wish to continue with acquisition talks in hopes of obtaining the necessary funding prior to closing the deal. They can make the seller aware of this difficulty with a *financing out condition*, which allows them to abandon the deal in the absence of funding. The point at which this condition is brought up is a delicate issue. The seller will want to address it in the term sheet (preferably with a clause requiring the buyer to pay a predetermined penalty in exchange for breaking off negotiations). Conversely, the buyer would prefer to avoid the issue until nearly the end of the acquisition discussions, so that it can avoid a penalty.

The next step in the acquisition process is due diligence. Thus far, the buyer has developed a valuation based on information supplied by the target, and which the target represents to be accurate. The buyer must now ascertain if this information is indeed accurate, and also investigate a variety of other financial and operational issues. This important area is discussed in greater detail in the Due Diligence chapter, with many review topics itemized in Appendix A.

Due diligence should be conducted by a large group of specialists with skills in such areas as accounting, human resources, legal, operations, and information technology. Not only does this allow for an extremely detailed and well-qualified review, but it also makes it easier to send informal messages to counterparties working for the target. This gives the buyer multiple channels of communication for an array of messages. In particular, it allows the company presidents to maintain cordial relations, while others engage in more difficult negotiations.

Based on the additional information collected in the due diligence process, the buyer can now construct a pro forma financial statement for the combined companies, so that it can see the net impact of the acquisition. The pro forma shows the income statements of both companies separately, and then adds or subtracts quantifiable additional costs or synergies to arrive at the most likely results of the combined entities. Some factors may require considerable additional analysis before inclusion in the pro forma. For example, the target's capitalization limit may differ from that of the buyer, so depreciation will vary. Also, the tax rate of the combined entity may differ from the individual ones of the separate entities. Further, the buyer may be able to refinance the target's debt at more advantageous rates. For these reasons, the pro forma requires considerable effort to attain a reasonable degree of accuracy.

If flaws or weaknesses in the target's finances or operations were found during due diligence, the buyer must decide if it should further negotiate the terms initially described in the term sheet. It is also quite possible that the problems discovered are of a sufficient level of severity to warrant abandoning the deal entirely. This is an excellent time for the buyer to stop and have the senior management team conduct a high-level review of the acquisition team's work, with the intent of making a go/no-go decision. The review should dig into the assumptions used for valuation modeling, the level and types of identified risks, competitor reactions, and so on. This is a valuable exercise, because too many buyers become caught up in the bureaucratic process of completing an acquisition, and do not stop to think about whether it still makes any sense to do so.

If the buyer elects to proceed, then the parties must negotiate a *purchase agreement*. This document, which is described in the Purchase Agreement chapter, describes the form of the acquisition, the price to be paid, and the representations of both parties regarding their condition and obligations prior to closing. Also, if the target is concerned about deferring income-tax recognition, then the purchase agreement can be structured to achieve that goal. This issue is addressed in detail in the Types of Acquisitions chapter.

If both parties prefer to conclude an acquisition with utmost dispatch, it is possible to simultaneously conduct due diligence and create the purchase agreement. However, both parties must be aware that problems found during due diligence will likely result in alterations to the purchase agreement of an iterative nature. Thus, what the parties save in time may be expensive in terms of additional legal fees. Under no circumstances should the purchase agreement be signed before the due diligence has been substantially completed, since major problems with the target company have a way of being discovered at the last moment.

The buyer's board of directors may hire an investment banking firm to render a fairness opinion about the purchase agreement. This opinion is an analysis of the deal being offered, and is intended to short-circuit any potential lawsuits from disgruntled shareholders. It is most useful when the acquisition involves some conflict of interest, when minority shareholders are being bought out, or when there will be a significant change in the target's organizational structure. The investment bank hired for this work should be demonstrably able to render an independent opinion, and should have sufficient technical and industry-specific skills to assemble an authoritative document. The investment bank's compensation should not be contingent upon closing the acquisition, since this would be a conflict of interest. In the vast majority of acquisitions, there is no need for a fairness opinion.

If the buyer is a larger company with a substantial ability to control market prices, then acquiring another company in the same industry may subject it to government anti-trust laws. If so, it must notify the federal government of the proposed acquisition, and wait for government approval before proceeding. The government may deny the transaction, or require some restructuring of the combined entity, such as the divestiture of specific assets. This issue is discussed in the Government Regulation chapter.

If the buyer is acquiring a business that deals in bulk sales (the sale of merchandise from inventory, such as a furniture retailer), then it may be subject to *bulk sales laws*. Under these laws, the buyer must give at least 10 days advance notice of the acquisition to each creditor of the seller, using a creditor list that is certified by the seller. The notice must identify the buyer and seller, and state whether the seller's debts will be paid as they become due. Some state laws even require the seller to retain its acquisition proceeds in escrow in an amount sufficient to pay any disputed debts.

The final step in the acquisition process is the integration of the two companies. This process, which is described in the Acquisition Integration Process chapter, is facilitated by an integration team, but the actual integration work is conducted at the line manager level, where those directly responsible for certain operations must integrate operations.

There are two types of buyers, and they treat integration in different ways. A *financial buyer* has only completed an acquisition in order to hold the company for a period of time, hope that it appreciates in value, and eventually sell it off at a profit. A financial buyer will conduct minimal integration activities. A *strategic buyer* will pay more for a target company than a financial buyer, because it intends to keep the most valuable parts of the acquiree and discard the rest. The strategic buyer is in a position to do this, because it has a significant knowledge of the industry in question, and of the acquiree's products, intellectual property, and processes. This frequently involves merging the acquiree's operations into those of another part of the buyer's portfolio of companies. Thus, a financial buyer will conduct extensive integration efforts in order to maximize any synergies to be found.

Integration is not necessarily a one-sided, traumatic integration of the acquiree into the buyer. If the acquiree is a vibrant, well-run company, it is entirely possible that the buyer will shift some of its operations into those of the acquiree, sometimes to such an extent that it is subsequently difficult to ascertain who acquired whom.

This discussion has assumed that two parties consummate an acquisition. However, in the vast majority of cases, the discussions fall apart, for any number of reasons. Because of this very high risk of deal failure, both parties should always publicly downplay any deal that may be in the works, and preferably keep it secret. In the event of failure, and if the discussions have been of a public nature, then both parties should jointly state that it was caused by unspecified differences that could not be reconciled, and issue no further information. Also, there is no point in publicly blaming the other party for a failed acquisition, since there is always a possibility that the parties will later make another attempt at an acquisition, and there is no point in having hard feelings between the companies.

Throughout this discussion, the assumption has been that the buyer is an independent third party. In reality, the target's management team may be taking an active role in the acquisition on behalf of the buyer, either to stay on with significant performance-based compensation packages, or to buy out the company themselves. If the later is the case, they usually put up a minimal amount of equity as part of the deal, accompanied by a massive amount of debt to fund the remainder of the purchase. Given the extraordinarily high leverage, the underlying business must have stable and predictable cash flows, within a secure market niche that does not require significant capital replacement costs during the loan payback period. If not, then the management team is at great risk of losing its investment, as well as its ownership of the company. A safer alternative for the management team is when a parent company wants to spin off a business unit, and it gives favorable payment terms to its management team, thereby enabling it to more safely carry out the acquisition.

In summary, the acquisition process flow involves an initial expression of interest, a valuation analysis that is likely to be repeated as more information about the target becomes available, a term sheet, due diligence, a purchase agreement, and finally the integration of the two entities. The odds of successfully completing each step decline as the process proceeds, so that a buyer may initially communicate with several dozen companies, issue term sheets to a quarter of them, and eventually conclude a purchase agreement with just one.

THE AUCTION PROCESS FLOW

A company's owners may elect to sell their business through an *auction* process. This may result in a higher price for their business, the commission of any brokers used to assist in the sale must be deducted from the eventual price. An auction also provides evidence that the seller's board of directors did its best to obtain the best possible price, thereby possibly averting any shareholder lawsuits claiming the contrary.

To initiate an auction, the seller's owners typically hire a broker to conduct the auction for them. Under this approach, the broker creates an *offering book* (also known as a *sales prospectus*) describing the company, but without revealing its name. The book usually contains the following information, which is designed to reveal the company's investment potential:

- *Investment summary.* A brief overview of how the seller would be an excellent investment opportunity.
- *Company overview.* A short list and extrapolation of the key reasons why the seller is worth acquiring.
- *Market analysis.* Describes the market in which the seller operates, and the seller's niche within that market.
- *Products and services.* Describes the key products and services offered by the seller, as well as their margins. This can also include a discussion of major customers and distribution channels.
- *Management.* Notes the qualifications of those managers expected to transfer to the buyer.
- *Historical and forecasted financial statements.* Includes audited financial statements (without footnotes) for at least the past two years, and preferably more. Should also include an estimate of

future financial performance for at least the current and following year.

- *Capitalization table.* Summarizes investor ownership by class of stock.
- *Asking price.* States the target price. If comparable sales have occurred recently, then note them in this section as justification for the asking price.
- *Concluding remarks.* Brings together all preceding sections into a one-page summary of the investment proposition.

The broker sends an auction notice to a broad array of possible buyers, and obtains an non-disclosure agreement from anyone who expresses interest. Despite the NDA, there is a strong likelihood that the seller's financial and operational information will soon find its way throughout the industry, and into the hands of competitors. Thus, anyone choosing to sell through an auction process should be ready to deal with broad distribution of potentially damaging information.

Confidentiality is a particular problem if the seller retains a broker that indiscriminately spreads the auction notice throughout an industry. The broker may gain a few more bidders, and certainly gives its own name better brand recognition in the industry—but the seller's privacy has vanished. It is better to conduct a low-key auction with a small group of pre-qualified bidders, so that noise about the auction is minimized. However, if an activist shareholder insists on a sale by auction, then it may be necessary to publicize the auction, so that the shareholders can be assured that a broad-based auction is indeed taking place.

Once the NDA is signed, the broker issues the offering book. The broker also sends additional information to those expressing interest in exchange for a letter of intent, with the intent of quickly whittling down the list of potential bidders to a group with the interest and wherewithal to make a valid bid for the seller. The broker then issues a purchase agreement (note that this varies from the normal acquisition approach, where the buyer controls the purchase agreement).

Bidders mark up the document with their changes, leading to further dickering with the broker. The broker will attempt to keep several bidders lined up, in case the bidder offering the best price backs out of the negotiations. However, if secondary bidders are shifted into the lead position, they now know that the broker has experienced some difficulty with their predecessor, which gives them greater bargaining power.

The broker may demand a cash deposit, cash escrow, or letter of credit from the highest bidder to ensure that it completes the deal. This is sometimes necessary because other bidders are likely to lose interest in the deal once it becomes apparent that another party is in the lead position to acquire the seller. As previously noted, the price tends to decline if negotiations fall through with the highest bidder, so the broker will be keenly interested in locking in this bidder.

Negotiations may break down with multiple bidders, so that the broker finds itself dealing with the last possible bidder. If so, the broker will not reveal that other bidders have dropped out, since this gives the bidder more negotiating power. Conversely, the bidder should always suspect that there are no other bidders, and be willing to walk away if the broker will not accept the bidder's best offer.

In general, the broker should always maintain confidentiality about the identities of all interested bidders. Not only does this give the broker a better bargaining position, as just noted, but it also prevents collusion among the bidders. For example, the bidders might allow one of their number to win with a low bid, in exchange for other concessions to be granted a later date, such as access to key seller technology, or the sale of selected seller assets to them.

Many experienced buyers are unwilling to take part in an auction, because they know the price at which the seller will eventually be sold is more likely to be at the high end of the price range. Instead, they may withdraw from the process, and wait to see if the auction falls through. If so, they can re-enter the bidding, and negotiate on a one-on-one basis, usually resulting in a lower price.

The auction process can also be used when the target company has entered bankruptcy protection. In this case, a court appoints a bankruptcy trustee, who runs the entity on behalf of its creditors. In many cases, the sale value of a bankrupt entity is worth more than its breakup value, so the trustee conducts an open auction to sell to the highest bidder. Once a winner is established, the trustee submits the winning bid to the bankruptcy court for approval. Though there are some extra steps to complete in a bankruptcy auction, the result can be a significantly low price for the buyer. However, the buyer must be willing to make significant changes to the acquiree to improve its profitability—after all, there is a reason why the company ended up under bankruptcy protection!

The auction process tends to take more time than a normal acquisition. It requires about one month for the broker to create an offering book and derive a list of potential buyers, another month to screen those buyers, one more month to receive bids and conduct due diligence, and a final six weeks to close the deal. Thus, given the number of parties involved and extra steps involved in an auction, the seller must be prepared to wait longer than during a normal acquisition transaction to complete a sale.

In summary, the auction process is time-consuming and expensive for the seller, but can also result in a higher sale price. Given the chance of obtaining an unusually high price, it is more common to see larger firms tread the auction path; not only are they better able to afford it, but brokers are more willing to represent them, in the expectation of considerable fees.

LOCATING AND CULLING ACQUISITION TARGETS

When a buyer decides to engage in an acquisition, it should do so in a methodical manner, and not in reaction to a sudden opportunity. This requires a long-term commitment to reviewing the range of possible acquisition opportunities, based on what it needs in an acquisition target. The first step in this process is to do a general review of the industry in which the buyer wishes to make acquisitions. The goal of this review is to determine the types of acquisition opportunities that exist, which other companies are completing acquisitions in the same market space, and what kinds of prices are being paid.

There are a number of ways for a buyer to identify possible acquisition targets. If it wants to make acquisitions in areas closely related to its existing operations, then its *sales department* very likely already has an excellent idea of who the best prospects might be, since they compete with them constantly.

Some of the best acquisition candidates are *current business partners*. They may be customers who work closely with the buyer to develop new products, or suppliers with whom the buyer has close, long-term relationships. However, these targets generally imply either upstream or downstream acquisitions, so that the buyer becomes more vertically integrated within its industry—which needs to be a strategy decision by senior management (see the Acquisition Strategy section).

Another option is to have the acquisition team regularly accompany the sales staff to the company's regularly scheduled *trade shows*. The acquisition team can tour the various company booths for ideas. A less time-consuming alternative is to obtain trade show directories, make lists of which companies attended, and investigate each one.

Another search method is to subscribe to all of the *industry publications*, and pore through them to determine which companies regularly advertise. This is also a good way to locate subject-matter experts at other companies, since they may write articles for the trade journals.

If a target industry has a large number of public companies, then go to Yahoo Finance or Google Finance, and review the *lists of competitors* that are listed next to each company. A more labor-intensive method is to access the annual 10-K reports of public companies and see who they list as competitors.

It is also possible to uncover targets through *special industry studies*. These studies may be created gratis by university professors as part of their research, but are more commonly made available through private studies that will cost the buyer anywhere from $5,000 to $20,000 to obtain.

Another alternative is *sell-side analysts*. These individuals work for banks, brokerage houses, and investment bankers, and usually specialize in the public companies located within a single industry. They are experts in those industries, and may be able to provide information about the more significant players within each one.

Standard & Poor's issues lengthy lists of companies through its *Industry Surveys*. Each report covers a specific industry, and is authored by a Standard & Poor's research analyst. The reports cover a great deal more than the names of the key players. They also note industry trends, how the industry operates, key ratios, additional references, and comparative company financial analysis. The reports cover over fifty industries, ranging from advertising to transportation.

If the buyer is searching for targets with valuable intellectual property, then it can develop its own *intellectual property study* of an industry. This study shows who is working on similar technologies, which ones are publishing authoritative literature on various studies, who is being cited as a reference, and who has filed for or received patents. Such a study requires a massive amount of work, and probably the retention of an intellectual property attorney to conduct investigations. Though expensive, it can reveal the direction in which technology is moving in an industry, so that a buyer can acquire key technologies in advance of its competitors.

Locating targets can be no trouble at all—they come to the buyer. The owners of privately-held firms may eventually want to cash out of their ownership positions, or do not have sufficient funds to keep plowing back into their businesses, or are running into regulatory problems—the reasons for sale are endless. Whatever the reason may be, company owners may make discreet inquiries among potential buyers, or through brokers.

All of the preceding methods should create a formidable list of acquisition targets; but how does a buyer winnow down the list to a qualified group of targets? The best method is to create a *fit matrix*. As shown in Exhibit 1.1, this is a matrix in which the buyer itemizes its main criteria for acquisition candidates, and how a target fulfills those needs. Common criteria are revenue size, profit size, market share, growth rate, and intellectual property. Other possible criteria are geographic location, product branding, types of distribution

Exhibit 1.1   Fit Matrix for ABC Company

Criteria	Fit	No Fit	Possible
Revenue > $10 million	√		
Revenue growth > 15%	√		
EBITDA > 15%	√		
Intellectual property			√
Growth stage		√	
Subject matter experts			√
Net cash flow positive		√	

channels, and corporate culture. The intent of this matrix is to eliminate targets from consideration, so its intent is essentially negative.

There is no scoring system involved in the fit matrix, since it is essentially subjective in nature. If a buyer were to set up a scoring system within a fit matrix, it should assign weightings to each criterion, since certain items usually outweigh the importance of others.

There is a price at which a buyer may find almost any target to be an attractive acquisition. However, it is only capable of digesting a certain number of targets per year, and it never has unlimited access to cash. Thus, the buyer must be extremely picky in determining which targets are worthy of a bid. A reason method for sorting through the list of targets is to adopt some simple cutoff criteria, below which a target will not be considered. For example, the target must have a revenue growth rate higher than that of the buyer, which ensures that the target's growth will incrementally increase that of the entire company. Similarly, the deal cannot dilute the buyer's earnings after a short acquisition integration period.

The buyer must also be extremely wary of any legal disputes in which a target is embroiled. It must evaluate each existing lawsuit for both the most likely and maximum payout possible. Of particular concern are lawsuits over the ownership of the target's intellectual property. If there is any hint of such an issue, and the buyer is basing much of the target's value on its intellectual property, then this can ruin the entire deal. Also, the due diligence team should review any lawsuits to which competing firms are being subjected, to see if the same problems could arise for the target. Given the severity of some lawsuit payouts, and the potential loss of control over intellectual property, litigation can be a prime reason to avoid an acquisition.

A key cutoff issue that many companies miss is the ability of the target to expand its underlying business concept. In many cases, the target is attempting to sell itself because it has completely filled its market niche, and no longer sees any way to grow further. The buyer must be very clear about its ability to expand the target's business. Otherwise, it is paying to acquire an entity with stale growth—and if a company is not growing, it only has one way to go—down.

Another cutoff issue is the proportion of sales among the target's customers. If a large proportion of sales is concentrated among a very small number of customers, then the buyer faces a high risk of major revenue declines if even one of these customers departs. This is a particular problem if there are only a handful of customers in total.

While not normally a cutoff criterion, the presence of a union shop can scare away the more skittish buyers. These buyers may have had unusually acrimonious union relations in the past, and have therefore imposed a ban on any new deals where a union is involved. Other buyers are aware that union relations *can* be managed properly, and do not consider this to be a significant issue.

One of the best cutoff criteria of all is to mention a potential price range to the target early in the discussions, and see if this meets with the approval of the target. If the target appears to have an inordinately high opinion of its value, then the buyer should allow it to obtain that price—from someone else.

By using these criteria to avoid unattractive deals, the buyer will have more resources available when the right target comes along, and can then offer a high price to obtain it.

THE OPTIMAL TARGET SIZE

One of the acquisition screening criteria that a buyer's acquisition team uses is a revenue size range. This range is based on the target's revenue, which is a useful (though rough) method for determining the approximate complexity of the acquisition transaction. The low end of this range is based on the legal and administrative costs of completing an acquisition. Given just these costs, few buyers will even consider an acquisition where the target has revenues of less than $5 million—it is simply not worth their time. Also, the acquisition team must consider how to best use its time in evaluating potential acquisition targets. It takes approximately as much time to conclude an acquisition deal with a $100 million target as it does with a $5 million target. Thus, there are multiple reasons why buyers tend to ignore smaller targets. The only case where an extremely small acquisition makes sense is when the target possesses unusually valuable intellectual property that the buyer can immediately use.

There is also such a thing as acquiring too large a target. If the buyer is nearly the same size as the target, then there is a good chance that the target, once acquired, will not feel obligated to replace its own systems and organizational structure with those of the buyer. Instead, there may be a protracted power struggle over a variety of issues, resulting in an extremely long time before the two entities are fully integrated (if ever).

The optimal acquisition size is in the general range of five to 15 percent of the size of the buyer. In this size range, the buyer can comfortably impose its will on the acquired company, resulting in rapid integration.

EVALUATE ACQUISITION TARGETS WITH ALLIANCES

Acquiring any company can be a significant risk, no matter how detailed the due diligence is. The problem is the difficulty of determining how the acquiree's employees handle themselves with customers, how they develop products, their level of ethics, and many other intangible issues that are critical to the success of an acquisition, but which are nearly impossible to measure. In addition, a buyer may pay for an acquisition based on the target's technology, only to find that the market shifts in a different direction, rendering its investment worthless.

The solution in some cases is to first enter into a business alliance with a target. By entering into a number of alliances, a buyer can essentially keep tabs on several potential acquisitions while a new market develops, and then make offers to selected alliance partners depending on which direction the market eventually turns. This is less of an advantage in industries where there is little technological innovation, in which case the acquirer can skip the alliance approach and proceed directly to an acquisition.

In addition, if a buyer makes a substantial investment in a target as part of the alliance agreement, then it may obtain a board seat. By doing so, it has full access to the target's financial information, and will have ready access to any financial or operational issues to which the target is being subjected. Some buyers have a formal process for such investments, where they establish in-house venture capital funds with authorization to make investments within a general range of investment criteria.

If the alliance involves cross-selling of each other's products, this gives the buyer excellent information regarding sales synergies that it can enter into its valuation model. Revenue synergies are among the most difficult synergies to realize, so using an alliance to obtain realistic synergy information can be a gold mine. Also, the buyer can use cross-selling to learn how to sell the target's products, which shows it how to integrate the sales and marketing organizations of the two companies.

The most important point in favor of the alliance approach is that the two companies have a chance over an extended period of time to examine any potential pitfalls that would interfere with an eventual acquisition, including issues with employees and a variety of communications-related topics. This approach also allows the target's employees to get to know their counterparts in the acquiring firm, which may reduce the amount of employee turnover that sometimes accompanies an acquisition.

The downside of the alliance approach is that a potential target may gain some prestige through the alliance, which can raise the price of the eventual acquisition. Also, taking additional time to work through an alliance arrangement gives the target time to be purchased by a competitor or at least set up a bidding war, though this danger can be mitigated by including a right of first refusal in the alliance agreement.

ACQUISITION RISKS FOR THE BUYER—VALUATION

Multiple studies have shown that, for between one-half and two-thirds of all acquisitions, the buying corporation's valuation declines to a level below that of the combined value of both the buying and selling entities before the acquisition took place. In essence, the acquisition transaction destroys value. However, this view avoids the buyer's alternative, which is to build the same expertise in-house. These endeavors are not as public as an acquisition, but may fail just as frequently. The difference is that acquisitions are conducted in the limelight, while organic growth is not. The open question, then, is whether a company really loses more value through acquisitions than through its other growth alternatives.

A variation on this problem is the "winner's curse," where the bulk of the value derived from the acquisition ends up in the hands of the seller's shareholders. This situation arises because selling shareholders sometimes have no risk at all—they are paid in cash, which means that the entire burden of making the transaction successful rests on the buyer. If the buyer cannot execute on its plan, then the shares held by the buyer's owners lose value. The winner's curse does not arise when the buyer pays with its own stock, since this means that the seller's shareholders will share equally in the risk of properly implementing the acquisition.

A major part of the valuation reduction conundrum is that the two entities are virtually never a perfect match for each other. Some aspects of the target company are of no use to the buyer, and may be actively counter-productive. In particular, the cultures of the two companies may clash so much that it is nearly impossible to achieve a seamless merger. Instead, the two companies operate together under a single corporate identity, but they do not create value. If anything, internal bickering shifts attention from servicing customers, resulting in lost sales and profits.

Of particular importance to valuation is factoring in the risk of acquiring an entity that is well outside the buyer's core competencies. An acquisition of this type contains a multitude of dangers, since the buyer's management has minimal experience in the target's operations. The best way to avoid this considerable valuation risk is to only acquire related businesses, where the buyer has sufficient in-house resources to deal with any problems that may arise.

The valuation reduction problem is much reduced for a serial buyer. A company that makes a practice of acquiring other entities has (presumably) learned from its mistakes through trial and error. It also has a rigorous system for evaluating and valuing targets, can identify and mitigate acquisition-related risks, and has excellent due diligence and integration systems in place. It is also much more decisive in its negotiations, being more willing to walk away from a deal if it cannot obtain a reasonable price.

In short, there is certainly a risk for the buyer of losing value from an acquisition, but perhaps no more than would be the case for an internally-funded project. If the buyer is uncertain of its ability to execute an acquisition, it can shift some of the risk to the seller, by paying with stock. The best way to mitigate valuation risk is to become a serial buyer of smaller companies, using each acquisition to gain acquisition skill.

ACQUISITION RISKS FOR THE BUYER—LEGAL

No matter how carefully managed an acquisition may be, there is still a significant risk of lawsuits. Of particular concern is the earnout provision, where the seller has an opportunity to be paid more by the buyer if it can achieve certain financial or operational targets during the year or so following the acquisition. The problem is that the buyer's and seller's goals may conflict following the acquisition, with the seller's management being solely focused on earning the maximum payment under the earnout provision, while the buyer wants to integrate the two entities together. A common result is complaints by the seller that the buyer is interfering with its right to earn a larger payment, followed by a lawsuit to obtain what the seller feels is due to its shareholders. The usual solutions for the buyer are to a) never agree to an earnout provision, or b) to budget for a maximum payment under the earnout, irrespective of the results that the seller actually posts.

Directors and officers are also more likely to be sued after an acquisition, if the transaction turns out to have less than stellar results. The grounds for such suits are that the buyer did not perform sufficient due diligence on the seller prior to closing the deal (such as ensuring that an audit was completed on the seller's financial records). Maintaining excellent due diligence records will create a defensible position for the buyer, since the presence of due diligence indicates the absence of negligence.

The buyer can also be sued if the acquisition transaction itself was faulty. This usually means that a key approval was not obtained (such as a shareholder vote), or a regulatory approval of the acquisition. The larger the business, the more likely it is that some legal slipup will occur that opens the door to a lawsuit. The buyer can mitigate this risk by using a high-end law firm with considerable acquisition experience, and even by hiring a second law firm to review the work of the first one.

Another legal problem is that, if the buyer acquires the seller's legal entity, it now becomes liable for *any* problems that the seller had. This can result in lawsuits several months or years after the acquisition, for issues that the buyer knew nothing about. The buyer can mitigate this risk by requiring the seller to indemnify the buyer for any undisclosed legal problems, but the buyer is still ultimately liable for these suits.

A buyer may think that it has avoided these legal problems by acquiring only selected assets of the seller. However, under some state laws, if a buyer acquires assets, then it must also assume liability for faulty products manufactured by the seller prior to the acquisition. Also in selected states, if the buyer pays with its own stock to acquire a seller's assets, then the legal system may construe the transaction as a merger, so that the buyer assumes the seller's liabilities.

The buyer also faces regulatory review by the government. As explained further in the Government Regulation chapter, the buyer must notify the federal government if it is contemplating an acquisition that will give it undue influence over a market. Based on an analysis of the submitted information, the government may conclude that the acquisition gives the buyer an excessively large market share, so it either prohibits the transaction or requires the buyer to sell off some assets in order to reduce its monopoly power. While this is rarely an issue for smaller firms, it effectively prohibits larger, market-dominating entities from completing any large acquisitions in the same market space.

In summary, there are a variety of legal issues arising from an acquisition, many of which can destroy any value created by the transaction. The buyer can mitigate some of this risk, but essentially an acquisition does increase the buyer's overall legal risk.

ACQUISITION RISKS FOR THE SELLER

While the buyer bears most of the risk in an acquisition, some also falls upon the seller—specifically, if it cannot complete an acquisition. The risk arises when a close competitor enters the bidding, and uses its due diligence investigation as a ploy to uncover the seller's competitive secrets. The competitor then backs out of the bidding, and uses the information to compete more effectively. For example, it can acquire the pay rates of the seller's key staff, and use this information to hire them away. It can also copy proprietary production or engineering information, and use it to develop competing products. Or, it can use sales information to approach key customers and offer alternative pricing or service arrangements. In short, a failed acquisition can be catastrophic for the seller.

It can use several techniques to mitigate this risk. The simplest is the standard "burn or return" provision in the confidentiality agreement that the buyer must sign before being given access to any seller information. This requires the buyer to either destroy or return any seller information that is marked "confidential." However, a less-than-ethical competitor could easily photocopy all such documents, and return the originals. A more secure alternative is to roll out information to bidders in stages. If the bidder displays continuing interest, then the buyer gives it access to increasingly proprietary information. It can also restrict copying of some documents, which are for "eyes only" review by the buyer.

Thus, the seller always runs the risk of having its proprietary information scattered among other companies. This is a significant problem if the seller can never seem to close a deal, so that it gains a reputation for always being for sale; this cheapens its perceived value.

ACQUISITION FOLLOW-UP ACTIVITIES

A serial buyer should always learn from its previous acquisition activities so that it can apply them to future deals. After concluding each deal, the buyer should ask itself these questions:

- How did what we bought compare to what we thought we bought? What investigative errors caused these differences?

- What problems at the target company did we miss, and how can we locate them in the future?

- How could we have spent less time on this transaction?

- Did our cut-off criteria function properly? Did we continue with a deal that should have been eliminated early in the process? Did we drop deals that could have been winners?

A buyer may not be able to answer some of these questions until many months have passed, since problems may not become immediately apparent. To ensure that these problems are still discussed, schedule review dates for three months and a year after the closing.

The earlier review will pick up most of the problems, while the later one can be used to address late-breaking problems.

The buyer should also create a standard list of key problems that have arisen in the past, and review this document prior to engaging in each subsequent acquisition. The intent is to look for these problems, and mitigate them wherever possible.

THE HOSTILE TAKEOVER

Most of this book assumes that the target company is interested in the buyer's offer, and is a willing participant in the acquisition process. This is not necessarily the case. The buyer may attempt a hostile acquisition, where it tries to make a purchase despite the wishes of the target's management team. This is extremely difficult to do when the target is privately held, since the management team usually owns the company, and can cheerfully spurn all offers. However, if the target is publicly held and ownership is widely dispersed, then the buyer may be able to complete a hostile takeover.

A buyer usually conducts a hostile takeover through a *tender offer*. This means that the buyer goes around the target's management to contact the target's shareholders, and offers to buy their shares. The rules for tender offers were defined in the 1968 Williams Act, which amended the Securities Exchange Act of 1934. In essence, the buyer sends a packet of information to the target's shareholders, includes a purchase offer, a deadline, and a letter of transmittal. The letter of transmittal outlines the method for transferring shares to the buyer. The buyer has the right to reject stock if an excessive amount is tendered, or if not enough is tendered (e.g., there are not enough shares to gain control of the target). The buyer also has the right to terminate its tender offer. A shareholder can withdraw any tendered shares during the tender offer period by submitting a letter of withdrawal, along with a signature guarantee verifying that the signature of the submitting party is that of the shareholder.

The tender offer contains a termination date, beyond which the buyer does not intend to accept additional shares of the target's stock. It can extend the tender offer, but must announce the extension no later than 9 A.M. on the business day following the date when the tender offer expires. The announcement must also state the approximate amount of securities that the buyer has already acquired, which gives everyone a good estimate of the progress of the tender offer, and the likelihood of the buyer's ultimate success.

If the buyer obtains at least 90 percent of the target company's stock, then it can adopt a merger resolution on behalf of the target company, accepting the takeover offer. Any uncommitted shareholders will receive the same compensation as all other shareholders who accepted the tender offer; however, these shareholders also retain appraisal rights, where a court can determine an objective fair value for their shares. A shareholder only exercises his appraisal rights if he feels that the tender offer undervalues his shares.

In addition, the buyer must document the tender offer in a filing with the Securities and Exchange Commission, including a term sheet summarizing the material terms of the tender offer, the buyer's identity and background, the source of funds for the acquisition, and the buyer's history with and plans for the target company.

As an alternative, the buyer may engage in a *proxy fight*, where it solicits proxies from the target's stockholders, and votes those shares at a stockholder's meeting that is called for the purpose of voting on the acquisition. The proxy solicitation must comply with federal securities laws, so it is best to hire a proxy solicitation service to handle this aspect of the acquisition on behalf of the buyer.

A hostile takeover is usually an intense and protracted affair, which fully involves the managements of both involved companies. This can be a major distraction from their conduct of daily business activities. Also, it is a reasonable assumption that the target's management will not be cooperative in the event of a takeover, so the buyer must be prepared to completely replace them, which will make subsequent integration efforts much more difficult. For these reasons, a buyer should have very good reasons for proceeding with a hostile takeover.

DEFENDING AGAINST A HOSTILE TAKEOVER

The target of a hostile takeover can defend itself by incorporating a variety of defenses into its bylaws, articles of incorporation, and employment agreements. The more common of these "poison pills" are:

- *Accelerated vesting.* This provision is located in the target's option and warrant grants, and provides that the vesting periods for all options and warrants shall accelerate in the event of a change in control of the company. This creates more stock for the buyer to acquire. This provision has become less useful of late, because it has become a standard feature of nearly all option and warrant grants, and so is no longer considered a specific protection against a hostile acquirer.

- *Back-end plan.* This provision is designed to ensure a minimum acceptable price for *all* of the seller's shareholders. It does so by giving each shareholder the right to exchange each share for either convertible stock, cash, or a note that matures within a short period of time. The conversion value can be for a fixed amount, or for a percentage of the price per share offered by the bidder. It does not necessarily prevent a hostile takeover, but will ensure a reasonable value for all shareholders whose shares might not otherwise be acquired by the bidder.

- *Dead hand provision.* This provision states that only the original directors who put a poison pill provision in place can remove it. This provision keeps a buyer from attempting to stack the target's board of directors with new nominees, since they will be unable to revise the provision.

- *Fair price provision.* This provision requires a supermajority of the shareholders (usually two-thirds) to approve a proposed acquisition unless the buyer pays all minority shareholders a fair price. A fair price can be defined as a price that equals or exceeds the price the buyer paid to acquire the target company's shares prior to its formal acquisition bid, or an average of the target's stock price on the open market for the preceding month. The intent is to provide fairness to the shareholders in a two-tier transaction, where the buyer acquires a majority interest, and later makes an offer for the remaining outstanding shares.

- *Flip-over plan.* This provision gives current shareholders the right to purchase shares of the company upon the occurrence of a triggering event. For example, shareholders may be able to buy additional shares at half-price if there is a hostile bid for the company. This right would "flip over" to the surviving entity if the target were acquired, so that the buyer would face substantial dilution of its shares. Obviously, additional language in the provision should not trigger the flip-over if the transaction is approved by the board of directors—otherwise, the company would never be able to sell itself, even if it wanted to.

- *Golden parachutes.* The employment plans of key managers may state that very large payouts to those managers will automatically be triggered if the company is acquired in a hostile takeover. While this will increase the acquisition cost of the buyer, it also raises the suspicion that the management team has included the provision for its own benefit.

- *Staggered director elections.* Most companies elect their entire board of directors once a year, which makes it easier for a buyer to acquire a sufficient number of shares to force its candidates onto the board during the annual shareholders' meeting, and gain immediate control of the company. However, if the target can alter the situation to allow multi-year staggered elections, this requires much more perseverance by the buyer over several years in order to obtain a majority of the director seats. An example would be a six-director board, with two directors being elected each year to a three-year term. This would require two years for a buyer to obtain a majority of seats.

- *Supermajority provision.* This provision requires that more than a simple majority of shareholders approve a merger—usually two-thirds. A buyer can get around this provision by gaining control of a simple majority of the outstanding shares, and then voting these shares to eliminate the supermajority provision. To prevent this, a company must also have a provision requiring a supermajority in order to modify the supermajority voting provision.

- *Voting in person.* This provision states that a shareholder cannot submit a written consent, but rather requires a shareholder meeting in which votes must be cast in person. This is a rare provision, since a widely distributed shareholder base may make it impossible to pass any shareholder resolution, much less an acquisition approval.

- *Voting rights.* A separate class of stock can be endowed with multiple votes per share, so that a small group of shareholders effectively wields control over the entire company. This goal can also be achieved by having a class of convertible preferred stock, where each share of preferred stock can convert into multiple shares of common stock.

Before company officers attempt to adopt any of these provisions, they must realize that their shareholders may very well not want any of them. After all, the intent of most shareholders is to eventually obtain the highest possible price for their shares, and a buyer is the one most likely to give it to them. Consequently, adopting anti-takeover provisions actually *reduces* the value of their company, because it drives away bidders. Thus, many astute shareholders will vote down such proposals. Anti-takeover provisions are most likely to be found in closely-held companies, where the owners are also members of management, and are more concerned with retaining control than with the value of their shares.

The target company can also elect to switch roles and make an offer to purchase the hostile buyer; a position from which it will back down only if the hostile buyer does so as well. In some cases, the target company may actually acquire the erstwhile hostile buyer. This is generally considered counterproductive to the target's shareholders; they will receive no payout premium, since they are the owners of the surviving company.

Another tactic is for the target to acquire a third company. By doing so, the combined entity may require so much difficult integration work that the hostile buyer now finds it to be a less attractive acquisition, and withdraws its offer. This is an especially attractive ploy if the new acquisition makes the target company so large that the hostile buyer might precipitate an anti-trust investigation if it were to follow through with its plans. However, the buyer can also sell off a sufficient amount of the newly acquired assets to bring it into compliance with anti-trust laws.

What if the target finds itself without any procedural defenses against a hostile buyer? It can bring a more suitable third party into the fray. One option is the *white knight*, which is a third party whom the target asks to make an offer for it, as an alternative to the hostile buyer. The target will still find itself owned by someone new, but presumably the white knight will be friendlier to management.

A less traumatic alternative is the *white squire*. This is a third party who agrees to buy a large block of the target's stock under a standstill agreement, whereby it cannot sell the shares to a hostile bidder. Alternatively, the target may require a right of first refusal if the white squire intends to sell the shares to another party. This tends to be a purely financial play for the white squire, under which the target essentially guarantees it a reasonable return on its invested funds in exchange for holding the stock for a certain period of time.

An alternative to the white squire is to shift stock into the hands of company employees through an employee stock ownership plan (ESOP). If the ESOP owns a sufficiently large proportion of company stock, a buyer will have an extremely difficult time rounding up enough stock elsewhere to obtain a majority of all shares held, thereby eliminating the acquisition threat.

The target also has the option of implementing a "scorched earth" policy, where it sells off its most valuable assets. The target is still valuable, since it has presumably now exchanged those assets for cash, which a buyer may still want to possess. Thus, the target must take the additional step of distributing the cash to its shareholders as a one-time dividend. By doing so, a hostile bidder has no point in continuing with an acquisition attempt. The considerable downside to this technique is that the target is now merely a shell of its former self, with little value.

There are many defenses against a hostile acquisition, but many of them damage the value of the underlying company by making it excessively difficult for *anyone* to eventually buy the company. If a company persists in implementing anti-takeover activities, then one must assume that it is more interested in maintaining independent control of the company than in maximizing shareholder value.

SUMMARY

This chapter has noted the reasons why people buy and sell companies, and revealed the basic process flow of an acquisition. In addition, we've covered a variety of ways to locate acceptable target companies, what special acquisition risks can occur, and how to engage in and defend against a hostile acquisition.

In the remainder of this book, we delve into much greater detail about the various stages of the acquisition process. There are separate chapters on how to create a valuation analysis, write a term sheet and a purchase agreement, how to conduct a due diligence review, and the steps that are required to fully integrate an acquisition. These chapters are in the approximate order that a buyer would follow for an acquisition, but they can be read independently of each other.

Chapter 2

Key Participants

This chapter describes the role of all key players in an acquisition. It begins with the buyer's acquisition team, since this group initiates the purchase transaction. We then proceed to the other players in alphabetical order, and end with the integration team, which is in charge of achieving synergies between the buyer and seller.

THE ACQUISITION TEAM

The buyer's acquisition team is listed first, since it initiates the purchase transaction. The team searches for acquisition targets, controls most contacts with those targets, and pitches prospective deals to the senior management team. The group is comprised of employees having considerable acquisition experience. They may be promoted from line manager positions, but are more commonly brought in from outside investment banking or legal firms. The group spends a great deal of time traveling to meet with prospective targets, and usually has minimal support staff at corporate headquarters. Due to the heavy demands on their time, team members tend to be relatively young.

The acquisition team must be sufficiently assertive, well organized, and politically connected within the company to keep the cumbersome acquisition process moving. It must also have a good grasp of the buyer's markets, business model, and strategy, so that it knows what potential acquisitions will be the best fit. The team's underlying skill set must include solid financial modeling, so that it can conduct a variety of purchase price analyses under multiple performance scenarios. It should also have a good grasp of the legal points of a purchase agreement, and be able to negotiate terms that yield a fair price and mitigate risk for the buyer.

The acquisition team may have a pay structure that rewards it for deals completed. Team members may also be more inclined to complete deals if they plan to work for other companies in the near future, and want to enhance their résumés with a long list of deals completed. Further, it is a rare buyer that links the subsequent results of an acquisition back to the acquisition team. For all these reasons, the team may complete deals that should have been avoided. Given the considerable risks associated with an acquisition, the team should actually be looking for reasons *not* to complete it, with successful deals being the exception. To foster this approach to deal reviews, the buyer should create incentives for the acquisition team that are based on its long-term success, and not award bonuses for initial deal completion.

ATTORNEYS

Because an acquisition is essentially a transfer of legal ownership, it involves attorneys at nearly every step of the process—in developing term sheets, reviewing due diligence documents, and crafting the purchase agreement. The contribution of a well-trained corporate attorney is absolutely critical to an acquisition. While many corporations have bemoaned the high prices charged by their legal advisors, they must remember that the attorneys are being paid to look out for the buyer's best interests, and so serve an essential protective role.

Attorneys are especially unbiased advisors, because their pay structure is not based on the success of the deal. They are paid by the hour, irrespective of whether the buyer completes the acquisition. However, *because* they are paid by the hour, they are more than happy to dig into the details of a deal to a much greater extent than is actually needed. Consequently, the acquisition team should ensure that all attorneys are aware of the business priorities underlying each deal, so that they focus their efforts in the right places. For example, if the buyer is contemplating an asset acquisition only, then the attorneys do not need to investigate the seller's legal entity, since the buyer does not plan to acquire it.

Unless a buyer engages in a substantial and ongoing amount of acquisition work, it will not have a need for a full in-house legal team. Instead, most buyers rely on outside attorneys who specialize in acquisitions. These people have engaged in many acquisitions, and so have significant skills that cannot be found in house. Usually, a number of attorneys are needed for an acquisition, each one specializing in a different area. While the primary task involves drafting the purchase agreement, there should also be a tax attorney who advises on how to make a deal more tax-efficient, as well as intellectual property attorneys who investigate the seller's copyrights, trademarks, and patents, and advise on how to protect any additional intellectual property.

In short, an excellent acquisitions attorney is literally worth his weight in gold, and the buyer may end up paying that much for his services.

BOARD OF DIRECTORS

Most acquisitions have a major impact on the results of both the buyer and seller, so the boards of both entities must approve the transactions; besides, corporate bylaws nearly always require it.

For smaller transactions, the board may readily accept management's recommendation to proceed, and approve the matter with minimal discussion. However, a larger transaction may spark a considerable amount of board debate. The board has a fiduciary responsibility to represent the best interests of shareholders, and so should take whatever steps it feels necessary to become comfortable with the proposed transaction. This can include hiring outside consultants to review and pass judgment upon it.

Despite the amount of review time that a board may invest in a proposed deal, it still has an essentially passive role—it does not actively scout for deals. If it were to force management to acquire a company, it must still rely upon the management team to integrate the two entities. Integration involves a massive amount of work, and if the management team resisted the initial deal, it is certainly less likely to invest the appropriate amount of time in an adequate integration effort.

The CEO is responsible for keeping the board apprised of all significant events leading to the purchase of a target company. This does not mean that the CEO must bury the board with information—far from it. The board is only interested in those deals that may close in the near future. This means that they do not need to hear about the latest "short list" of favorite targets, nor the progress of due diligence, nor of deals where the two parties are still far apart on terms. Conversely, the CEO should not present the board with information at the last minute, either—the board does not want to think that it is rubber-stamping a transaction that is essentially complete. If potential deals are especially large or involve a fundamental strategy shift by the buyer, the board may want to be involved earlier in the process, and be updated at more frequent intervals.

BROKERS

Brokers work for companies that are trying to sell themselves. A broker will contact the buyer's CEO to see if there is any interest in acquiring the company that he represents. If so, the broker will send a brief summary of the selling entity, and the buyer will likely join in an auction with other interested parties to see who is willing to pay the most for the selling company. The broker will do everything possible to maximize the price for the seller's shareholders, since he will be paid a percentage of the final price obtained.

The broker's job is also to pre-screen potential buyers, to see if they have the financial resources to pay for an acquisition.

From the buyer's perspective, it is generally not a good idea to work with a broker. First, this will probably lead to a bidding war with other potential buyers, so that the winner may pay an excessive price. For this reason alone, many buyers refuse to participate in auction bidding. Also, it is better for a buyer to proactively use its own acquisition strategy to approach other companies, rather than to passively wait for brokers to send deals its way. By waiting for brokered deals, a buyer is essentially placing its acquisition strategy into the hands of a broker who works for someone else.

From the seller's perspective, a broker can be quite useful. Selling companies likely have no experience with the selling process, so they can tap the broker's expertise in creating marketing materials and negotiating the purchase agreement. The seller can also shift the harder negotiations to the broker, leaving more time to run the underlying business.

However, the seller must be cognizant of how the broker deal is structured. Brokers usually insist upon an exclusive arrangement, where they are entitled to a percentage of the sale price, even if they are not directly involved in locating the buyer. They may also want a fee if the seller eventually sells to a company that the broker initially contacted; this "tail" arrangement typically lasts for one year after the brokering agreement is terminated.

The seller can insist on a number of changes to the brokering agreement. One issue is the fee collected by the broker. If the seller knows he can sell his business for a certain amount without any broker assistance, then he can insist that any broker commission be based on a sale price above that amount. The seller can also insist on a maximum fee, though it is generally better to incentivize the broker to obtain a high price by using an uncapped commission structure. Another possibility is to shrink the term of the brokerage agreement to a short interval, such as from three to six months. If the broker cannot achieve a sale by that time, then the seller should consider a different broker who has access to an alternative set of potential buyers.

A seller who wants to use a broker can find broker lists through the International Business Brokers Association. Many more brokers can be found on the Internet by entering "mergers and acquisitions brokers" in a search engine.

THE CHIEF EXECUTIVE OFFICER

The Chief Executive Officer (CEO) plays a conflicted role in acquisitions. While he must look at acquisitions as a possible option for improving his company, he is also well aware that he can personally benefit from the transaction. Simply put, a CEO usually draws a larger salary if the underlying company is bigger, so they have a tendency to complete acquisitions, even if the transactions are not economical to the company. In addition, the CEO may hold a large number of stock options whose value may rise considerably in the event of a successful acquisition. Aside from pay, there is also the ego boost that a CEO gets from making an acquisition and thereby managing a larger entity.

Also, company directors are increasingly displaying impatience with CEOs who do not perform immediately, so CEO tenures are getting shorter. In order to retain their jobs, CEOs are pushing for acquisitions that will contribute immediate gains in the scale and performance of their companies. This tendency is most common in underperforming entities with new CEOs, and less so where companies are already performing well, and are therefore inclined to be more selective in their acquisitions.

For these reasons, the CEO should not lead the acquisition team. Instead, he should delegate the acquisitions role to a group of professionals who can more dispassionately evaluate target companies. He should only be consulted in order to set the overarching strategy, and later to evaluate proposals brought to him by the acquisitions team.

In addition, the CEO is extremely useful for making initial and ongoing contacts with his counterpart at the target company. The acquisition team would otherwise have to deal with lower-level people at the target who might shunt aside any potential deal before the target's

CEO ever hears about it. Instead, the CEO can deal directly with his counterpart, which at least allows the acquisition team to have a hearing at the top level of the target.

INVESTMENT BANKERS

Investment bankers are highly networked financial experts who handle debt and equity placements, initial public offerings, acquisitions, and divestitures. They identify acquisition targets, determine appropriate purchase valuations, set up meetings between interested parties, and structure acquisition financing. They do not necessarily put their own funds into a deal. Instead, they initiate deals and bring parties together to consummate those transactions. Investment bankers spend a great deal of their time pitching prospective deals to clients.

Investment banking firms are specifically designed to support acquisitions. The larger ones have well-trained employees with considerable experience in deal making, and should have sufficient staff to ensure 24/7 support in case a deal must be concluded on short notice. This staff is comprised of junior analysts who work on valuation models, associates who deal with the more complex financial modeling, vice presidents who manage acquisition deals, and directors who pitch deals to prospective buyers, and also manage the most complex acquisitions.

Investment bankers do not have as much in-depth industry knowledge as their clients, but may have substantially more contacts within that industry. They usually have strong financial analysis skills and a deal-making background. Besides giving a great deal of technical support to an acquisition transaction, they can also provide much broad strategic advice to the buyer, as well as information about which industry players may be up for sale, and who is buying.

Investment bankers are paid based on the success of the transaction, not on an hourly basis. These fees can be (and usually are) huge. Because of the success-based nature of their compensation, they have a strong incentive to push the buyer to close deals, irrespective of the merit of those transactions. Thus, strictly because of their compensation, it is unwise to acquire a company based solely upon the recommendation of an investment banker.

Though they are not a major source of their profits, investment bankers also provide fairness opinions. A fairness opinion is a documented study in which the investment banker provides its opinion about the fairness and reasonableness of the financial terms of an acquisition. While the fairness opinion is of no use from an operational perspective, it does provide legal support for the buyer's board of directors, which might be sued by shareholders for its approval of an acquisition.

There is some gamesmanship that goes on with fairness opinions. An investment banker will only agree to work on a fairness opinion if it believes in advance that the deal was fair. If not, it will not take on the work, and the buyer's board must search for a more risk-tolerant investment bank to issue the opinion. Even if investors were to attack the investment bank on the grounds that it issued a flawed opinion, the bank usually covers itself by stating that it only created the opinion based on information supplied to it by the buyer and other sources—thereby neatly shifting any legal liability elsewhere. Thus, there will only be a fairness opinion if the deal was clearly fair, which obviates the need for the opinion!

It is by no means necessary for a buyer to employ the services of an investment banking firm, especially if it is large enough to employ in-house expertise on a full-time basis. Larger buyers will only employ investment bankers for peak load situations. It is also possible for a buyer's top management to occasionally employ an investment banker as a reward for gratis work done in the past. It is in hopes of such work that some investment bankers give away a limited amount of free advice or research.

INVESTOR AND PUBLIC RELATIONS

A public company that acquires another entity must report on the transaction in its filings with the Securities and Exchange Commission (SEC). When doing so, the buyer should clearly state its reasoning for completing the acquisition. In addition, many public companies conduct quarterly conference calls, where they report on the most recently completed quarter's results and respond to questions from anyone attending the call. Attendees are frequently analysts who follow the company's stock, and who may alter their buy/sell recommendations to the investing public as a result of that call.

The investor relations officer (IRO), who is responsible for the conference call, must be extremely well-prepared for analyst questions regarding an acquisition. If not, analysts and major shareholder will note any inept preparation, which reduces their trust in management's ability to make the acquisition a success, and which in turn may lead to a sell-off of the company's stock. Thus, the IRO should over-communicate about the acquisition, and be willing to thoroughly discuss the primary terms of and rationale for the deal. Those attending the call on behalf of the company (generally the CEO, CFO, and IRO) must also be prepared to discuss in broad terms how the company intends to integrate the acquiree into its operations, and what types of synergies it plans to achieve.

The IRO must extend this level of conference-call preparation to other acquisitions that the company has made in the recent past. Listeners may ask how well preceding acquisitions have been integrated, so the IRO should prepare answers in advance, describing those integration activities, and remaining integration tasks to be completed. If an acquisition is not going well, then don't hide it—be honest with listeners, state the situation, and note what the company is doing to mitigate the problem. By doing so, the company's stock price may still slide, but less than would be the case if it hid the problem until the situation had worsened.

The IRO must be in continual communication with those people involved in acquisitions for the company, in order to create well-supported communications with the investment community about why the company has completed an acquisition, and how well the subsequent integration activities are progressing.

Relations with the outside community are still important even if a company is privately held, especially if the buyer is in the retail business. If an acquisition can potentially cause controversy, then customers could boycott the company. While it may not be possible to entirely sidestep such problems, the buyer should involve its public relations staff in the acquisition process as early as possible. This group can develop a range of possible scenarios, as well as a variety of pre-packaged responses. This level of preparation keeps the buyer from appearing to be a lumbering and insensitive corporate monolith.

LENDERS

Lenders play an extremely important role in an acquisition, and frequently from a negative perspective. Many debt agreements contain a provision stating that the lender can accelerate the loan if there is a change in control of the borrower. Thus, if an acquisition target has debt and the buyer cannot afford to pay off the debt at the point of purchase, the lender effectively has control over the acquisition. It can delay an acquisition by negotiating at length with other lenders to see whose debt has a senior position, and can also require extensive additional guarantees.

Lenders may also be involved in an acquisition from a positive perspective; they lend funds to the buyer specifically to acquire a target. This is particularly common when management initiates a leveraged buyout (LBO), where nearly the entire payment comes from debt. If so, the senior lender takes a senior position in the company's assets and in exchange lends roughly 50 to 60 percent of the total purchase price. Subordinate lenders issue about 20 to 30 percent of the total purchase price in exchange for a higher interest rate and a junior collateral position, while the remaining funding comes from new equity.

In short, approval from either the target's or buyer's lenders is commonly needed for many acquisitions, and can significantly slow down deal completion.

LINE MANAGERS

The buyer's line managers will probably be responsible for managing any newly acquired company. Upon them falls some of the more technical due diligence activities, substantially more integration work, and virtually all of the subsequent day-to-day management tasks. Despite this level of tactical support, the acquisition team does not always ask the line managers what their opinions are regarding the advisability of a purchase. The reverse should be the case; line managers can be extremely knowledgeable about the reputations, strengths, and weaknesses of target companies, and may have close ties to a number of their employees. The sales manager can be an especially valuable source of information, since his salespeople may be competing against the target on a regular basis.

However, before relying entirely on the opinions of line managers when approving acquisitions, there are three issues to consider. First, a line manager may be threatened at the prospect of merging with another company, if there is any probability that he will be pushed aside in favor of the manager occupying his position in the target company. Second, he may be comfortable in his position, and not want to go through the annoyance of a broad-based integration that may require a considerable amount of travel. However, a line manager may actively support an acquisition for the sole reason that it rapidly expands his personal empire (quite possibly with an associated pay raise). In this last case, line managers tend to be especially acquisitive if the buyer's senior managers do not charge the line manager for the cost of capital used for any acquisitions; in this case, they have a stronger tendency to advise overpaying for a target. In order to gain a more balanced view of the situation, the acquisition team should consider the opinions of the line managers alongside those of other sources.

While the primary focus of this book is on *acquisitions*, it is worth noting that line managers have a strong tendency to advise against *divestitures*. Any divestiture of an area under a line manager's control reduces his area of responsibility, which may therefore lead to a cut in his compensation.

SPECIALIST CONSULTANTS

Though the acquisition participants noted thus far are the primary players in acquisition transactions, there is also a need for specialist consultants who are experts in areas that could cause major liabilities for the buyer—specifically, in the areas of environmental, human resources, and regulatory liabilities.

If the buyer is considering acquiring a company that owns property or deals with hazardous materials, then it absolutely must engage the services of an environmental consultant, who can test for and evaluate the extent of any pollution. As explained further in the Government Regulation chapter, the Comprehensive Environmental Response, Compensation, and Liability Act (CERCLA) allows the government to attach liability to the current owner or operator of a polluted site, the owner or operator at the time when hazardous disposal occurred, the entity that arranged for disposal, and the entity that transported the substance to the site. In short, CERCLA was designed to cast a very wide net in search of anyone who can pay for a cleanup operation. Even if the buyer thinks that the probability of environmental liability is quite low, the amount of payout associated with that risk is inordinately high, so it makes sense to use an environmental consultant to evaluate the situation.

Liabilities for human resources problems are vastly smaller than for environmental issues, but when multiplied by the number of employees involved, can still result in excessive potential liabilities. A human resources consultant can assist in a number of ways. One skilled in labor relations can review a target's history of dealing with unions to estimate any labor relations problems that the buyer may be inheriting. Other consultants can provide advice on outstanding or potential suits related to wrongful discharge or discrimination, while others can provide guidance related to human resources issues in foreign countries, or the cost of a target's benefit and pension plans.

If a target company operates within a highly regulated industry, the buyer should hire a regulatory expert who can advise on how regulations will affect the acquisition. The buyer will also want to plan for any expected changes in current regulations, for which the expert can provide advice. If the buyer is likely to run into regulatory problems as a specific result of the contemplated acquisition, this is also an area about which to obtain advice.

In all three cases, the level of loss experienced by a buyer can be considerable, and so warrants the use of experts. These individuals may be expensive, but their advice can help a buyer avoid some cavernous pitfalls.

PLAYERS IN HOSTILE TAKEOVERS

The cast of characters changes somewhat when a buyer attempts an acquisition despite the wishes of the target's management team and board of directors. This scenario arises only for public companies with a broad shareholder base, allowing the buyer to directly appeal to the target's shareholders. To do so, the buyer hires a proxy solicitation firm, which solicits proxies from the target's shareholders. The buyer then votes the proxies at a stockholders' meeting that is called for the purpose of voting on a change in directors. If the buyer can place a majority of its directors on the target's board, then it can have them vote in favor of the acquisition.

This process can involve a great deal of investor lobbying. In particular, the buyer must be willing to present its case directly to any institutional investors in the target company, since they are most likely to have the most significant stockholdings. Also, it is much easier to contact a few institutional investors than the thousands of retail investors who may own a similar number of shares.

The target company can bring in additional players to avoid an unwanted acquisition. One option is to have a third party, known as a "white squire," purchase a large block of the target's stock and hold those shares until the acquisition threat has passed. This usually requires a standstill agreement by the white squire, so that it does not sell its stock to the prospective buyer. The target may also ask for a right of first refusal, so that it can buy back the stock if another party attempts to buy the white squire's holdings.

The target can take a step further and approach a more acceptable third party about buying it. This entity, known as a "white knight," generally has better relations with the target than the buyer. This is a last resort for the target, since it will unquestionably lose its independence to someone.

INTEGRATION TEAM

The integration team is mentioned last, because the bulk of its activities begin after the other players have departed. The integration team is responsible for creating and monitoring an integration plan that maximizes the value of the acquiree to the buyer by implementing a variety of synergies. It does this by facilitating changes that are the responsibility of line managers to implement. This group is described in much greater detail in the Acquisition Integration chapter.

SUMMARY

The CEO should set a general acquisition strategy for the corporate acquisition team, and then get out of the way and let the team search for prospects that fall within the strategy. The team will return to the CEO from time to time with prospects. If he approves of a prospect, then the team brings in a variety of specialists, such as tax attorneys and environmental liability consultants, to conduct due diligence and hammer out a purchase agreement. If the deal is a major one or steps somewhat outside the boundaries of the original acquisition strategy, then the buyer's board of directors may be notified early for their opinions. Otherwise, the board must still pass judgment when the purchase agreement is ready for signing. Once the agreement is signed, the integration team takes over, and is responsible for merging the acquiree into the rest of the company to whatever extent will maximize synergies. Thus, many parties are involved in an acquisition. The bulk of all tactical activities are handled by the acquisition and integration teams, while strategy-setting and the ultimate purchase decision fall within the control of the CEO and board of directors.

Chapter 3

Valuing an Acquisition Target

Once a buyer has identified a prospective target, it needs to establish an initial valuation for it. Once the buyer has done so, the two parties discuss the various factors used to establish the valuation, as well as the manner of payment. If they are both reasonably satisfied with the proposed price to be paid, then the buyer issues a term sheet to the seller (see the next chapter), and the buyer then engages in a great deal of due diligence work. Thus, the valuation process is an early-stage bottleneck in the acquisition process.

In this chapter, we describe a variety of valuation methods, the concept of the control premium, the discounted cash flow model, a variety of qualitative factors that can influence the valuation, and reasons for using different forms of payment.

ALTERNATIVE VALUATION METHODS

There are a number of ways to value a target company. While the most common is discounted cash flow, it is best to evaluate a number of alternative methods, and compare their results to see if several approaches arrive at approximately the same general valuation. This gives the buyer solid grounds for making its offer.

Using a variety of methods is especially important for valuing newer target companies with minimal historical results, and especially for those growing quickly—all of their cash is being used for growth, so cash flow is an inadequate basis for valuation.

If the target company is publicly held, then the buyer can simply base its valuation on the *current market price per share*, multiplied by the number of shares outstanding. The actual price paid is usually higher, since the buyer must also account for the control premium (see the following section). The current trading price of a company's stock is not a good valuation tool if the stock is thinly traded. In this case, a small number of trades can alter the market price to a substantial extent, so that the buyer's estimate is far off from the value it would normally assign to the target. Most target companies do not issue publicly traded stock, so other methods must be used to derive their valuation.

When a private company wants to be valued using a market price, it can use the unusual ploy of filing for an initial public offering while also being courted by the buyer. By doing so, the buyer is forced to make an offer that is near the market valuation at which the target expects its stock to be traded. If the buyer declines to bid that high, then the target still has the option of going public and realizing value by selling shares to the general public. However, given the expensive control measures mandated by the Sarbanes-Oxley Act and the stock lockup periods required for many new public companies, a target's shareholders are usually more than willing to accept a buyout offer if the price is reasonably close to the target's expected market value.

Another option is to use a *revenue multiple* or *EBITDA multiple*. It is quite easy to look up the market capitalizations and financial information for thousands of publicly held companies. The buyer then converts this information into a multiples table, such as the one shown in Exhibit 3.1, which itemizes a selection of valuations within the consulting industry. The table should be restricted to comparable companies in the same industry as that of the seller,

Exhibit 3.1 Comparable Valuations Table

| | | ($ Millions) | | EBITDA* | Revenue | EBITDA* |
	Market Capitalization	Revenue	EBITDA*	Percentage	Multiple	Multiple
Large Caps (>$5 billion)						
Electronic Data Systems	$ 9,720	$ 22,134	$ 1,132	5%	0.4	8.6
General Dynamics	$ 36,220	$ 27,240	$ 3,113	11%	1.3	11.6
Lockheed Martin	$ 43,020	$ 41,862	$ 4,527	11%	1.0	9.5
Northrop Grumman	$ 25,350	$ 32,018	$ 3,006	9%	0.8	8.4
Medium Caps (<$5 billion)						
ManTech International	$ 1,630	$ 1,448	$ 114	8%	1.1	14.3
Perot Systems	$ 1,850	$ 2,612	$ 184	7%	0.7	10.1
SAIC, Inc.	$ 3,640	$ 8,935	$ 666	7%	0.4	5.5
SRA International	$ 1,540	$ 1,269	$ 93	7%	1.2	16.6
Small Caps (<$1.5 billion)						
CACI, Inc.	$ 1,470	$ 1,938	$ 146	8%	0.8	10.1
ICF International	$ 258	$ 727	$ 71	10%	0.4	3.6
SI International	$ 299	$ 511	$ 39	8%	0.6	7.7
Stanley, Inc.	$ 570	$ 409	$ 25	6%	1.4	22.8

(Continued)

59

Exhibit 3.1 (Continued)

	Market Capitalization	Revenue	EBITDA*	EBITDA* Percentage	Revenue Multiple	EBITDA* Multiple
	($ Millions)					
Micro Caps (<$250 million)						
Dynamics Research Corp.	$ 92	$ 230	$ 13	6%	0.4	7.1
Keynote Systems	$ 210	$ 68	$ (5)	–7%	3.1	(42.0)
NCI, Inc.	$ 249	$ 304	$ 22	7%	0.8	11.3
Tier Technologies	$ 152	$ 111	$ (22)	–20%	1.4	(6.9)
Averages by Capitalization						
Large caps	$ 28,578	$ 30,814	$ 2,945	10%	0.9	9.7
Medium caps	$ 2,165	$ 3,566	$ 264	7%	0.6	8.2
Small caps	$ 649	$ 896	$ 70	8%	0.7	9.2
Micro caps	$ 176	$ 178	$ 2	1%	1.0	87.9

*EBITDA = Earnings before interest, taxes, depreciation and amortization.

and of roughly the same market capitalization. If some of the information for other companies is unusually high or low, then eliminate these outlying values in order to obtain a median value for the company's size range. Also, it is better to use a multi-day average of market prices, since these figures are subject to significant daily fluctuation.

The buyer can then use this table to derive an approximation of the price to be paid for a target company. For example, if a target has sales of $100 million, and the market capitalization for several public companies in the same revenue range is 1.4 times revenue, then the buyer could value the target at $140 million. This method is most useful for a turnaround situation or a fast-growth company, where there are few profits (if any). However, the revenue multiple method only pays attention to the first line of the income statement and completely ignores profitability. To avoid the risk of paying too much based on a revenue multiple, it is also possible to compile an EBITDA (i.e., earnings before interest, taxes, depreciation, and amortization) multiple for the same group of comparable public companies, and use that information to value the target.

Better yet, use the revenue multiple and the EBITDA multiple in concert. If the revenue multiple reveals a high valuation and the EBITDA multiple a low one, then it is entirely possible that the target is essentially buying revenues with low-margin products or services, or extending credit to financially weak customers. Conversely, if the revenue multiple yields a lower valuation than the EBITDA multiple, this is more indicative of a late-stage company that is essentially a cash cow, or one where management is cutting costs to increase profits, but possibly at the expense of harming revenue growth.

The revenue and EBITDA multiples just noted are not the only ones available. The table can be expanded to include the *price/earnings ratio* for a public company's traded stock. Also, if the comparable company provides one-year projections, then the revenue multiple can be re-named a *trailing multiple* (for historical 12-month revenue), and the forecast can be used as the basis for a *forward multiple* (for projected 12-month revenue). The forward multiple gives a better estimate of value, because it incorporates expectations about the future. The forward multiple should only be used if the forecast comes from guidance that is issued by a public company. The company knows that its stock price will drop if it does not achieve its forecast, so the forecast is unlikely to be aggressive.

Revenue multiples are the best technique for valuing high-growth companies, since these entities are usually pouring resources into their growth, and have minimal profits to report. Such companies clearly have a great deal of value, but it is not revealed through their profitability numbers.

However, multiples can be misleading. When acquisitions occur within an industry, the best financial performers with the fewest underlying problems are the choicest acquisition targets, and therefore will be acquired first. When other companies in the same area later put themselves up for sale, they will use the earlier multiples to justify similarly high prices. However, because they may have lower market shares, higher cost structures, older products, and so on, the multiples may not be valid. Thus, it is useful to know some of the underlying characteristics of the companies that were previously sold, to see if the comparable multiple should be applied to the current target company.

Another possibility is to replace the market capitalization figure in the table with *enterprise value*. The enterprise value is a company's market capitalization, plus its total debt outstanding, minus any cash on hand. In essence, it is a company's theoretical takeover price, because the buyer would have to buy all of the stock and pay off existing debt, while pocketing any remaining cash.

Another way to value an acquisition is to use a *database of comparable transactions* to determine what was paid for other recent acquisitions. Investment bankers have access to this information through a variety of private databases, while a great deal of information can be collected online through public filings or press releases.

The buyer can also derive a valuation based on a target's *underlying real estate values*. This method only works in those isolated cases where the target has a substantial real estate portfolio. For example, in the retailing industry, where some chains own the property on which their stores are situated, the value of the real estate is greater than the cash flow generated by the stores themselves. In cases where the business is financially troubled, it is entirely possible that the purchase price is based entirely on the underlying real estate, with the operations of the business itself being valued at essentially zero. The buyer then uses the value of the real estate as the primary reason for completing the deal. In some situations, the prospective buyer has no real estate experience, and so is more likely to heavily discount the potential value of any real estate when making an offer. If the seller wishes to increase its price, it could consider selling the real estate prior to the sale transaction. By doing so, it converts a potential real estate sale price (which might otherwise be discounted by the buyer) into an achieved sale with cash in the bank, and may also record a one-time gain on its books based on the asset sale, which may have a positive impact on its sale price.

An acquiree's real estate may even be the means for an acquirer to finance the deal. For example, if the acquiree owns property, it may be possible to enter into a sale-and-leaseback transaction which generates enough cash to pay for the acquisition. Another possibility is to look for property leases held by the acquiree that are below current market rates, and sublease them for a profit. Finally, it may be possible to consolidate acquiree locations and sell any remaining properties that are no longer needed.

If a target has products that the buyer could develop in-house, then an alternative valuation method is to compare the *cost of in-house development* to the cost of acquiring the completed product through the target. This type of valuation is especially important if the market is expanding rapidly right now, and the buyer will otherwise forgo sales if it takes the time to pursue an in-house development path. In this case, the proper valuation technique is to combine the cost of an in-house development effort with the present value of profits forgone by waiting to complete the in-house project. Interestingly, this is the only valuation technique where most of the source material comes from the buyer's financial statements, rather than those of the seller.

The most conservative valuation method of all is the *liquidation value* method. This is an analysis of what the selling entity would be worth if all of its assets were to be sold off. This method assumes that the ongoing value of the company as a business entity is eliminated, leaving the individual auction prices at which its fixed assets, properties, and other assets can be sold off, less any outstanding liabilities. It is useful for the buyer to at least estimate this number, so that it can determine its downside risk in case it completes the acquisition, but the acquired business then fails utterly.

The *replacement value* method yields a somewhat higher valuation than the liquidation value method. Under this approach, the buyer calculates what it would cost to duplicate the target company. The analysis addresses the replacement of the seller's key infrastructure. This can yield surprising results if the seller owns infrastructure that originally required lengthy regulatory approval. For example, if the seller owns a chain of mountain huts that are located on government property, it is essentially impossible to replace them at all, or only at vast expense. An additional factor in this analysis is the time required to replace the target. If the time period for replacement is considerable, the buyer may be forced to pay a premium in order to gain quick access to a key market.

It is also possible to create a *hybrid valuation model* that mixes several of the above methods. For example, the buyer could calculate the liquidation value of a target, and then add to that number the next two or three years of free cash flow (as described later in the Discounted Cash Flow Model section). This method yields a conservative valuation that the buyer would be hard put *not* to realize, and which might form the basis for a minimum bid.

While all of the above methods can be used for valuation, they usually supplement the primary method, which is the discounted cash flow (DCF) method. That method will be discussed shortly in the Discounted Cash Flow Model section.

THE CONTROL PREMIUM

Why does a buyer offer to pay more for a target than the price at which the target's shares currently trade? One reason is certainly to keep other potential bidders from entering the fray. However, the real reason is that shares trade based on their value to individual shareholders, who have no control over the business; thus, a share price is only based on the prospective financial return that a shareholder expects to achieve. However, if a buyer wishes to obtain control over the target, then it should expect to pay a control premium over the current stock price. By doing so, it has complete control over the potential size and timing of cash flows. Historically, this has made the control premium worth somewhere in the range of 35 to 50 percent of a target's freely traded stock value. Recent control premiums for the purchase of publicly traded companies can be found in the annual *Control Premium Study* that is published by Mergerstat (located at www.mergerstat.com).

SYNERGY GAINS

If the buyer pays the full share value of a target, as well as a control premium, then how does it expect to earn a return? The target's existing shareholders appear to be receiving all of the value inherent in the business. There are certainly cases where the target's stock price may be unusually low, such as when industry is at the low point of a business cycle, where profits are minimized. In such cases, the buyer snaps up deals based on timing. However, these are isolated instances. In most cases, the buyer is depending on the realization of synergies between its own company and the target, which may be considerable.

A buyer with expert knowledge of potential synergy gains can earn substantial amounts that comfortably exceed the purchase price. However, a buyer may run into an experienced seller who wants a share of those synergy gains. If the seller wants payment for an excessive portion of the expected gains, the buyer must walk away from the deal—there is simply no way to earn a profit from the transaction.

Synergies are only realized by strategic buyers, not financial buyers. A financial buyer simply buys a business in order to hold it and gain appreciation value from its internal growth over time. A strategic buyer, on the other hand, is willing to pay a higher price in the knowledge that it can squeeze out extra value. Thus, the strategic buyer may be willing to pay a higher price than a financial buyer, perhaps in the range of a 5 to 20 percent premium over what a financial buyer would pay.

Thus, a canny seller will court strategic buyers in order to maximize the price paid, but must be aware that it has to leave a generous amount of the potential synergies to the buyer, in order to make the acquisition sufficiently tempting.

THE DISCOUNTED CASH FLOW (DCF) MODEL

The best possible reason to buy a company is for the cash that it can generate. The DCF model is designed to reveal the *free cash flow* that is available for distribution to investors at the end of each year shown in the model. This means that the model must not only reveal the cash generated by ongoing operations, but also subtract out all planned capital expenditures and tax payments, so that completely unrestricted cash surpluses or shortfalls are revealed for each year in the model.

The typical DCF model includes a projection of the target's cash flows for the next five years, plus a terminal value for what the target theoretically could be sold for at the end of that time period (which is based on prices currently being obtained for comparable companies). An example of a DCF is shown in Exhibit 3.2.

The buyer should beware of models where the terminal value is by far the largest component of the model; the terminal value is the least predictable part of the valuation, because it is the furthest into the future and assumes a specific sale price that is very difficult to justify. If the terminal value comprises the bulk of the DCF, then the buyer will

Exhibit 3.2   Discounted Cash Flow Model

(000s)	Year 1	Year 2	Year 3	Year 4	Year 5	Terminal Value
+ Revenues	$ 438	$ 473	$ 511	$ 552	$ 596	
− Cost of goods sold	$ 175	$ 189	$ 204	$ 221	$ 238	
= Gross margin	$ 263	$ 284	$ 307	$ 331	$ 358	
− General and administrative	$ 171	$ 184	$ 199	$ 215	$ 232	
= Earnings before interest and taxes	$ 92	$ 99	$ 107	$ 116	$ 125	
− Interest	$ 5	$ 5	$ 5	$ 5	$ 5	
− Taxes	$ 33	$ 35	$ 38	$ 41	$ 44	
− Incremental working capital change	$ 22	$ 24	$ 26	$ 30	$ 33	
− Incremental fixed asset change	$ 15	$ 16	$ 18	$ 19	$ 20	
+ Depreciation	$ 14	$ 15	$ 17	$ 18	$ 19	
= Cash flow	$ 31	$ 34	$ 37	$ 39	$ 42	$ 120
Discount rate	10%	10%	10%	10%	10%	
Annual discount rate	0.90909	0.82645	0.75131	0.68301	0.62092	0.56447
Discounted cash flows	$ 28	$ 28	$ 28	$ 26	$ 26	$ 68
Net present value	$ 204					

need to supplement the DCF analysis with other forms of valuation analysis.

A major part of the DCF analysis is the interest rate that is used for discounting the value of future cash flows to the current period. This interest rate is equivalent to the buyer's incremental cost of capital. The cost of capital is the weighted average cost of the buyer's debt, preferred stock, and equity. The cost of equity is the most difficult to

Exhibit 3.3   Weighted Average Cost of Capital Calculation

Capital Type	Amount Outstanding	Interest Rate	Cost
Debt	$25,000,000	7%	$1,750,000
Preferred stock	10,000,000	10%	1,000,000
Equity	30,000,000	14%	4,200,000
Totals	$65,000,000	**10.7%**	$6,950,000

determine, but usually involves the capital asset pricing model (see the author's Financial Analysis book for an explanation). On an extremely simplified basis, the cost of equity is at least 5 to 7 percent higher than the current interest rate on U.S. government treasury notes, and can be substantially higher. As an example, the following table shows the dollar amount of the three components of a company's cost of capital, yielding a weighted average cost of capital of 10.7 percent.

It is preferable to use the *incremental* cost of capital, which incorporates the buyer's most recent cost of debt. The incremental rate is better, because that is the rate at which the buyer will need to obtain funding to pay for the target.

It is also possible to adjust the cost of capital for the perceived risk of the target company. For example, if the target is a well-established one with predictable cash flows, the buyer can simply use its cost of capital as the discount rate. However, if the target's cash flows are more uncertain, the buyer can add a risk percentage to its discount rate. By doing so, cash flows that are further in the future will be worth less in the DCF, resulting in a lower valuation for the target.

The buyer may also adjust the discount rate downwards for any especially valuable characteristics that the seller may have, such as subject-matter experts or patents on key technology. However, this is an entirely subjective reduction. The buyer would do better to attempt to quantify these characteristics of the seller elsewhere in the model, such as an increase in revenues from company-wide use of the seller's patented products.

The interest rate used in the debt portion of the cost of capital can vary considerably, resulting in significant changes in the value of the target company. For example, if interest rates increase, the buyer's cost of capital also increases. When the buyer then uses this increased cost of capital as its discount factor in the DCF model, target company valuations will decline. Conversely, if interest rates drop, then target values increase. Thus, external economic factors driving interest rates are directly related to acquisition prices.

Also, the size of the target can alter the buyer's cost of capital. For example, if the prospective deal would require a large amount of financing by the buyer, it is likely that its incremental debt cost will increase, which in turn affects its cost of capital. If this is the case, then use the projected increase in the cost of capital as the most appropriate discount rate in the DCF model; this will make the acquisition look less attractive.

The DCF is the most reliable method for valuing a mature, slow-growth company with established cash flows. It is not applied so frequently to high-growth entities that are using all available cash to support their increasing working capital needs. Instead, buyers tend to use comparable valuations for these targets. However, it is always of some value to also run a DCF, because it reveals a reliable minimum valuation for the target. The buyer can also create a variety of cash flow projections for the target that are further out in the future than the usual five years used for the model, to get some idea of what the target's cash flows will be like once its high-growth period is over.

CONSTRUCTING CASH FLOW SCENARIOS

Where does the buyer obtain the information needed to construct a cash flow analysis? The seller will prefer to show estimates of future sales, which inevitably reveal an optimistic "hockey stock" of sudden growth in "just a few more months." If the buyer were to use just these projected numbers, it would likely arrive at a valuation that is too high, and overpay for the seller. A better method is to create multiple scenarios, where the seller's estimates are reserved for the most optimistic version. Another "most likely" estimate should be based on the seller's most recent historical results, while a conservative version assumes that the seller's historical results worsen significantly.

While the use of three cash flow scenarios certainly shows some valuation prudence, it can hide unsupported assumptions within the scenarios. For example, an analyst might assume a simplistic revenue decline of 10 percent in the conservative version, which is not based on any concrete risk analysis. Instead, use documented changes in specific variables in the three versions. For example, if there appears to be a risk of soft pricing in the market, then use the conservative scenario to specifically model price declines of various sizes. Similarly, if there is a risk of supplier bottlenecks, then model the impact of price increases for key materials. Also, if the target must match research expenditures elsewhere in the industry, then review percentage changes in these expenditures. By taking the time to document these more detailed analyses, a buyer can determine the price points, volume levels, and cost structures at which a target breaks even, and when the target can potentially earn a great deal of money.

Another factor to consider in one or more of the valuation scenarios is the presence or absence of seller risk guarantees. For example, if the seller is guaranteeing to pay for any undocumented lawsuits or payouts related to documented lawsuits, then the buyer can eliminate this factor from its conservative scenario. In essence, the more risks the seller guarantees, the lower the expenses shown in the model, and the higher the valuation that the buyer can offer to the seller.

Once constructed, the buyer should multiply each of these cash flow versions by a weighting factor, and not simply average them. The most likely scenario should receive the bulk of the weighting, such as 60 or 70 percent, with the outlying conservative and optimistic versions receiving the remainder. Thus, a 20–60–20 or 15–70–15 weighting essentially assumes that the seller's most recent historical results are most likely to continue into the future.

A more conservative method of cash flow analysis is to construct an estimate based entirely on historical results, with a weighting system that favors the most recent year. For example, if the buyer wants to model the target's past five years of results, it can multiply the target's cash flows by five for the most recent year, by four for the immediately preceding year, and so on. Once all five years have been added together, divide by 15 to arrive at the weighted cash flow for the five-year period. The resulting 5,4,3,2,1 weighting system thereby gives some credence to relatively old cash flows, and great merit to recent results. This method is not recommended, since it is entirely based on prior results, and gives no weighting at all to a target's future prospects.

CASH FLOW ADJUSTING FACTORS

The buyer cannot simply run a DCF of a target's existing operations and consider the job done. This would imply that the buyer intends to make virtually no changes to the target once it has completed the acquisition. In reality, there are multiple changes to be considered, many of which should be included in the projected cash flow.

In many acquisitions, the buyer assumes that the combined entities will be able to increase revenues beyond what the companies were achieving separately. However, revenue synergies are notoriously difficult to achieve, because they require the cooperation of a third party (customers). An experienced buyer usually reduces or even eliminates any revenue synergies in the cash flow model. Instead, it focuses on cost reductions, which are entirely within its control.

Not only should the buyer *not* budget for revenue gains, but it should strongly consider modeling for a modest revenue *decline* at the target that is caused by some degradation in its customer base. This is caused by any changes in service levels, sales people, or products that customers may experience as a result of the acquisition. Also, competitors will likely be circling the target's customers like sharks, hoping to pick off a few. Further, if the buyer is only planning to acquire a single division of a larger company, the target may lose some customers simply because the associated services or products of its parent company will no longer be sold, or not as a package. Thus, a reasonable modeling technique is to incorporate a modest decline in the target's customer base, especially during the initial year of the acquisition. A common reduction in the customer base is in the range of 2 to 5 percent.

The buyer must also assume a variety of acquisition expenses, including legal fees, valuation services, appraisals, environmental audits, and financial audits. If the buyer has engaged in a number of acquisitions, then it can easily compile a database of what these costs have been in the past, and use it to estimate such costs in a prospective valuation. If the buyer anticipates diverting a substantial amount of management time toward the integration of the target's operations into those of the buyer, then it can also estimate the impact of this "soft" cost on the entire business.

One likely cost-control scenario is that some employees will be let go. If so, there will be some cost savings by eliminating their positions, but there will also be a short-term additional costs associated with severance pay. If the buyer is taking on this obligation, then it must factor severance pay into its cash flow assumptions.

A special case is adjustments to the cash flows associated with a target's defined-benefit pension plan. These costs can vary substantially over time, so an analyst should intensively review the actuarial assumptions underlying any such plans. For example, if the buyer believes that the plan is underfunded, it has reasonable grounds for demanding a reduction in the purchase price, so that it can offset the imminent funding liability. Conversely, if the plan is overfunded, the seller can bargain for a purchase price increase, which effectively pays it back for the amount of the overfunding. The funding status is by no means obvious, since it is driven by the future interest-rate assumption used by the plan actuary; the higher the rate, the fewer existing assets are needed to offset projected plan liabilities. Consequently, arguments over the correct interest-rate assumption will alter the purchase price, and will result in changes to the DCF.

Another issue is the cyclicality of the industry in which the target is located. If there are strong historical cycles, then the buyer should assume that there will be a recurrence. This requires that the cash flow model assume the presence of both the upside and downside of that cycle, using historical information for both the duration and size of the cycle. This gives the buyer a reasonable idea of how cash flows will change over time. In many instances, highly variable cyclical results will force the buyer to abandon a deal, because the downside of the cycle eliminates or reverses the profits generated during other years.

An area missed by many cash flow models is the immediate sale of some assets following the acquisition. Either party may have duplicative or obsolete assets that can be dispositioned for immediate cash. If the buyer can pre-sell some assets before a purchase agreement even closes, then this is a "hard" cash inflow to include in the cash flow model.

The buyer should also be aware of the seller's fixed asset replacement cycle. It is entirely possible that the buyer has delayed key asset purchases in order to give the appearance of having excellent cash flow. However, its equipment and facilities may now be so run down that the buyer must expend significant amounts over multiple years to replace the assets. The dollar value of the replacement amounts should be gleaned during the due diligence stage, and entered into the DCF.

The buyer should also include in the DCF the impact of any cost escalation clauses in the seller's contracts with its suppliers. For example, there may be a series of scheduled annual increases in a building lease, or a price increase in a raw materials contract. As was the case with fixed asset replacements, these costs are not readily apparent, and must be found during the due diligence process.

Finally, the buyer may have some concern about the accuracy of the financial statements it is using to compile a cash forecast, if the target cannot provide audited financial statements. If there has never been an audit, and especially if the buyer's due diligence indicates some issues with the presented financial information, then it may have to adjust cash projections downward, or only base a valuation on the most conservative scenario. To avoid this, the target should have its books audited for the past year (and preferably two years), in order to qualify for high cash flow assumptions in the buyer's valuation model.

THE EARNOUT

There are times when the buyer and the seller have entirely different concepts of the valuation to be used for the acquisition, usually because the buyer is basing its valuation on the seller's historical performance, while the seller is using a much higher forward-looking view of its prospective performance. The *earnout* is frequently used to bridge the valuation perception gap between the two parties. Under an earnout, the seller's managers and/or shareholders will be paid an additional amount by the buyer if upon the achievement of specific performance targets (usually the same ones the seller has already claimed it will achieve during the acquisition negotiations).

The earnout is also a useful tool for the buyer, because the seller's management team has a strong incentive to grow the business for the next few years. In addition, the buyer can shift a portion of its purchase price into a future liability that can likely be paid from cash earned in the future by the seller. It is also useful for the seller's shareholders, since it defers income taxes on the payment.

However, many earnouts also result in lawsuits, because the buyer merges the acquiree into another business unit, charges corporate overhead to it, or shifts key staff elsewhere in the company—all factors making it extremely difficult for the acquiree's management team to still earn the additional payment, or even to determine what its performance has become. Even if there are no lawsuits, the acquiree's management team may be so focused on achieving their earnout that they do not assist the rest of the buying entity with other matters, so that corporate-level goals are not reached. Also, if the earnout award is based strictly on the achievement of revenue, rather than profit, then the acquiree's management team may pursue unprofitable sales in order to meet their earnout goals.

The problems with earnouts can be mitigated by continuing to track the acquiree's performance separately in the financial statements, carefully defining the earnout calculation in the original acquisition document, requiring earnouts to be based solely on net income achieved, and by adding an additional layer of compensation that is based on working more closely with the rest of the buying company, such as commissions for cross-selling. Also, to keep the acquiree happy, do not institute a "cliff" goal, where no bonus is paid unless the entire target is reached. Instead, use a sliding scale, so that some bonus is paid even if only a portion of the performance target is achieved.

QUALITATIVE FACTORS

Thus far, the valuation discussion has centered entirely on a quantitative analysis of how much to pay for the selling entity. While quantitative analysis certainly forms the core of a valuation, the buyer must also consider a broad array of qualitative factors. Here is a sampling of the more common ones:

- *Difficulty of duplication.* If a buyer perceives that the barriers to entering a seller's field of operations are high, or if the cost of duplicating the seller's operations is excessive, the buyer may be more inclined to pay a premium for the business. For example, a proprietary database may take so long to duplicate that a buyer will value the seller just based on the cost it would otherwise incur to create the database from scratch.
- *Risk of expiring contracts.* A seller whose revenues are tied to short-term sales, without immediate prospects for renewing the backlog, will be perceived to have a lower valuation than an entity possessing a strong backlog and clear evidence of long-term sales agreements with its customers.
- *Management.* A seller's cost structure, perception in the marketplace, and customer relations are driven in large part by the quality

of its management team. If this group is perceived to be first class, it can increase the corporate valuation, since these people typically have exceptional skill in growing businesses and in anticipating and overcoming operational problems.

- *Client base.* A significant factor in determining valuation is the size, type, and distribution of clients. For example, a seller with a single client will be perceived to be at great risk of losing all of its sales if the client is dissatisfied. Alternatively, a broad mix of clients, particularly those large enough to support multiple sales, will reduce the perceived risk of sales loss.

- *Inherent risk.* A seller whose financial performance can be dramatically affected by adverse situations will have a comparatively lower valuation. For example, farm businesses can be severely affected by drought conditions.

- *Disaster analysis.* Even beyond the inherent risk just noted, the buyer should closely review the characteristics of the seller's business to see if there is any risk of a truly catastrophic failure, such as a facility being destroyed because it is situated on an earthquake fault line. Even if the probability of a disaster is low, the consequences may be so large that the buyer must either walk away from the deal or find a mitigating action to offset the risk.

- *Lawsuits.* Nothing will drive a buyer away faster than an unresolved lawsuit, especially one with a demand for a large settlement. Even if there is no lawsuit, the prospect of one, as evidenced by lawsuits targeted at others in the same industry, can have a negative impact on valuation.

- *Patents.* If a seller has established key patents or processes that give it a clear competitive advantage, this can increase its valuation level.

- *Branding.* If a seller has invested a great deal of time and effort in creating brands for its products or services, this can give it a significant boost in valuation. However, if the seller has not continued to invest in its brand, then there is a risk of brand degradation that will require years to rebuild.

It is best to wait until the quantitative analysis has been completed, and then adjust the baseline quantitative results with estimates of the additional impact of the items just noted.

WHICH VALUATION METHOD IS BEST?

The buyer should use a number of different valuation models. By doing so, it can obtain a high-low range of estimates that gives it the general boundaries for a valuation. The best valuation estimate usually begins with a DCF analysis, adjusted for comparable transaction multiples. For example, a standard DCF analysis may reveal that a target is worth $15 million which is approximately 8 times its most recently reported EBITDA. However, because the target is located in a "hot" industry, with unusually high multiples of 12 times EBITDA, the buyer should consider increasing the size of its offer to match the going rate. Its alternative is to wait until such time as the industry valuation gradually declines, at which point the DCF results and comparables are in closer alignment.

An example of what a range of values could look like is shown in Exhibit 3.4, where several methods are used that were discussed earlier in the Alternative Valuation Methods section. In the example, note that the revenue multiple method yields a clearly outsize valuation, while the real estate values method results in an excessively low one. Since these valuations are clearly beyond what the other methods are indicating, the high-low valuation extremes are excluded from the likely valuation range.

The buyer should also create a hard cap on the valuation, beyond which it will not go under any circumstances. To derive it, the buyer should have a higher-level executive review all of the valuation models, and use them to set a price ceiling. This executive should not be directly involved in the prospective acquisition, and so has no personal interest in whether the buyer acquires the target. The resulting price cap is the absolute maximum that the buyer will pay. By establishing such a cap, the buyer can avoid overbidding in the heat of negotiations.

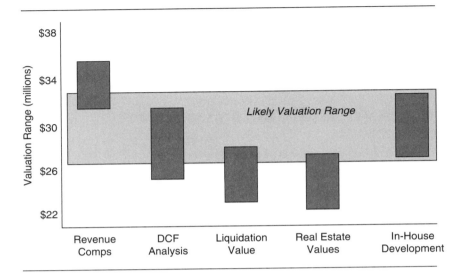

Exhibit 3.4 Valuation Range Analysis

Also, though it may initially seem odd to do so, the buyer should consider establishing a floor price. By establishing a price that is reasonably fair to the seller, there is less risk that the seller will back out at the last moment and court other bidders. Also, the seller is more cooperative with subsequent integration efforts if it believes it was paid a fair amount. Of course, if the seller is in desperate straits and wants to sell at any price, then the buyer should hardly balk at paying too little!

THE METHOD OF PAYMENT

The buyer can pay the seller in cash, debt, or stock. If the seller accepts *cash*, then it must immediately pay income taxes on its gain. However, the seller also obtains an entirely liquid asset, and is no longer tied to the future results of its business. Generally speaking, the buyer is willing to pay less if the payment is in cash, since the buyer will have to dip into its capital resources to obtain the funds, rendering it less able to deal with other issues that may require cash funding. If the buyer goes on to achieve significant synergy gains, then its shareholders will receive the entire benefit of the gains, while the seller's shareholders will receive no gain. Finally, the buyer may want to pay cash simply because it can, and other bidders cannot. If the buyer is cash-rich, and interest rates are so high that the cost of debt is prohibitive for other bidders, then it can make an offer that the seller literally cannot refuse.

If the buyer pays in *stock*, the seller gains tax-deferred status on the payment (subject to the form and amount of the payment, as described later in the Types of Acquisitions chapter). If the seller is in no immediate need of cash, this might make a stock payment a reasonable form of compensation. The other consideration in a stock payment is the buyer's expectation that it will create sufficient synergies to improve the value of its stock. By paying the seller in stock, the buyer's shareholders are forgoing some of the synergy gains to be achieved, and giving them to the seller. Conversely, if the seller suspects that it cannot achieve sufficient synergies, then it can offload some of the risk to the seller by issuing stock. Finally, if the buyer is a private company, the seller has no clear path to eventually liquidating any shares paid to it, which makes this an extremely unpalatable option.

The buyer's payment behavior is also driven by its perception of how fairly the market is currently valuing its stock. If the buyer feels that its stock price is currently trading at a maximum level, then it will be more inclined to use its stock for acquisitions, and will act in the reverse manner if its stock is trading at a low price. If the buyer consistently uses its stock to acquire multiple companies in succession, the market may feel that this is a sign that the buyer's management is of the opinion that the stock has reached a maximum valuation, and so will tend to trade down its price.

If the buyer pays with *debt*, the seller is in the worst position of all three payment scenarios. The seller's shareholders do not obtain any liquid assets in the short term, they do not share in any upside potential caused by synergy gains that would have been realized by stock ownership, and they are totally dependent on the buyer's management team to create enough cash flow to pay them. If the seller has collateralized the assets of the sold business, this is still not adequate, since the buyer may have stripped the entity of assets by the time the seller obtains possession of it.

In short, the seller prefers cash for its liquidity value, but forgos the opportunity to share in any synergy gains that stock ownership would have provided. The buyer prefers a cash payment if it is sure of its ability to achieve significant synergies, which it wants to retain through stock ownership. A debt payment is the worst-case scenario for the seller, who obtains neither liquidity nor appreciation value. While these choices are frequently driven solely by the financing available to the buyer, this is not always the case. If the buyer has the option of paying in stock or cash, but pays in cash, then this is a significant indicator that it believes it can reserve significant synergy gains for its shareholders. If the buyer has the same option but pays in stock, then it may be more concerned with its ability to achieve synergy gains, and so is offloading some of the risk onto the seller.

The buyer can model its payment options with a pro forma spreadsheet, such as the one shown in Exhibit 3.5. The exhibit contains an example of a 100% stock payment, followed by a 100% cash payment. The key financial information for the buyer and seller are identical in both scenarios. In the stock payment scenario, the buyer plans to achieve $535,000 in savings through various cost reductions. However, because it plans to pay in stock, it is passing some of the gains over to the selling shareholders, as reflected in the earnings per share figure. In the cash payment scenario, the buyer plans to achieve the same savings, but must also incur the interest cost of a loan that it uses to pay cash to the seller's shareholders. Though the added interest burden drags down the net earnings of the combined entities, the buyer's existing shareholders receive the entire synergy gains, resulting in an impressive earnings per share boost.

Exhibit 3.5 Payment Scenarios

(000s)				Adjustment	Combined
Stock Payment Scenario	Buyer	Seller	Adjustment	Notes	Results
Revenues	$24,000	$3,000			$27,000
Cost of sales	$16,000	$2,000	−$360	(1)	$17,640
Administrative	$6,000	$500	−$175	(2)	$6,325
Interest	$100	$50			$150
Income before tax	$1,900	$450			$2,885
Income tax at 34%	$646	$153			$981
Net income	$1,254	$297			$1,904
Outstanding shares	400	100			
Seller shares retired			−100		
Buyer shares issued			150	(3)	550
Earnings per share	$ 3.14	$ 2.97			$ 3.46

				Adjustment	Combined
Cash Payment Scenario	Buyer	Seller	Adjustment	Notes	Results
Revenues	$24,000	$3,000			$27,000
Cost of sales	$16,000	$2,000	−$360	(1)	$17,640
Administrative	$6,000	$500	−$175	(2)	$6,325
Interest	$100	$50	$180	(4)	$330
Income before tax	$1,900	$450			$2,705
Income tax at 34%	$646	$153			$920
Net income	$1,254	$297			$1,785
Outstanding shares	400	100			
Seller shares retired			−100		
Buyer shares issued					400
Earnings per share	$ 3.14	$ 2.97			$ 4.46

(1) 2% reduction in purchasing costs for the combined entities.

(2) Overlapping administrative costs eliminated.

(3) Share exchange is 1.5 buyer shares for each seller share.

(4) Sale price is 1x revenues, financed with 6% loan.

SUMMARY

There are multiple ways to create a valuation for a target company, and the buyer should consider using several of them to do so. This results in a range of possible values, usually yielding a relatively narrow range of prices within which the buyer should place a bid. While there are a number of qualitative factors that can result in significant changes to the values, the buyer should be wary of unsupported changes yielding substantial boosts in the valuation. When these additional factors are introduced, the buyer will likely find itself paying too much, and never achieving an adequate return on its investment.

The buyer should track performance information on its acquisitions, to see how the projected valuations actually turned out. If there were significant differences between the model and reality, then the buyer should be willing to constantly adjust the model to bring it closer to reality. This feedback loop is extremely valuable for obtaining more accurate valuations in the future.

Chapter 4

The Term Sheet

The term sheet clarifies the initial terms of a possible deal between the buyer and seller. It is the first documented evidence of a possible acquisition, and establishes the foundation for continued discussions between the buyer and seller, which may eventually result in a purchase agreement. The buyer controls this document, but accepts input from the seller as the two parties work together through several iterations to arrive at a mutually agreeable set of terms.

There is no legal requirement that a term sheet be used in a transaction, but there are still several excellent reasons for doing so, which are covered in the next section. We then describe the various elements of a term sheet, and give examples of each one.

REASONS FOR USING A TERM SHEET

A term sheet is non-binding, so why issue one at all? There are several excellent reasons for doing so. First, it prevents misunderstandings. The buyer and seller are about to embark on a number of review iterations of a purchase agreement and a significant amount of due diligence effort. Given the amount of labor and related expense that the parties will incur, it makes a great deal of sense to mutually agree on the general outlines of the deal, and to put those terms on paper. This greatly reduces the odds that the parties will later have a falling-out about general conceptual issues that would have otherwise appeared in the term sheet. This is especially important for an inexperienced buyer or seller (usually the seller), who is not familiar with the acquisition process.

Second, the term sheet creates a moral commitment for good faith efforts by both parties to complete the deal. Once the parties have agreed to the general structure of the deal, there is a tendency to assume that the deal will be completed, and that a party would be remiss if it did not take all reasonable steps to follow through on its "commitment." For larger companies, where the various steps of the transaction are usually handled by a team of experts, a term sheet typically sets the acquisition bureaucracy in motion, which builds momentum to get the deal done, barring considerable effort by a top executive to stop it.

Third, if the seller is conducting an auction, the term sheet is used as an intermediate step to narrow the list of potential suitors. After potential buyers have had time to review a standard packet of information describing the seller's company, the seller requests a term sheet from suitors by a specific date; anyone not submitting a term sheet is barred from further consideration in the auction process.

Fourth, some elements of the term sheet can be binding on the parties. The term sheet can define obligations for confidentiality regarding the information exchanged between the parties, though this is normally handled separately in a non-disclosure agreement. It can also specify that each party will bear its own expenses associated with the acquisition, or that each party will pay for a specific proportion of costs. The most common binding provision is a no-shop clause, where the seller agrees to deal exclusively with the buyer through a relatively brief negotiation period that typically lasts a few months. This reduces the buyer's risk that the seller will shop the purchase price specified in the term sheet to other potential suitors.

Finally, the term sheet can even be structured as a fully binding document. Under this approach, the term sheet tightens the range of excuses that either party can use to avoid consummating the purchase agreement. This format is not fair to the buyer, who has not yet completed a due diligence review of the seller, and so has no idea of what undisclosed problems the seller may have. Consequently, a seller who insists on a binding term sheet may find that the pool of potential buyers has narrowed considerably.

In summary, the term sheet is primarily useful as an initial summary of the terms of a deal. If the parties cannot agree on the contents of a term sheet, then there is no point in proceeding with any due diligence work or legal activity regarding the purchase agreement. By agreeing to a term sheet, there is a heightened probability that the parties will work together to complete the deal.

COMPONENTS OF A TERM SHEET

A term sheet outlines the general structure of a proposed deal. As such, it should mimic the more important elements of a purchase agreement, while avoiding an excessive level of detail. The letter usually begins by identifying the two parties, and then proceeds to the legal structure of the transaction. An example follows:

Date: October 10, 20__

Participants: Buyer Corporation, a Delaware corporation ("Buyer") and Seller Corporation, a Delaware Corporation ("Seller")

Transaction Structure: Buyer will acquire all of the outstanding capital stock of Seller in a Type B acquisition. This is a tax-free reorganization, with Buyer issuing its common stock to Seller's stockholders in an unregistered private placement.

The term sheet then reveals the expected amount and type of payment that the buyer intends to give to the seller's stockholders, usually with a caveat that this payment is subject to adjustment, based upon what the buyer finds during the due diligence process. This is where the buyer will state if there is any restriction on sale of the stock being used as payment. The term sheet can also stipulate any adjustments, such as reductions based on an excessive amount of outstanding payables or debt. Further, the term sheet can stipulate an "earnout" payment, where selling stockholders receive an additional payment based on the subsequent performance of the selling company. It can also describe a "true-up" provision, where selling stockholders can receive additional shares if the buying company's stock price subsequently drops. An example follows:

Payment: Barring discovery during due diligence that significantly impacts the valuation, it is anticipated that Buyer will pay to the stockholders of Seller $5,000,000 in shares of Buyer's restricted common stock, based on the average closing price of Buyer's common stock for the 10 trading days prior to closing. This price will be reduced by the amount of any outstanding debt or payables more than 30 days old as of the transaction closing date. All issued stock will be restricted for a period of 12 months from closing.

In addition, in recognition of the potential for substantial improvements in Seller's performance during 20__, Seller's stockholders will receive 8.0x of Seller's incremental EBITDA earnings in excess of $__, in the form of Buyer's restricted common stock. This payment will be based on the average closing price of Buyer's common stock for the 10 trading days prior to the end of 20__.

In addition, in recognition of the significant price swings experienced by Buyer's stock, Buyer will compute the average daily closing price for its stock for the last 10 trading days in the month of _____ and compare that to the closing price. If the closing price is less than the subsequent market price, then Buyer will issue additional stock so that the total dollar value of the closing shares and the additional shares is equal to the valuation of the stock of Seller set forth above, and as adjusted pursuant to the terms of the definitive agreement.

There may be some confusion regarding the bearing of acquisition-related expenses between the buyer and seller. In particular, an inexperienced seller may attempt to foist its acquisition-related expenses onto the prospective buyer. A brief statement should clarify that each party is responsible for its own expenses. An example follows:

Expenses: The Buyer and Seller will each be solely responsible for their respective legal, accounting, and other expenses associated with the transaction contemplated herein, including investment banking fees.

If a publicly held company purchases the selling entity with its stock, it usually does so with unregistered stock, which the selling stockholders cannot initially sell. The selling stockholders may insist on registration rights, obligating the buyer to register its shares for sale. Since registration is a cumbersome and expensive process, buyers prefer to avoid this clause, on the grounds that selling stockholders can sell their shares under Securities and Exchange Commission Rules 144 and 144(k) within six and 12 months, respectively. An example follows:

Registration Rights: The Buyer stock to be issued in connection with the transaction is restricted stock that has not been registered under the Securities Act of 1933, as amended ("Act"). In the transaction, persons receiving Buyer stock will be granted registration rights obligating Buyer to use its reasonable efforts to register the Buyer stock issued in the transaction with the Securities and Exchange Commission, with such registration rights to terminate when the Buyer stock can be sold pursuant to Rule 144.

Of significant concern to the seller is how its employees are to be treated subsequent to the acquisition. This can be as simple as a statement that they will be retained, or can be expanded to discuss their compensation. An example follows:

Personnel: It is anticipated that Buyer will hire the employees of Seller. All retained employees will receive a retention bonus in the form of Buyer stock in the amount of 50% of their base pay, with three-year vesting.

Many stock option plans automatically accelerate vesting in the event of a change in control. If not, the term sheet can specify how outstanding seller options and warrants are to be treated. A significant issue to clarify is how the exercise prices of options and warrants will change to match the price at which the seller is being sold. Alternatively, the term sheet can specify that all options and warrants will be exercised prior to the purchase agreement. Two examples follow:

Options and Warrants (1): The Buyer will assume all outstanding Seller options and warrants, adjusted for the stock-for-stock exchange ratio. All existing vesting periods will be retained.

Options and Warrants (2): All Seller "in the money" options and warrants will be exercised prior to closing.

The term sheet should describe those conditions that must take place before the parties will agree to the purchase agreement. These "conditions precedent" reveal the general boundaries within which the parties are most likely to come to an agreement. The seller tries to reduce the number of conditions precedent, thereby giving the buyer fewer excuses to back out of the deal. However, this only matters if the clause is binding. An example follows:

Conditions Precedent: The purchase transaction contemplated under these proposed terms is subject to the following conditions:

1. Two years of audited financial statements
2. Successful completion of due diligence
3. Approval of all government regulatory bodies
4. Receipt of outside opinions regarding the tax-free nature of the transaction
5. Successful completion of debt or equity financing by the seller to provide funding in the amount of the payment
6. The business, assets, financial condition, operations, results of operations and prospects of Seller being substantially as have been

represented to Buyer and no change having occurred which, in the sole judgment of Buyer, is or may be materially adverse to purchase

7. Negotiation and execution of a definitive agreement setting forth representations and warranties of the two entities, covenants, and any other provisions customary in transactions of this nature

8. Approval of this sale and purchase by the Boards of Directors of both the Buyer and Seller

In addition to the conditions precedent, the buyer also wants to warn the seller that it will require additional representations and warrants as part of the purchase agreement. These are too numerous to mention in a term sheet, so a brief clause merely points out their existence. The clause states that representations and warranties apply to both parties (which is true), but the real liability rests upon the seller. An example follows:

Representations and Warranties: This sale of Seller to Buyer will be made by a purchase transaction, which shall contain appropriate representations and warranties of the companies, covenants of the companies reflecting the provisions set forth herein, as well as any other provisions typically found in such agreements and appropriate conditions of closing.

While negotiations are proceeding between the buyer and seller, the seller may be tempted to engage in activities to improve its payout, such as dividends to stockholders or equity issuances to employees. To prevent this behavior, the term sheet can include a restrictive covenant. An example follows:

Preclosing Covenants: Prior to closing, the Seller will only undertake those transactions required in the ordinary course of business, and will preserve its relations with key business partners. Seller will not engage in any equity or debt-related activities, divestitures, or acquisitions without first notifying the Buyer.

A buyer does not want to issue a term sheet and then see the seller promptly shop the offer among other potential buyers in search of a higher bid. To avoid this behavior, the buyer may want a binding no-shop clause through the negotiation period, with 90 days being a common no-shop duration. Even if the seller has no intention of shopping the offer, it still wants to minimize the duration of the no-shop provision, in case its negotiations with the buyer break down. An example follows:

> **No-Shop:** The Seller will not enter into any material discussions relating to the subject matter of this term sheet with any other person or entity, nor will Seller negotiate with any persons or entities with respect to the sale, exchange or other transfer of its assets or stock during such period. The no-shop period will commence upon the buyer's written acceptance of these terms, and will expire 90 days later.

The term sheet should include a binding clause that both parties not disclose to third parties that an acquisition is being discussed. Any discussion in the press about an acquisition can be damaging to the seller's prospects, since it forewarns competitors of the transaction. An example follows:

> **Announcements:** The Buyer and Seller agree not to make any disclosures concerning this contemplated sale to any non-related parties without the express written consent of the other party. Third parties who are expressly exempted from this prohibition are any professionals used by either party to assist in evaluating or closing the transaction, as well as those employees of the Buyer or Seller who are part of the due diligence process.

A key part of the term sheet is a statement that it does not bind either party to a purchase agreement. This is of particular importance to the buyer, since subsequent due diligence may reveal a significant flaw in the seller that will cause the buyer to stop any further negotiations. However, there may still be some sections of the term sheet that are intended to be binding, such as the no-shop or expenses sections. Two examples follow, where the first version references several binding sections of the letter, and the second version does not:

> **Non-Binding (1):** Except with respect to the sections entitled "No-Shop" and "Expenses," this term sheet reflects the parties' intentions only and is not a legally binding commitment or agreement with respect to either party. The parties shall enter into good faith negotiations to establish the terms of a legally binding definitive purchase agreement and other agreements necessary to give effect to the intentions expressed herein. This term sheet is subject to satisfactory completion of due diligence.

> **Non-Binding (2):** This term sheet reflects the parties' intentions only and is not a legally binding commitment or agreement with respect to either party. The parties shall enter into good faith negotiations to establish the terms of a legally binding definitive purchase agreement and other agreements necessary to give effect to the intentions expressed herein. This term sheet is subject to satisfactory completion of due diligence.

The term sheet may also include an acceptance period, during which the selling entity must indicate its acceptance. By including this clause, the buyer is limiting the duration of its offer. This keeps the seller from insisting on retaining the general terms outlined in the term sheet during some later time period, when its financial circumstances may have changed significantly. An example follows:

> **Acceptance Period:** The conditions and intent of this term sheet will expire if not accepted by Seller on or before October 31, 20__.

In addition, the term sheet may include a confidentiality agreement. However, this is generally handled in a larger, separate document that more thoroughly addresses every detail of what information the parties will not disclose, and how due diligence information is to be dispositioned following any termination of discussions.

SUMMARY

The term sheet is an extremely useful document, usually just a few pages long, that outlines the basic points of a possible purchase agreement. It defines the boundaries within which the buyer and seller will subsequently negotiate, thereby controlling the expectations of both parties. As such, it is an inexpensive and easily produced document that initiates the acquisition transaction. A buyer with acquisitions experience will likely have developed a boilerplate term sheet document that it can easily modify to match the requirements of a specific seller.

Chapter 5

Due Diligence

A buyer performs due diligence on the target company in order to assess the benefits and liabilities of the proposed acquisition. The buyer does this by investigating all relevant aspects of the target that could present risks or opportunities to it.

For a full acquisition of the target's legal entity, involving the assumption of all financial, environmental, and legal liabilities, as well as all assets, there are a great many sub-sets of analysis to perform. However, for a minor acquisition, such as the purchase of all or specific assets, the number of analyses is substantially less. In this chapter, the types of acquisition analysis are broken down into a wide range of categories, which makes it easier to select only those needed for a specific type of acquisition.

Despite being lengthy, this chapter does not address the full range of due diligence topics. For a longer checklist, see Appendix A.

DUE DILIGENCE TEAM STAFFING

Performing due diligence on a potential acquisition is like no other type of financial analysis—not because the analysis itself is different, but because of the logistics of the situation. Typically, a potential acquisition situation arises suddenly, requires the fullest attention of the buyer for a short time, and then subsides, either because the buyer elects not to pursue the acquisition, or because the deal is completed, and an integration team takes over the activities of melding the organizations together.

Because of the suddenness of an acquisition evaluation, a company must be fully prepared to switch from into a full-bore analysis mode. However, due diligence team members have other duties, and cannot leave them in order to conduct an investigation. Accordingly, the capacity of the various buyer departments to complete a potentially massive analysis chore may not be possible, if they are to operate in anything close to a normal and efficient manner. Accordingly, a company must make one of three choices. First, if there are very few acquisition evaluations to make and the potential acquirees are small ones, then it may be possible to accept some degree of disruption within the company and perform all the work with the existing staff. A second alternative is to form an acquisition analysis group that does nothing but evaluate potential candidates on a full-time basis. This is an excellent approach if the buyer grows primarily by acquisition. The third alternative is to hire an outside auditing firm to conduct the financial analysis on behalf of the company. This is a good alternative if the in-house staff does not have sufficient time or training, and if there are not enough acquisitions to justify hiring a full-time team of analysts. However, using outside auditors can be an expensive proposition, and the audit staff used must be of a high enough level of training and experience to conduct a thorough review. Thus, the number of potential acquisitions and the ability of the internal staff to complete acquisition analysis work will dictate the method used to conduct a due diligence analysis.

Because of the total time commitment required for due diligence work, there is a tendency to shift people in and out of the team, as they are pulled away for other projects. This yields minimal continuity in following up on open items of investigation, and it is more likely that key review items will be missed entirely, or not thoroughly reviewed.

To avoid these problems, the buyer should insist on keeping the same people on the team until their assigned tasks are complete.

Where possible, some members of the team should come from the managers and their staffs who will eventually run the target company. These employees will exercise the utmost care in making inquiries, because they know that, once the acquisition is completed, they will be responsible for cleaning up any messes that are not uncovered. They also realize that the target's performance will factor into the cal-culation of their bonuses. Though this group will not have all of the expertise needed for the entire due diligence program, they are invalu-able for investigating operational issues.

The due diligence team does not simply work on a prepared list of questions, submit their results to the team manager, and go home. The process is more interactive. The team should meet regularly and share their results. By doing so, everyone can hear about issues and concerns that have arisen, and see how that affects their own area of investigation. For example, if one person talks to customers and learns that there has been a product recall, this leads the engineering due diligence people to determine why the recall occurred and what was done to fix it.

The acquisition integration team that eventually takes over from the due diligence team will also monitor the findings. The integration manager must be ready with a reasonably well thought-out integration plan as soon as the acquisition transaction is completed, and can do this most effectively by learning about the issues spotted by the due diligence team. For example, if the cultural investigation reveals an autocratic management structure at the target company, the integration team will need to spend considerably more time installing control sys-tems, which are more likely to be flouted in such an environment.

DUE DILIGENCE INTERVIEWS

While the bulk of due diligence efforts involve document review, sig-nificant information can also be gleaned from a variety of interviews of target company employees. Some due diligence teams make the mistake of only interviewing senior managers. Though this group may be well-intentioned, they do not normally have a detailed knowledge of specific processes, products, contracts, and so forth. For this information, it is better to interview division and plant managers, division accountants, sales managers, purchasing agents, and people in similar positions. These employees are most familiar with the details of company operations, and also have the least incentive to lie, since they probably don't own many shares of the target's stock. Also, if there is evidence of senior management fraud, this is the group most likely to know about it and also the most likely to talk about it.

DUE DILIGENCE—OVERVIEW

With the acquisition analysis team in place, a buyer can then compile a list of due diligence questions that are tailored to the precise circumstances of the target company. The main analysis areas are as follows:

- *Market.* If the buyer is new to the industry in which the target is located, it should inquire about a variety of fundamental competitive issues, such as the ease of entry into the market, any excess capacity that may drive down prices, and the general size and growth rate of the market.
- *Culture.* The buyer must understand how the target operates. Corporate culture involves the integration of numerous elements, such as its organizational structure, sense of community, and decision-making systems. The mark of an experienced buyer is one that spends considerable time investigating this area, because it knows that some cultures are strongly resistant to subsequent integration.
- *Personnel.* If a potential acquiree has one or more departments that are justly famous for their work, then buying the company may be worthwhile in order to obtain those specific departments. The main analysis needed here is to determine the current compensation levels of the people being acquired, as well as how these pay levels

compare to both internal and industry pay standards, and the presence and cost of any long-term compensation agreements.

- *Intellectual property.* A target company may possess one or more valuable patents, especially ones that can be used to enhance the value of the buyer's products. The primary analysis focuses on the number of years remaining prior to patent expiration and (especially) the expected cash flows to be obtained from them prior to expiration.

- *Brands.* A brand name is immensely valuable if it has been carefully maintained for many years, has been strongly supported with proper marketing, and is used on excellent products. This is a good reason to acquire a target company, and is most common in the consumer goods field. The investigation focuses on the incremental profits to be gained by use of the brand name in relation to the cost of acquiring and maintaining the brand.

- *Risk management.* A well-run target will have systems in place for evaluating and mitigating those areas in which it is most at risk of loss. A target with an excellent risk management program is more valuable to the buyer, because the buyer is less likely to incur unexpected losses following the acquisition transaction.

- *Capacity.* If a company is faced with a long lead time or technological challenges to acquire greater production capacity, it may be worthwhile to purchase a production facility from another company. The analysis focuses on the age and usefulness of the machinery and facility purchased.

- *Assets and liabilities.* When an entire company is purchased, the acquiring organization is taking over virtually all assets and liabilities. In this instance, a comprehensive review of all balance-sheet line items is mandatory.

- *Equity.* Buyers tend to focus the bulk of their efforts on asset and liability investigation, and are then surprised when they realize that a key shareholder has super-voting rights, and must be appeased in order to approve the acquisition. This can be avoided by investigating a short list of ownership topics.

- *Profitability.* The bottom line on any acquisition is the bottom line—the buyer must expect to increase its earnings per share as a result of the transaction. This requires a detailed review of the target's income statement, broken down by subsidiary, customer, and product.

- *Cash flow.* If a company has a large store of cash or continuing cash flows, it is a prime target for purchase by companies that need the cash, possibly to fund further acquisitions. For this type of acquisition, an intensive review of the balance sheet, income statement, and statement of cash flows is necessary.

- *Customers.* The relationship that a target has with its customers is a key concern to the buyer, but is frequently not investigated in detail. The buyer should review the length of relationships, profitability by key customer, complaint records, contracts, and related issues.

- *Product development.* A target with a long-term commitment to product development is quite valuable. Relevant topics of investigation are the size and quality of the target's product pipeline, as well as the presence of any failed products, target costing, and an effective development plan.

- *Production process.* A target's production process can hide considerable synergies. The buyer should examine its work flows, throughput philosophy, and industrial engineering capabilities.

- *Information technology.* A target's information technology systems can be a barren wasteland of ancient legacy systems and overburdened infrastructure. The buyer should be willing to conduct an in-depth investigation of this area to root out the worst problems.

- *Legal issues.* The buyer's attorneys are an important part of the due diligence team, because they protect it from a broad range of legal hazards. They are among the first to begin due diligence work and the last to leave, and can be expected to spot numerous legal problems in such areas as contracts, licensing deals, liens, and pending litigation.

All of these areas are described in more detail in the following sections. In addition, the due diligence team should be on the lookout for indicators of major problems, as discussed later in the Red Flags section. Also, after reviewing these areas, the due diligence team manager must look at the sum total of all issues uncovered, and decide if the target's problems simply make it too complex of an acquisition to contemplate. This topic is addressed later in the Complexity Analysis section.

DUE DILIGENCE—MARKET OVERVIEW

In most cases, the buyer is located within the same market as the target, and so is already extremely knowledgeable about the structure and level of competition within the target's market. However, if the target is located within a different market, the buyer should conduct a high-level overview of how the market operates. Here are some issues to consider:

- *Ease of entry.* If there are strong barriers to entry, then the buyer has less reason to worry about competition from new market entrants. Examples of entry barriers are significant government regulation and high capital costs (both occurring in the utilities industry) and continuing research and development expenditures (such as in the pharmaceuticals industry). Conversely, almost anything involving the Internet has low barriers to entry, since a company can create a Web site in a very short period of time and at minimal cost.

- *Excess capacity.* Does the market have a boom-and-bust history of building too much capacity and then suffering through a pricing crash until demand catches up with supply? This has been a common problem in the semi-conductor market for many years. Alternatively, can extra capacity be brought into the market on short notice, thereby also imposing negative pricing pressure? This has been a continuing issue in the airline industry, where new market entrants can use the credit offered by leasing companies to quickly buy excess airplanes and put them back into service.

- *Level of expertise.* Are there any market leaders who have bought into the market through an acquisition, but who really don't know the market very well? If the buyer has a greater level of expertise, or is willing to rely on the target's management team, then it may have a significant competitive advantage. These competitors may be too slow or ineffective in responding to market changes, thereby allowing others to rapidly expand their market share.

- *Market growth trend.* If the market is growing rapidly, this does not mean that it will continue to do so. At some point, the growth rate of all markets declines to roughly match the growth rate of the world economy (or shrinks, as new markets replace them). Consequently, the buyer should make an estimate of whether it is in the dangerous position of buying at the top of the market.

- *Pricing sensitivity.* How sensitive are customers to price increases? In some industries, products are considered non-essential, so customers simply stop buying them if the price increases too much. This is a particular problem if there are substitute products to which customers can easily switch.

- *Total market size.* The market must be large enough to allow for significant growth by multiple players. If not, then many companies will fight over too small an amount of sales, resulting in severe price competition and multiple bankruptcies.

The topics noted here are extremely broad issues—so broad that many buyers ignore them completely, preferring instead to focus on the specific attributes of individual target companies. Nonetheless, these factors have a considerable impact on the long-term profitability of any company. Thus, the buyer should consider these issues for its target markets at least once a year, to see if it should continue or change its existing acquisition strategy.

DUE DILIGENCE—CULTURE

One of the most important due diligence areas is the target's culture, since this is the fundamental basis upon which the target operates. However, very few buyers investigate culture to any extent, on the grounds that culture is not quantifiable. What they miss is that integration of the target into the buyer's organization will be extraordinarily difficult unless the buyer works within the restrictions of the buyer's culture while making changes. In some cases, the cultures of the two companies are so incompatible that a successful integration is almost impossible. Thus, a due diligence review of culture should be one of the first and most important items completed, so that the team can quickly determine if it should recommend immediately abandoning the acquisition. Here are several core culture areas in which conflicts can lead to acquisition failure:

- *Organizational structure.* When one entity has a highly structured command-and-control environment and the other pushes decision-making down to lower-level employees.
- *Bureaucracy.* Where one entity requires the use of rigidly defined policies, procedures, and forms, while the other allows a variety of systems as long as the overall strategy is achieved.
- *Innovation.* Where one entity takes action despite uncertainty, while the other engages in long-term planning, extensive market studies, and incremental product extensions.
- *Employee focus.* Where one entity fosters a strong sense of community through a broad array of social events, benefits, and retention policies, while the other focuses more on cost reduction.
- *Not invented here.* Where one company only develops new products in-house and manages all functions internally, while the other emphasizes a lean staff and outsourcing of all non-key functions.

While it is entirely possible to work around one of these conflicts, having multiple ones will likely cause the acquisition to fail. Though the buyer can conduct a massive management purge in order to eliminate the existing culture, this also destroys a great deal of value, and so is rarely worth the effort. Consequently, the due diligence team should pay a great deal of attention to the differences between the cultures of the buyer and the target, and how they will affect the acquisition.

DUE DILIGENCE—PERSONNEL

The core asset of many companies is its employees, so the due diligence team should focus a considerable proportion of its time in this area. Here are the key review topics:

- *Compare employee pay levels to industry and internal averages.* Obtain the pay rates for the target company, and review them for inordinately high or low pay levels. Then compare these rates not only to the industry average, but also the buyer's average, to determine the difference between the existing and incoming pay levels.
- *Compile pay histories.* The target may have recently given pay raises to key (or all) employees, in hopes of conning the buyer into continuing these pay levels. Conversely, it may have reduced salary levels in order to make itself appear more profitable. By creating a three-year salary history for all employees, the due diligence team can spot both issues. In the first case, the analysis presents a cogent argument for reducing wages. In the later case, the buyer is forewarned that it may have to raise employee pay back to earlier levels.
- *Review bonus and commission plans.* Obtain copies of all bonus and commission plans. Assemble into a table the criteria used to trigger payments, and the size of those payments. Also, note whether payments are based on "hard" quantitative performance criteria, such as attaining specific revenue numbers, or "soft" qualitative measures. Also, what is the payment history under these

plans? If there is a long history of paying bonuses using "soft" criteria, the buyer may face turnover problems if it switches to plans that are triggered by more quantitative measures.

Review commission plans to see if the target pays upon invoicing, or upon receipt of cash from customers. If the target pays based on invoicing and the buyer wants to switch it to cash-based payments, this will cause trouble with the target's sales staff, who may suffer a short-term drop in compensation. Also, compare commission percentages to those paid elsewhere in the company for reasonableness.

- *Investigate special pay situations.* There may be special pay situations for the target's employees that are triggered by an acquisition, and which could make it far more expensive for the buyer. For example, there may be golden parachute clauses, loan forgiveness, or option auto-vesting in their employment or option agreements triggered by a change in control of the target. Auto-vesting is a nearly universal feature of option agreements.

- *Review long-term compensation agreements.* If a target company has obtained the services of a number of exceptional employees, it is quite possible that it has done so by offering them expensive, long-term employment contracts. Locate these contracts and categorize their key components.

- *Determine the current turnover rate.* If there is a high turnover rate at the target, then the cost of acquisition may not be worthwhile if the buyer cannot find a way to retain employees.

- *Review benefits.* There are a broad range of benefits, some of which may be specifically tailored to individuals within the target company, and which those people want to keep. For example, if employees are older, benefits may include free medical insurance, a supplemental pension plan, or long-term disability. Conversely, benefits for a more youthful group may include a flexible work schedule. If the buyer plans to merge the target's benefits into its own company-wide plan, it should estimate the amount of employee turnover caused by the elimination of these special benefits.

If the buyer intends to retain the target's benefits, then it should summarize their total annual incremental cost over those of the rest of the company. For this purpose, a good source of information is the target's employee manual, which usually includes a comprehensive list of all benefits offered. Even more important, if the buyer decides to roll out company-wide a new benefit that is currently only offered within the target, it must determine the incremental cost to the entire company.

- *Investigate principal employees.* The buyer is fully justified in conducting a database search of all available court records on the target's owners and key managers. The objective is to spot any felonies, especially those involving fraud.

- *Verify collective bargaining arrangements.* If there is a union, then review the dates, duration, issues, and settlement terms of any prior strikes for at least the past five years. Be sure to go back a long way to verify strike history—just a few years is not sufficient. Union members have long memories, and will adversely recall a strike from many years in the past. Also, make inquiries about the current status of negotiations with any unions, and what the most likely settlement terms will be.

- *Review grievance records.* If some employees are represented by a union, then review grievance records for the past few years to see if there is a continuing history of problems. If so, this increases the probability of a strike or prolonged contract negotiations when the next labor contract is due for renewal.

- *Investigate employee names listed on patents.* If individual employees are named on patents or patent applications filed by the target company, then it is a good bet that those employees may be in a revenue-sharing arrangement with the company employing them. If so, determine the amounts paid to the employees for use of the patents, such as a fee per unit sold, or an annual payment.

These patent payments must be added to the employee salaries to determine the true cost of acquiring the new personnel.

• *Interview customers and suppliers about employees.* If there are problems with the desired employees, the target company is almost certainly not going to reveal this information, since it is trying to obtain payment for "selling" them to the buyer. Accordingly, it may be necessary to interview the target company's suppliers or customers to get their opinions about the people under consideration.

An example of the analysis report that the buyer should issue for a due diligence on employees is as follows:

Analysis Report for Acquisition of Personnel

Description	Additional Information	Summary Costs
Total cost of incoming staff (15 staff)		$1,237,500
Average cost of incoming staff	$82,500	
Average cost of in-house staff	73,000	
Prior year employee turnover level	10%	
Additional cost to match in-house salaries to incoming salaries (13 staff)		123,500
Net present value of projected patent payments to employees		420,000
Cost of employment contract buyouts		250,000
Total cost of employee acquisition		**$2,031,000**
Total cost per employee acquired (15 staff)		**$135,400**
Industry Average Pay Rate Per Person		$80,000
Percentage premium over market rate		**69%**

Note that the cost of acquisition has been converted at the bottom of the example into a cost per employee, which is then compared to the average market rate. The premium to be paid over the market rate gives the buyer its best idea of the true cost of the staff it is acquiring, and therefore whether it should proceed with the acquisition.

DUE DILIGENCE—INTELLECTUAL PROPERTY

Due diligence for intellectual property largely focuses on the existing costs and revenues currently experienced by the target's patent and copyright holdings. The buyer should review the estimated additional revenues and costs that will subsequently be incurred by its use of the patent, which may vary from the use to which it has been put by the current patent owner. The primary analyses are as follows (references are to patents, but by inference include copyrights):

- *Determine annual patent renewal costs.* Annual patent costs are quite minimal, but should be included in any patent analysis in order to present a comprehensive set of cost information.
- *Determine current patent-related revenue stream.* Obtain revenue information for the last few years, to see if there is an upward or downward trend line for the revenues; if the trend is downward, then the revenue stream for which the company is paying is worth less.
- *Ascertain extent of current litigation to support patents.* A major issue for any patent holder is the legal expense required to keep other entities from encroaching on the patent with parallel patents, or by issuing products that illegally use technology based on the patent.
- *Verify the patent application process.* The target should have a process in place for documenting and applying for patents on a regular basis. Otherwise, it may develop an excellent product, only to see a competitor patent the underlying concept.

An example of the analysis report for a patent purchase is shown below:

Analysis Report for Patent Acquisition

Description	Additional Data	Summary Revenues & Costs
Years left prior to patent expiration	10 years	
Net present value of cash inflows		$1,200,000
Discounted cost of remaining filing costs		−42,000
Discounted cost of expected annual legal fees		−375,000
Net present value of patent		**$783,000**

The bottom line of the patent acquisition analysis report is the net present value of all cash flows, which the buyer can use as the highest recommended amount to pay for the patent. However, given alternative uses for the patent that it may be contemplating, the buyer may anticipate a higher cash inflow that will allow it to pay a higher price.

Besides a net present value calculation for patents, due diligence should also encompass patent risks. Some problems may not be immediately obvious. For example, have other companies in the same industry experienced problems enforcing their patent rights? If so, how likely is it that the target will eventually confront the same issues? Also, are any key patents held by entities or individuals other than the target? If so, verify that the documents giving the target access to the patents will not terminate in the near future, and give the target rights to obtain usage extensions.

DUE DILIGENCE—BRANDS

A brand name can be immensely valuable, but its true value can be subject to a broad range of interpretation. Use the following steps to arrive at a more quantitative view of brand value:

- *Determine the amount of annual trademark fees.* This is a very minor item, but can grow to considerable proportions if the brand trademark is being maintained worldwide, which requires filings and maintenance fees in a multitude of jurisdictions.

- *Determine clear title to the brand name.* This is not just a matter of paying for a small amount of research by a legal firm to determine the existence of any countervailing trademarks, but also requires a search in multiple jurisdictions if the buying company wants to expand the brand to other countries.

- *Ascertain the amount and trend of any current cash inflows from the brand name.* The two best analysis options are to either measure just that portion of sales that are specifically due to licensing agreements (and therefore easily traceable) or by measuring the incremental difference in cash flows from all products under the brand name, in comparison to those of the industry average or specific competitors.

- *Note the amount and trend of any legal fees needed to stop encroachment.* A quality brand frequently attracts competitors that build inexpensive knock-offs, and illegally sell them for vastly reduced prices. Given the reduced quality and prices, the net impact of these fake goods is to cheapen the brand's image. Constant legal pursuit of these companies is the only way to keep imitating products off the market, so compile the target company's related legal costs.

In the following exhibit, we itemize the financial analysis associated with a brand name acquisition:

Analysis Report for Brand Acquisition

Description	Additional Data	Summary Revenues & Costs
Net present value of current cash inflows		$500,000
Discounted cost of annual trademark fees		−65,000
Cost of trademark search (for clear title)		−175,000
Discounted cost of annual legal fees		−780,000
Cost to purchase competing brand names	See note	−2,250,000
Total net cost of brand name		**$−2,770,000**

Note: A competing trademark has already been filed by company XYZ in all countries of the European Community and Japan. The cost required to purchase this trademark is included in the analysis.

DUE DILIGENCE—RISK MANAGEMENT

The risk management policies of the target company can be of significant concern to the buyer, because inadequate risk management leaves it open to possibly enormous additional expenditures. While a buyer will rarely find an environment where the target completely ignores all forms of risk, there are some areas in which risk coverage is likely to be inadequate. Here are some areas to investigate:

- *Claim terms.* If the target's various policies stipulate that they only cover "claims made," this means that they only cover claims actually made to the insurance company during the policy term. Thus, if claims are made *after* the policy term that relate to the covered period, the insurance company is not required to reimburse the company for them. A less risky policy is one that allows "claims incurred," so that claims will be allowed even if they are filed after the policy period. The buyer can convert a "claims made" policy into a "claims incurred" policy by requiring the target to purchase "tail" insurance, which extends coverage for a "claims made" policy into future periods.

- *Deductibles.* Is the target assuming large deductibles or self-insured retentions on its insurance? If the target uses risk analysis to deliberately set deductibles where its overall cost is lowest, then such behavior is perfectly acceptable. However, if the target is doing so simply to reduce its up-front insurance cost, then the buyer must conduct its own risk analysis to determine the potential increased liability arising from the situation.

- *Penetrated aggregates.* Does the target have inadequate insurance coverage, such that the aggregate amount of claims exceeds the aggregate amount allowed by its coverage? If so, the target is essentially uninsured for any additional claims.

- *Premium adjustments.* The target may be claiming inordinately low transaction volumes in order to reduce its up-front insurance costs in such areas as workers' compensation insurance and business interruption insurance. The issue is most easily spotted by reviewing the size of any premium adjustments made after insurance carriers conduct end-of-period audits.

- *Self-insurance.* The target may be self-insuring those claims that arise less frequently, which is perfectly acceptable as long as it has umbrella coverage that is triggered once a certain aggregate claim level is exceeded. If the umbrella is not present, then the buyer may have a substantial unaddressed risk.

- *Site security.* If there are assets on site that are valuable and easily removed, does the target have adequate security to ensure that they are not stolen? In many cases, companies do not install such security until they have already suffered a significant loss.

- *Uninsured risks.* Has the target completely ignored insurance coverage to some major risk areas, such as environmental liabilities or damage to its inventory? This is essentially self-insurance (see the earlier point), but in this case, the target is simply unaware of the missing coverage or the underlying risk. The buyer may have to conduct its own risk investigation to uncover uninsured risks.

While the above points will reveal areas of significant risk, the due diligence team should also make note of the target's overall commitment to a risk management program. This is evidenced by a high-level officer who is charged with risk management, strong management support of the program, and extensive employee training in those aspects of risk management over which they have an impact.

DUE DILIGENCE—CAPACITY

When a buyer purchases a manufacturing facility from another company, it is usually doing so to increase its capacity. With this end in mind, the key analyses revolve around the condition and cost of the facility, to determine the amount of replacement machinery to install, as well as the actual production capacity percentage, the cost per percent of capacity, and the facility's overhead cost. For many of the analyses, the information assembled must be for three activity levels—minimum, normal, and maximum capacity levels. The reason for the three-fold format is that management may not use the facility as much as it anticipates, in which case it must be aware of the minimum costs that will still be incurred, as well as the extra costs that must be covered if the facility runs at the highest possible rate of production. The primary analyses are as follows:

- *Determine the facility overhead cost required for minimum, standard, and maximum capacity.* Any facility requires a minimum maintenance cost, even if it is not running. Such costs include taxes, security, insurance, and building maintenance. Also, current accounting records will reveal the overhead needed to run the facility at a normal level, while the industrial engineering or production personnel can estimate the additional costs needed to run the plant at full capacity.

- *Ascertain the amount of capital replacements needed.* Some machinery will be so worn out or outdated that it must be replaced. A qualified industrial engineer or production manager can determine the condition of the equipment. If this is not readily apparent, then perusing the maintenance records will reveal which machines require so much upkeep that a complete replacement is a more efficient alternative.

- *Find out the periodic maintenance cost of existing equipment.* Even if equipment does not require replacement, it must still be maintained, which can be a considerable cost. Obtain this information for the normal run rate, and estimate it for the maximum capacity level.

- *Determine the maximum production capacity.* The industrial engineering staff must estimate the maximum capacity level at which the facility can run, subject to expenditures for equipment replacements and facility modifications.

- *Investigate any environmental liabilities.* Environmental liabilities can be extraordinarily expensive, and may sometimes exceed the cost of the entire facility. To guard against this problem, conduct an environmental investigation, and also determine the cost of insurance to provide coverage in case such damage is discovered after the purchase date.

- *Determine the cost of modifications needed to increase the capacity of the facility.* Unless a facility has been very carefully laid out in the beginning to maximize throughput, it is likely that it can use a layout overhaul. Accordingly, the industrial engineering staff should review the current situation and recommend necessary changes.

The preceding analyses are summarized in the sample capacity analysis report shown below, which includes low-medium-high categories for costs that are based on projected capacity utilization levels.

Analysis Report for Capacity Acquisitions

Description	Costs at Minimum Capacity Usage	Costs at Normal Capacity Usage	Costs at Maximum Capacity Usage
Facility overhead cost	$1,000,000	$3,500,000	$5,000,000
Capital replacement cost*	0	0	400,000
Equipment maintenance cost	0	450,000	600,000
Cost of environmental damage insurance	50,000	50,000	50,000
Cost to investigate possible environmental damage	100,000	100,000	100,000
Facility modification costs	0	0	700,000
Total costs	**$1,150,000**	**$4,100,000**	**$6,850,000**
Percent capacity level	0%	50%	85%
Cost per percent of capacity	**N/A**	**$82,000**	**$81,000**

*Note: Represents the depreciation on capital replacement items.

At the bottom of the example, all costs are converted into a dollar amount for each percent of capacity used. Note that there is no utilization listed for the minimum level, since the facility is shuttered under this assumption.

DUE DILIGENCE—ASSETS

A company will sometimes acquire just the assets of another organization. This is most common when there is some risk associated with the liabilities of the target, such as lawsuits, environmental problems, or an excessive amount of debt. When assets are purchased, the buyer can be quite selective in buying only those assets that are of the most value, such as patents, brands, or personnel (which have been covered in previous sections). At this point, we note only the following additional analyses needed to ensure that all other assets are properly reviewed prior to an acquisition:

- *Conduct a fixed asset audit.* Before paying for an asset, make sure that the asset is there. The fixed asset records of some companies are in such poor condition that assets still on the books may have been disposed of years before. An appraiser or an internal audit team can conduct this review.

  While conducting this audit, also make inquiries about which assets will require near-term replacement (a particular problem with computer equipment). Compare the resulting total replacement cost to the target's longer-term replacement expenditures to see if an unusually large number of replacements are needed. This can be an indication that the target has been strapped for cash, or that it has restricted asset replacements to give the appearance of having exceptional cash flow.

- *Appraise the value of fixed assets.* Even if an asset exists, it may have far less value than the amount listed in the fixed asset database. To be sure of the current value of all assets, have an appraiser review them and determine their value. The final appraisal report should contain two values for each asset—the rush liquidation value, and a higher value based on a more careful liquidation approach. These two values can be the focus of a great deal of negotiating between the buyer and the target company, since the buyer will want to pay based on the rush liquidation value, and the target will prefer to sell at the price indicated by the slower liquidation approach.

- *Ascertain the existence of liens against assets.* A company should not purchase an asset if there is a lien against it. This usually occurs when the target has used the assets as collateral for loans, or used leases to finance the purchase of specific assets. The standard procedure in an acquisition is to have lenders remove liens prior to the completion of an acquisition, which frequently requires paying off those lenders with a new bridge loan that covers the period of a few weeks or days between the removal of liens and the transfer of payment from the buyer to the target, which is then used to pay off the bridge loan.

- *Determine the collectibility of accounts receivable.* If the purchase includes all current accounts receivable, then trace the largest invoices back to specific shipments, and confirm them with the customers to whom the invoices were sent. Also, trace the history of bad debt write-offs to determine an appropriate average amount that will reflect the amount of the current accounts receivable that will become bad debt.

- *Verify the bank reconciliation for all bank accounts.* For any checking or investment account, verify the amount of cash at the bank and reconcile it to the amount listed in the corporate accounting records. Also, investigate any reconciling items to ensure that they are appropriate.

- *Review existing product line.* Consider how the target's products fit into the buyer's product line from several perspectives. First, must they still be manufactured from separate facilities, or can the facilities be consolidated? Also, can they be supported by a single combined engineering staff, or are the two teams too disparate to meld? Do the two sets of products slot into different price points, or are there products competing at the same price point? Is there any documented evidence of design flaws or other defects that will call for extensive replacements under warranty?

- *Investigate inventory.* Companies have a strong tendency to re-tain inventory long after it has lost some or all of its value. To see if this is the case, review the inventory for obsolescence, utilizing a usage frequency report from the target's inventory tracking system. Also, see if the company has a history of regu-larly writing down or disposing of inventory—if not, there is an increased chance of obsolescence. Also, if there has been a product recall or excessive warranty returns, the flawed inven-tory might have been returned to stock. Finally, compare the target's inventory to that of the buyer; if the two inventories will be consolidated, then some items may become overstocked, resulting in dispositioning costs.

- *Audit the existence and valuation of remaining assets.* There are usually a number of smaller-dollar assets on the books, such as the payoff value of life insurance, deposits on rentals and leases, and loans to employees or officers. All of these items must be audited, both through investigation of the original contracts on which they are based and through confirmations from those entities who owe the target company money.

- *Determine the value of any tax loss carry-forward.* If the buyer is acquiring a tax loss carry-forward from the target company, it can use this to reduce its own tax burden. Use a tax specialist to review the validity of the target company's tax returns to ensure that the reported loss on which the carry-forward is based is valid, and re-view the tax laws to ensure that the company is qualified to use the loss carry-forward (which under current laws can only be recog-nized over a very long time period).

A sample of an analysis report for assets is noted below:

Analysis Report for Assets

Description	Slow Liquidation Value	Rapid Liquidation Value
Appraised value of assets (rapid liquidation)	$18,500,000	$16,000,000
Book value of accounts receivable	5,500,000	5,350,000
Value of cash and investments	750,000	750,000
Life insurance cash value	125,000	125,000
Loans to employees	80,000	60,000
Total asset valuation	**$24,955,000**	**$22,285,000**

The preceding report shows separate columns and totals for quick and longer-duration asset liquidation periods. These columns can be used as the upper and lower boundaries of the price it should pay for the target company's assets.

The asset analysis report can also be used to determine which assets to sell off to help pay for the acquisition. If the buyer intends to fully integrate the target company into its operations, then there is a good chance of asset duplication, where something can be sold off. Conversely, if the buyer intends to run the target as a free-standing entity, then there are unlikely to be many opportunities for asset liquidation.

DUE DILIGENCE—LIABILITIES

If the buyer decides to purchase a target as a complete legal entity, rather than buying pieces of it, then it must also review the target's liabilities. The main liability analyses are as follows:

- *Reconcile unpaid debt to lender balances.* There may be a difference between the amount recorded on the target's books as being the debt liability, and the lender's version of the amount still payable. If there is some doubt regarding whose version is correct, then use the amount noted by the lender, since this entity will not release its lien on the target's assets until it believes itself to be fully paid.

- *Look for unrecorded debt.* A target company may have incorrectly reported a capital lease as an operating lease, or is recording some other form of debt payment as an expense, without recording the underlying debt liability. Review the target company's stream of payments to see if there are any continuing payments, most likely in the same amount from period to period, that indicate the presence of a debt paydown.

- *Review debt terms.* An experienced due diligence team will review a target's debt agreements as soon as possible, because it knows that the lending institutions are the most likely to cause trouble when the buyer acquires the target. Bankers may call their loans at once, or squabble with other lenders over the seniority of their claims on collateral, or want the buyer to guarantee the debts of the new subsidiary. They may have also imposed unusually restrictive covenants, or limitations on the accumulation of additional debt.

- *Audit accounts payable.* Verify that all accounts payable listed on the target company's books are actual expenses and not duplicates of earlier payments. Also, investigate the unvouchered accounts payable to see if these are approved and binding expenses, and if there are additional receipts for which there are no existing accounts payable listed in the accounting records.

- *Audit accrued liabilities.* A target company that wants to obtain the highest possible selling price will downplay accrued expenses, so be—ful to verify the existence of all possible accruals. The following accruals are among the more common ones:

  ○ Income taxes

  ○ Payroll taxes

  ○ Personal property taxes

○ Warranty costs

○ Product recalls

In particular, review the target's history of product recalls and warranty replacements. Even a single significant product flaw may require such an inordinately high replacement expenditure that the economics of the proposed deal will no longer work.

All of the above analyses are summarized in the following sample analysis report for liabilities. Of particular interest are the line items for reconciliation problems, such as extra debt and accounts payable, as well as corrections to the accrued expenses. All of these adjustments are used to negotiate a lower price for the target company, since the higher liabilities reduce its net value.

Analysis Report for Liabilities

Description	Additional Data	Summary Revenues & Costs
Book balance of debt		$3,750,000
Add: Additional lender balance due	See Note 1	15,000
Add: Unrecorded capital leases	See Note 2	175,000
Book balance of accounts payable		2,200,000
Add: Unrecorded accounts payable	See Note 3	28,000
Subtract: Duplicate accounts payable	See Note 4	−2,000
Book balance of accrued liabilities		450,000
Add: Additional accrual for property taxes	See Note 5	80,000
Add: Accrual for workers' compensation insurance	See Note 6	15,000
Total liabilities valuation		**$6,711,000**

Note 1: Company recorded $15,000 in late interest payments as a debt reduction.

Note 2: Capital leases for six forklifts recorded as expenses.

Note 3: No supplier invoice recorded for maintenance supplies received on last day of the month.

Note 4: Supplier invoices for in-house construction work recorded under both vouchered and unvouchered accounts payable.

Note 5: Original accrual did not reflect an increase of 2.3 percent in the tax rate.

Note 6: Original accrual based on a payroll level that is 15 percent lower than the actual payroll amount.

DUE DILIGENCE—EQUITY

At a minimal level, a due diligence team can simply request the target's current shareholder list, and assume that it will pay the people itemized on that list. While this may be sufficient for a very small target company having a simple capital structure, a great deal more investigation is needed for larger firms that have issued special classes of voting stock, options, registration rights, and more. Here are additional areas to investigate:

- *Calculate exercisable options and warrants.* A large number of options or warrants may have been issued. If the buyer's expected price per share for the target's stock is below the exercise price of the options and warrants, the buyer may find itself saddled with a large number of additional shareholders.

- *Investigate registration rights agreements.* Some shareholders may have registration rights, under which the target is required to include them in any stock registration that it files with the Securities and Exchange Commission (SEC). While this does not usually involve any significant additional expense to the target, it can result in an extremely large registration, which may draw the adverse attention of the SEC.

- *Obtain the shareholder list.* Verify the number of shares outstanding, and to whom they were issued. Also, if the target is using a stock transfer agent to issue its stock certificates, have the agent provide a list, and look for discrepancies between it and the list provided by the target.

- *Investigate special voting rights.* Examine the bylaws and articles of incorporation to determine if any stock has been issued that has unusual voting rights. In particular, the holders of convertible stock may have the right to approve any sale of the target, irrespective of the votes of common stockholders. More unusual is the presence of a separate class of super-voting stock, for which each share has multiple votes.

In brief, the due diligence team must determine who needs to vote for the acquisition, how many shares it must purchase, and whether the buyer will inherit any registration obligations as part of the acquisition.

DUE DILIGENCE—PROFITABILITY

There are several ways to review the profitability of a target company. One is to track the trends in several key variables, since these will indicate worsening profit situations. Also, it is important to segment costs and profits by customer, to see if certain customers soak up an inordinate proportion of total expenses. Further, it may be possible to determine the head count associated with each major transaction, to determine the possibility of reducing expenses by imposing transaction-related efficiencies. The intent of these analyses is to quickly determine the current state and trend of a target's profits, as well as to pinpoint those customers and costs that are associated with the majority of profits and losses. The main analyses are as follows:

- *Review a trend line of revenues.* If there has been a decline in the rate of growth or an overall decline in revenues, then review the target's percentage of the total market to see if the cause might be a shrinkage in the overall market. If not, then review sales by product and customer to determine the exact cause of the problem.

- *Review a trend line of bad debt expense.* As a market matures and additional sales are harder to come by, a company's management may loosen its credit terms, which allows it to increase sales, but at the cost of a higher level of bad debt. This may exceed the additional gross margin earned from the incremental sales that were added. To see if a target has resorted to this approach to increasing sales, review the trend line of bad debt expense to see if there has been a significant increase. Also, review the current accounts receivable for old invoices that have not yet been written off as bad debt, and also see if there are sales credits that are actually bad debts. The sum of these items constitutes the true bad debt expense.

- *Review a trend line of sales discounts.* As a follow-up to the last item, management may offer discounts to customers in advance to generate additional sales, or add customers who are in the habit of taking discounts, whether approved or not. These issues are most common when a company's sales are no longer trending upward, and management is looking for a new approach to spur sales, even at the cost of reduced margins due to the discounts. These discounts may be stored in a separate account for sales discounts, or mixed in with sales credits of other kinds.

- *Review a trend line of direct costs.* For most organizations outside of the service sector, this is the largest cost, and so requires a reasonable degree of attention. The due diligence team cannot hope to delve into all possible aspects of labor and material costs during a due diligence review, such as variances for scrap, purchase prices, or cycle counting adjustments. However, it is easy to run a trend line of these costs for the last few years, just to see if they are changing as a proportion of sales. A small increase in costs here can relate to the entire cost of a department in other areas of the company, so a change of as little as one percent in this expense category is cause for concern.

- *Review a trend line of gross margins.* Compare this measure to industry averages or to the gross margins of specific competitors, so the buyer can gain some idea of the production efficiencies of the company it is attempting to purchase.

- *Ascertain the gross profit by product.* Review the gross profit for each product at the direct cost level, to determine which ones have excessively low profit levels, and are targets either for withdrawal from the market or a price increase. If possible, also determine the cost of fixed assets that are associated with each product (i.e., product-specific production equipment), so that the buyer can budget for an asset reduction alongside any product terminations.

- *Review a trend line of overhead personnel per major customer.* Determine the overhead needed to support a profitable base of customers with a ratio of overhead personnel to the number of major customers. This review can extend much more deeply to determine which customers require inordinate amounts of time by the support staff, though this information is rarely available.

- *Review a trend line of overhead personnel per transaction.* Determine the number of personnel involved in all major transactions, such as accounts payable, accounts receivable, receiving, and purchasing, and divide this number into the annual total of these transactions. If there appears to be an excessive number of employees per transaction, then the buyer may be able to reduce personnel costs in these areas.

- *Look for delayed expenses.* It is extremely common for a target to enhance its profitability just prior to a sale, usually by deferring non-critical expenses. These deferrals may include maintenance, advertising, research and development, and pay raises. However, the buyer may have to pay out extra amounts to bring these expenses back to normal, resulting in reduced short-term profitability. Deferred costs can be most easily found by tracking individual expense line items on a trend line for the last few years.

As part of a due diligence analysis, these measures and trend lines will reveal where to focus the bulk of the analysis team's attention in determining the extent of problem areas and their impact on profitability. In the following analysis report, a qualitative review of each analysis area is noted, since this review is intended to find further problems, not to devise a valuation for the target.

Conclusion and recommendations: The target company has experienced flattening sales, and so has shifted new sales efforts to low-end customers who cannot pay on time and will only accept lower-priced products, which also increases the overhead needed to service these accounts. Recommend dropping all low-margin, low-credit customers, as well as all associated overhead costs to increase profits.

Analysis Report for Profitability

Type of Analysis Conducted	Notes
Review a trend line of revenues	Percentage rate of growth has declined in last two years
Review a trend line of bad debt expense	Bad debt expense has increased, due to relaxation of credit standards
Review a trend line of sales discounts	80% of the newest customers have all been given sales discounts of 10%–15%
Review a trend line of material costs	No significant change
Review a trend line of direct labor costs	No significant change
Review a trend line of gross margins	The gross margin has dropped 13% in the last two years, entirely due to increased bad debts and sales discounts
Review a trend line of net margins	Slightly worse reduction than indicated by the gross margin trend line analysis
Ascertain the gross profit by product	All products experienced a reduction in gross profit in the last two years
Ascertain the gross profit by customer	Sales to older customers have retained their gross margin levels, but newer customers have substantially lower margins
Review a trend line of overhead personnel per major customer	There has been a slight increase in the collections staffing level in the last two years, due to the difficulty of collecting from newer customers
Review a trend line of overhead personnel per transaction	No significant change

DUE DILIGENCE—CASH FLOW

The analysis of a target's historical and projected cash flows is of major importance, since the buyer must know if the purchase transaction will result in a new source or use of corporate cash. The key cash flow analyses on which to focus are as follows:

- *Review trend line of net cash flow before debt and interest payments.* Begin with the cash flows shown on the statement of cash flows. Then ignore the impact of debt and interest payments, since inordinately high cash flows to pay for these two items may mask a perfectly good underlying business. If there is a pronounced additional requirement for more cash to fund either the acquisition of fixed assets or working capital, then identify the culprit and proceed with the following cash flow analyses. This first trend line, then, was to determine the existence of a problem, and to more precisely define it.

- *Review trend line of working capital.* Poor customer credit review policies or inadequate collection efforts will lead to an increased investment in accounts receivable, while excessive production or product obsolescence will increase the inventory investment. Also, a reduction in the days of credit before payments are made to suppliers will reduce the free credit that a company receives from them. To see if there is a problem in this area, add the total accounts receivable to inventory and subtract the accounts payable balance to arrive at the total working capital amount. Then plot this information on a trend line that extends back for at least a year. If there is a steady increase in total working capital, determine which of the three components has caused the problem.

- *Segment working capital investment by customer and product.* Focus on the accounts receivable and finished goods inventory investments to see if there is a specific customer who is responsible for a working capital increase, or review just the inventory investment to see if a specific product is the cause. Then cross-reference this information against analyses for profitability by customer and product to see if there are any combinations of low-profit, high-investment customers or products that are obvious candidates for termination.

- *Review trend line of capital purchases.* This is a simple matter to investigate by general fixed asset category, since this information is reported on the balance sheet. However, there may be good reasons for large increases in fixed asset investments, such as automation, the addition of new facilities, or a general level of competitiveness in the industry that requires constant capital improvements. Only by being certain of the underlying reasons for cash usage in this area can one suggest that cash can be saved here by reducing the volume of asset purchases.

The report that the due diligence team issues as part of the cash flow analysis is primarily composed of judgments regarding the need for historical cash flows, estimates of future cash flows, and how the buyer can alter these flows through specific management actions. A sample of such a report is shown below:

Analysis Report for Cash Flow

Type of Analysis Conducted	Notes
Review trend line of net cash flow before debt and interest payments	The target company is experiencing a massive cash outflow in both the working capital and fixed assets areas.
Review trend line of working capital	There is a severe cash outflow, due to $2,000,000 in accounts receivable invested in the Gidget Company, as well as a large investment in five distribution warehouses for its Auto-Klean product, each of which requires $1,500,000 in inventory.

(Continued)

| Segment working capital investment by customer and product | The main cash outflows are due to the Gidget Company customer and the Auto-Klean product. |
| Review trend line of capital purchases | Has purchased $10,000,000 of automation equipment to improve margins on its sales to the Gidget Company. |

Conclusions and recommendations: There is a major investment in sales to the Gidget Company, which is not justified by the 5% return on sales to that customer. The receivable investment of $2,000,000 can be eliminated by stopping sales to this customer, while $5,000,000 can be realized from the sale of automation equipment used for the production of items for sale to it. Also, the number of distribution warehouses for the Auto-Klean product can be reduced by two, which will decrease the inventory investment by $3,000,000. The amount of cash investment that can be eliminated as a result of these actions is $10,000,000.

DUE DILIGENCE—CUSTOMERS

Some buyers focus only on the existence of a sales history and outstanding receivables, without conducting any significant investigation of the underlying customer base. This is a serious mistake, since some types of customers may not yield continuing revenues once the acquisition has been completed. Here are some issues to investigate:

- *Concentration analysis.* A target company with a broad base of customers is a far more palatable acquisition opportunity than one whose sales are derived from a small cluster of large customers, since the departure of even a single large customer could have a major negative impact. A simple analysis of the prior year's sales by customer will reveal if the customer base is heavily concentrated.

- *Customer markets.* How well are customers performing? If their markets are suffering through a decline or increased competition, it is entirely possible that they will soon cut back on their orders, or demand price reductions. Also, is there a merger trend among customers that may eventually cut into sales? While this level of investigation does not need to encompass all of a target's customers, it should include those comprising the bulk of its sales.

- *Customer relationship duration.* Do customers show loyalty to the target by having made purchases for many years? If there is a high churn rate, then the target is not taking care of its customers, or there is simply no customer loyalty in the industry (which is indicative of competition based largely on price).

- *Maintenance revenues.* If customers pay an annual fee for product maintenance, and there is a long history of these recurring payments, then this is extremely valuable revenue. The buyer is essentially acquiring a long-term and very reliable revenue annuity. However, also compare the offsetting cost of servicing customers under the maintenance agreements, to ensure that the target is actually turning a profit. Also, review the maintenance agreements to see if there are limitations on the size or frequency of maintenance price increases; some agreements will restrict increases to the rate of inflation, or freeze increases for the first few years.

- *Customer complaints.* If there are a large number of returned products or complaints, then there is a significant risk of customer departures. There should be a customer support database in which all complaints are recorded, as well as the target's responses to these complaints.

- *Personal relationships.* If customers have direct and long-standing relations with particular sales people, the buyer needs to know this in order to target employee retention efforts at those individuals. This analysis can be quite a revelation if the primary customer contact is the target company's owner, who may be leaving at the time of the acquisition. If this is the case, contact the largest customers to see how they will react to the prospect of an acquisition.

- *Profitability analysis.* A common scenario is for a small company to stumble into a profitable niche market, and then incrementally expand into other areas that require more customer support and lower profit margins. The buyer can delve into the amount of "hand holding" required for certain customers, as well as margins on products they buy, and any special payment terms. The likely result will be a set of customers who contribute nothing to the target's profits, but which also consume an inordinate amount of its resources.

- *Customer contracts.* Some customer contracts specify that they are voided by a change in control of the target. If so, the due diligence team needs to itemize the waivers that the target must obtain from these customers as part of the acquisition agreement. Without waivers, the buyer could face a significant shortfall in expected revenues from the target.

In essence, the best scenario is to have a broadly distributed group of customers with a long history of purchases from the target, who appear to be well taken care of, and are not especially price-sensitive.

DUE DILIGENCE—PRODUCT DEVELOPMENT

In industries where competition is based primarily on innovation, the true driver of profitability is the target's product development process. It requires a special skill set to evaluate a target's development efforts, so the due diligence tram should bring in the buyer's product development manager or an outside specialist to conduct an investigation. Some of the key items to investigate are:

- *Product pipeline.* Does the target have a robust stream of incoming products? For each one, determine the amount of remaining time required before it can be launched, as well as any technical, pricing, or safety hurdles yet to be surmounted.

- *Hanging products.* Many product pipelines contain one or two products that seemingly never reach market, but which continue to absorb time and money for long periods of time. To determine if this is the case for the target, summarize the cost invested in each product, and the time period during which it has been in development. This is a key synergy area, since the buyer can easily cut a product in which it has no emotional investment.

- *Key development personnel.* There are usually a small number of key people who are responsible for most of the products delivered to market. Find out who these people are, and what it will take to retain them. An excellent sign of a successful development team is one with minimal turnover and considerable longevity with the target company.

- *Incremental product launches.* A target may have a long track record of product launches, but they may be incremental spin-offs of existing products. This is not necessarily bad, since the odds of success for incremental upgrades are generally good. However, there are only so many upgrades that can be launched.

- *Funding.* How much does the target invest in new product development each year? This is generally measured as a percentage of total revenues, but also be sure to compare the total annual expenditure to that of the target's competitors. A key finding may be that the target is being massively outspent by a rival, so that there is no way it can compete over the long term based on its future product stream.

- *Product flaws.* Does the target have a history of issuing inadequately engineered products that fail? The best source of information for this investigation is warranty claim records. It may also be possible to determine how many products are returned for rework by examining the receiving log. A large number of engineering change orders clustered soon after a product launch is another telling indicator.

- *Development plan.* Is there a product development plan that the target closely adheres to, or does it follow a more casual approach?

Having a plan speaks well of the target's ability to create products in new markets where it can grow.

- *Target costing.* Does the target use the target costing methodology, where it develops products to match specific costing targets? If so, it is probably realizing above-average profit margins. If not, the buyer has an excellent opportunity to impose the methodology and reap additional synergies.

In short, the buyer is looking for a few key success factors when reviewing a target's product development efforts: an ongoing funding commitment, a development strategy, a strong team to carry out that strategy, and a record of consistently bringing new products to market in a timely manner and within budget.

DUE DILIGENCE—PRODUCTION PROCESS

In industries where competition is based primarily on cost, a strong driver of profitability is the target's production process. If so, the due diligence team should spend a considerable amount of time here, delving into the following issues:

- *Work flow.* Does the target produce to a forecast or to actual demand? The first scenario involves large assembly lines that produce to inventory, while the second scenario typically involves the use of cellular manufacturing layouts and minimal on-hand inventory.

- *Throughput philosophy.* Does the target focus its efforts on its bottleneck operations, to ensure that products with the highest throughput are manufactured first? Does it create products that maximize throughput? For more information on this topic, see the author's Throughput Accounting book.

- *Industrial engineering.* Does the target have an active industrial engineering staff that is constantly upgrading the work flow of the production environment? Irrespective of the type of work flow, there should be an enduring commitment to achieving high levels of production efficiency.

- *Engineering change orders.* When the engineering staff creates product changes, what is the procedure for instituting the change? Does the target use up its remaining finished goods and raw materials prior to implementing the change, or is there a significant amount of excess inventory on hand related to these changes?

- *Safety.* A production area that is poorly managed and improperly set up is more likely to have an ongoing record of safety problems. This in turn results in higher employee absenteeism, workers' compensation premiums, and a greater likelihood of unionization.

- *Shipping delays.* If the production area is incapable of meeting demand, there will be a continuing series of missed ship dates, partially filled orders, or substituted orders, with a lengthy backlog.

- *Cost estimating procedures.* If the target is creating customized products, then how effective are its cost estimating procedures? Does it fully factor in all costs to its pricing decisions? Are overhead costs incorrectly allocated? These issues could mean that the target is unnecessarily driving away business, or accepting jobs for which it has no chance of earning an adequate profit.

- *Pricing procedures.* If the target creates standard products, then how does it set prices? Are they based on a cost-plus model, or what the market will bear? Does the target set low prices in order to gain market share, or high prices in order to squeeze all possible profit from a declining market position? If the buyer's pricing philosophy varies from that of the target, pricing could change dramatically after the acquisition.

The review of a production system will very likely yield a number of problem areas. However, this is not necessarily bad, and should certainly not be grounds for terminating an acquisition. On the contrary, the buyer may be able to achieve massive profit improvements in the production area. If anything, the presence of significant problems in the production area may be the key determining factor in deciding to *acquire* a target.

DUE DILIGENCE—INFORMATION TECHNOLOGY

The information technology (IT) systems of a target company are likely to play a pivotal role in its operations, so they represent a significant risk that bears in-depth investigation. Given the complexity of IT systems and the time required to properly evaluate them, IT due diligence will likely span the entire length of the due diligence effort.

Many smaller buyers do not have sufficient IT expertise to properly evaluate the systems of a target company. As a result, it is common for them to ignore the target's IT systems entirely, and deal with them after the deal is closed. This introduces significant risks, since the buyer will be completely unaware of the real state of the target's IT systems, which may be at the point of failure.

The best alternative is to bring in an IT consulting firm to conduct a complete review of the target's IT infrastructure, software applications, network, policies, and procedures. This review can be extremely expensive, since it must be completed on a rush basis and requires the services of high-end IT experts. However, it can mitigate a considerable amount of risk.

Once the due diligence is complete, it may also make sense to retain the consulting firm to assist in integrating the target's systems into those of the buyer. There is some efficiency to be gained by doing so, since they are already familiar with the target's systems.

DUE DILIGENCE—LEGAL ISSUES

There is a wide array of legal issues that the buyer must review. In most cases, the analysis issues noted here are related to various kinds of contracts. When these arise, a key analysis point is to see if they can be dissolved in the event of a corporate change of control. Key legal reviews are as follows:

- *Articles of incorporation and bylaws.* This document will include any anti-takeover provisions that are intended to make a change of control very expensive.

- *Board minutes.* This review should cover the last five years, and address whether stock issuances have been authorized, equity compensation plans have been properly approved, and so on.

- *Certificate of incorporation, including name changes.* This is used to find the list of all names under which the target company operates, which is needed for real estate title searches.

- *Certificate of good standing.* Verify that the target has filed its annual report with the secretary of state of the state within which it is incorporated on a timely basis.

- *Employment contracts.* Key employees may be guaranteed high pay levels for a number of years, or a "golden parachute" clause that guarantees them a large payment if the company is sold.

- *Engineering reports.* These documents will note any structural weaknesses in corporate buildings that may require expensive repairs.

- *Environmental exposure.* Review all literature received from the Environmental Protection Agency, as well as the Occupational Safety and Health Administration, and conduct environmental hazard testing around all company premises to ascertain the extent of potential environmental litigation.

- *Expiring contracts.* Summarize the expiration dates of all contracts, to determine which ones are expiring soon. While many will be renewable at approximately their current terms and conditions, the buyer should be aware of any unusually favorable contracts that are about to terminate, as well as any situations where the replacement contract is likely to be significantly more expensive (such as a below-market office lease).

- *Insurance policies.* Verify that the existing insurance policies cover all significant risks that are not otherwise covered by internal safety policies. Also, compare these policies to those held by the buyer to see if there can be savings by consolidating the policies for both companies.

- *Labor union agreements.* If the target company is a union shop, the union contract may contain unfavorable provisions related to work rules, guaranteed pay increases, payouts or guaranteed retraining funds in the event of a plant closure, or onerous benefit payments.

- *Leases.* Creating a schedule of all current leases tells a buyer the extent of commitments to pay for leased assets, as well as interest rates and any fees for early lease terminations.

- *Licenses.* A license for a target company to do business, usually granted by a local government, but also by another company for whom it is the distributor or franchisee, may not be transferable if there is a change of ownership. This can be quite a surprise to a buyer that now finds it cannot use the company it has just bought.

- *Liens.* A creditor may have a lien on the target's assets until such time as a debt is repaid. Liens may also exist because of a prior debt, and the creditor forgot to remove it once the debt was repaid. If so, the target is responsible for lien removal.

- *Litigation.* This is a broad area that requires a considerable amount of review before legal counsel can be reasonably satisfied as to the extent and potential liability associated with current and potential litigation. This review should encompass an investigation of all civil suits and criminal actions that may include contract disputes, fraud, defamation, discrimination, harassment, breach of employment contract, wrongful termination, inadequate disclosure issues, insider trading, debt collection, deceptive trade practices, antitrust suits, environmental practices, or other issues. It should also include tax claims and notices of potential litigation received from any of the following government agencies:

  ○ Department of Justice

  ○ Department of Labor

  ○ Equal Employment Opportunity Commission

  ○ Federal Trade Commission

- ○ Internal Revenue Service
- ○ Securities and Exchange Commission (applies only to a publicly held entity)

  Litigation analysis can also encompass a review of liability trends within the target's industry, to see what types of lawsuits may be filed against the target in the near future.

- *Marketing materials.* The target company's advertising of its product capabilities can be a source of potential litigation, if the publicized product claims are overstated.

- *Pension plans.* Determine the size of the employer-funded portion of the pension plan. This will require the services of an actuary to verify the current cost of required future funding.

- *Product warranty agreements.* Review the published warranty that is issued alongside each product to verify its term, as well as what specific features it will replace in the event of product failure.

- *Related party transactions.* In closely held companies, it is not unusual for top managers to treat the companies like their personal banks, shifting money in and out for a variety of non-business purposes, including payments to other companies that they also own. While this may not be illegal, the due diligence team should model the target's results to see how it would have performed without these transactions.

- *Sponsorship agreements.* A target company may have a long-term commitment to sponsor an event that will require a significant expenditure to maintain or terminate.

- *Supplier or customer contracts.* A target company may be locked into a long-term agreement with one or more of its suppliers or customers, possibly guaranteeing unfavorable terms that will noticeably affect profits if the buyer purchases the company.

- *Trade secrets.* There are a variety of trade secrets, such as unpatented inventions and manufacturing processes, for which confidentiality has been strictly maintained. While it is extremely difficult to quantify the value of trade secrets, the due diligence team can at

least investigate how well the target uses access restriction procedures and confidentiality agreements to protect its secrets, as well
as how vigorously it pursues violators of its trademarks, copyrights,
and patents.

In a few cases, it is possible to quantify the legal problems arising
from this analysis. For example, one can quantify the extra cost required to fulfill any "poison pill" provisions, or the net present value
of all employment, labor union, and lease provisions that require a
specified minimum set of payments for a designated time period. An
example of the format used to summarize these expenses is shown
below:

Analysis Report for Contractual and Legal Issues

Description	Additional Information	Summary of Costs
Poison pill payout provision	Bylaws section 2, clause 14	$12,500,000
Golden parachute provision	For all officers	3,250,000
Discounted cost of all lease provisions	Copiers, forklifts	320,000
Discounted pension plan funding requirements		4,750,000
Discounted cost of sponsorship agreement		220,000
Termination payment for long-term supplier contracts		540,000
Total cost of contractual and legal issues		**$21,580,000**

DUE DILIGENCE FOR A BUSINESS SEGMENT

If the company being sold is a spin-off from a larger business, it is
entirely possible that the buyer must be prepared to immediately step
in with a variety of replacement services. For example, the selling

parent company may provide shared office space, accounting and legal services, and information technology support. It may also provide access to crucial manufacturing or research facilities. If so, due diligence must ascertain the extent of these services, and how difficult they would be to replace.

This is a prime area in which the due diligence team must share its findings with the integration team, which must determine how long the selling parent company is willing to provide services and at what cost. The team must then be ready with a services replacement plan as soon as the purchase transaction is finalized.

DUE DILIGENCE—FORECASTS

It is extremely unwise for a buyer to evaluate a target company based solely on a forecast provided to it regarding future results. Any target company attempting to maximize its valuation will dream up every possible revenue increase for the next year, which inevitably yields a "hockey stick" jump in revenues. Needless to say, these gains rarely materialize.

However, the due diligence team should make *some* estimation of what the target's results may be over the next few years, and the target's forecasts are at least a starting point for making this determination. To do so, the due diligence team needs some investigative tools to verify how the forecasts were constructed. Here are some useful tips:

- *Backup for revenue changes.* All too frequently, revenue forecasts are based on nothing more than a percentage change over the previous year (usually in an upward direction). Instead, look for written market assessments by the target's sales department that itemize exactly what changes are expected by geographic region and product.
- *Capacity changes.* Does the forecast note when current capacity levels will be exceeded, so that it incorporates additional expenditures for new equipment and personnel?

- *Competitive reactions.* If the target company expects to gain market share, then it can expect a strong adverse reaction from its competitors. Does the forecast contemplate how the target will react to such issues as price declines, faster delivery, or improved product quality by competitors?

- *Estimate participation.* How far down in the corporate hierarchy does the target's budgeting team go in order to obtain input for forecasts? For the best information, it should ask every manager about future revenue and cost estimates for his or her areas of responsibility. If, on the other hand, the forecast is based largely on the opinions of the target's president, then consider the results to be suspect.

- *Working capital.* If the forecast assumes a large jump in revenues, then there should also be a corresponding increase in working capital, since the target company must somehow fund the related accounts receivable and inventory.

Of the greatest importance in evaluating a forecast is the target's historical ability to meet forecasts. If it has set unrealistic expectations in the past and failed, then the due diligence team should rightfully assume that the target will fail again with the current forecast.

DUE DILIGENCE—MISSING INFORMATION

In a hostile takeover attempt, the target company may be quite diligent in blocking attempts at obtaining information about it. This results in a significant loss of information, so that the buyer cannot complete a full analysis of the situation. If so, it is very useful to make a list of what information has not been obtained, and what the risk may be of not obtaining it. For example, if there is no information available about a company's gross margin, then there is a risk of making too large an offer for a company that does not have the margins to support the price. Once all these risks are assembled into a list, determine the level of risk the company is willing to bear by not having the information, or in deciding to invest the time and money to obtain it. This will be an iterative process, as the number of open questions gradually decreases, and the cost and time needed to find the answers to the remaining questions goes up. At some point, the buyer will decide that enough information is available to proceed with making an offer, or that the risk is too great to do so.

If the target is a publicly held company, the risk of not having key information is somewhat lessened, since it is required to reveal a great deal of information in its quarterly and annual reports. In particular, the Management Discussion and Analysis (MD&A) section can be most illuminating, since it itemizes such factors as key risks, how the target makes money, key indicators that it uses to monitor the company, financing arrangements, material commitments, key competitors, and so forth.

COMPLEXITY ANALYSIS

The primary objective of complexity analysis is to determine if it will be too difficult to integrate a target company, with a secondary objective of determining the level of risk posed by its general level of complexity.

One area to consider is the sources of the target's revenue. The level of complexity and risk is increased when revenue is derived from multiple businesses, since the buyer must devote additional levels of management resources to each of those businesses. Complexity and risk also increase when a significant percentage of revenue is derived from a small number of large transactions that are custom-tailored to individual customers. These transactions tend to be highly volatile in their amount and frequency, making it difficult to estimate future revenue levels and attendant cash flows.

The tax rate can also contribute to complexity and risk. This is especially true if the target company has located its headquarters in a tax haven, since this indicates a strong interest in tax avoidance that has likely led to the use of a variety of complicated tax avoidance schemes. A further indicator of tax complexity is a substantial difference between the reported level of book and tax income. Finally, a volatile effective tax rate indicates that the target company is engaged in a variety of one-time tax dodges. While all of these issues may be caused by completely legal transactions, it clearly indicates that the company has altered its operations in a variety of ways to take maximum advantage of the tax laws, and this will require considerable ongoing effort to maintain.

Another indicator of complexity is the presence of off-balance sheet assets and liabilities, such as variable-interest entities, research and development partnerships, and operating leases. While the intent of these transactions may have little to do with dressing up the balance sheet and may be based on solid operational reasons, they are still more likely to cause sudden changes in the reported condition of the company if underlying accounting rules are altered to require their full presentation.

DUE DILIGENCE—RED FLAGS

When conducting a due diligence review, the review team will inevitably find some items that will be of concern to the buyer. However, some concerns are more significant than others, and are indicative of a lax control environment that may pose major risks to the buyer. Some of the most important issues are as follows:

- *Auditor resignation.* There are valid reasons why auditors may resign from the ongoing audit of a company, but it is still a significant indicator that the auditors found objectionable practices at the target company.

- *Change in accounting methods.* If the target has changed to an accounting method that leads to better financial results, this is a strong indicator of financial chicanery. This is an especially strong indicator if the company has a history of making such changes on a continual basis, creating significant changes to its financial results.

- *Complex business arrangements.* If the target controls a number of business entities for which there is no apparent business purpose, it may be using inter-company transactions to avoid income-tax payments, or siphoning off funds to officer-controlled entities.

- *Covenant problems.* If the target barely meets its loan covenants on a recurring basis, this is a strong indicator of earnings management.

- *Criminal records.* If an owner or key manager of the target has committed a felony, the buyer should at least conduct an especially vigorous due diligence examination, if not back out at once, on the grounds that the risk of fraud is enhanced. However, a personal bankruptcy is *not* grounds for pulling out of an acquisition, since this is an occasional trait of a serial entrepreneur—some business ventures will fail, but this does not necessarily reflect on the owner's current business operations.

- *Insider stock sales.* If a number of stockholders are selling their stock at approximately the same time, they may have inside information that future operating results will be poor, which will drive down the stock price. However, if only a few people are selling, and not in great volume, then it may only mean that they are obtaining liquidity for specific needs, such as college or house payments.

- *Internal audit scope restrictions.* If the internal audit department is barred from investigating certain areas of the company, this is a massive warning sign that management may be hiding information. An indicator is when senior managers are allowed to review and change the annual internal audit plan before it is approved by the audit committee.

- *Minimal operational reports.* A well-run company should have a variety of operational reports. If there are few such reports, either the management team does not have proper control over its business, or it is a sham operation for which there are no operations of significance.

- *Month-end shipping surge.* If the target has a persistent habit of shipping the bulk of its orders within the last few days of a month, there may be a dangerous "make the numbers" environment in which employees are accustomed to process shipments past the month-end deadline, or ship damaged goods, or make shipments when there are no firm orders.

- *Non-standard accounting practices.* Within most industries, competitors account for a variety of accounting transactions in about the same way. When a company departs from standard practice, and especially when the results yield more aggressive revenue or earnings results, this may indicate that other accounting practices are also being stretched. This scenario may yield an earnings restatement if the buyer acquires the company and then imposes its own (and presumably more conservative) accounting practices.

- *Previous failed sale attempts.* Prior to the current acquisition discussions, the target may have repeatedly tried to sell itself. If so, the previous buyers found something that caused them to cancel further acquisition discussions. While this could have simply been excessively high pricing demands by the target, there also could be some other issue that the current buyer should be aware of.

- *Regulatory warnings.* If the target has received several regulatory warnings in the recent past, this may simply indicate that the government has spotted a specific safety or environmental problem, and wants it fixed at once. However, it may be indicative of a more deep-rooted problem, such as an emphasis on cost reduction over regulatory compliance, or a culture of only barely meeting regulatory requirements.

- *Reserve changes.* There are a small number of expense reserves that companies use, such as a bad debt allowance, or a reserve for warranty expenses. If it appears that these reserves are being frequently adjusted in order to enhance or smooth out the target's reported results, the due diligence team can reasonably assume that earnings management is pervasive.

The presence of red flags in one or two of these areas may not be cause of overwhelming concern. However, if problems crop up in many areas, the due diligence manager should consider a strongly-worded recommendation to walk away from the deal. This may call for a detailed analysis of the reasons behind the recommendation, since the buyer may have already agreed to a breakup fee that requires it to pay the seller if it backs out of the purchase transaction.

DUE DILIGENCE—SELLER'S PERSPECTIVE

The discussion of due diligence is of greatest concern to the buyer, who must probe deeply to determine the extent of any underlying risks. However, it is also useful to consider the problems experienced by the seller in responding to requests for information.

If the seller is actively selling itself, then it has a good idea of what information prospective buyers need, and will have already accumulated a set of documents that addresses nearly all of the questions that anyone is likely to ask. If the buyer persists in asking for additional items that have no great bearing on either risk or price analysis, this could annoy the seller enough to eliminate the buyer from consideration. At a minimum, it creates a high annoyance level that may carry over into subsequent integration efforts. Thus, the due diligence team should compare its information requirements to what the seller has already accumulated, and consider throwing out incidental requests that have marginal value to the buyer, but which will require considerable effort by the seller.

Under no circumstances should the buyer pepper the seller with a perpetual stream of requests. Instead, present due diligence requests in clusters. There should be a single large set of requests at the start of the process that contains nearly all of the information the buyer needs. Once the due diligence team has reviewed this information, it may have additional questions, which it should compile into another list, and so on. By structuring requests in this manner, the seller can collect information more efficiently. Also, the due diligence team manager should review all subsequent requests for information, and eliminate them if they will only yield marginally useful information. Otherwise, information requests may trickle on for some time.

The seller faces a particular problem with due diligence investigations of its customers. A prudent buyer will want to speak with the seller's largest customers, but this means that the seller must parade a number of potential buyers past those customers. If this happens, the seller should warn in advance all customers to be contacted, and reassure them that the seller will continue its operations as usual irrespective of any sale transaction. These reassurances will sound less valid if a large number of buyers appear, so the seller should try to spread contacts around among multiple customers.

What if the buyer is a competitor of the target company? If so, the target will be rightfully concerned about handing over confidential information that the buyer could use against the target if the acquisition falls through. One option is for the buyer to volunteer to bring in a third-party consulting firm, such as its auditors, to review the target's more confidential information. This independent firm can then verify and summarize the information, stripping out key competitive data, have the target approve it for distribution, and then send its report to the buyer. Another option is to require the buyer to pay a breakup fee if it backs away from the acquisition. A third variation is to only release the most sensitive information once the deal is far advanced, when the parties are less likely to back away from the acquisition. However, if the target wants to be sold, then at some point it must issue a certain amount of confidential information, and so must be willing to trust in the intentions of the buyer.

DUE DILIGENCE—DOCUMENTATION

Most companies undertake due diligence because they want to learn more about the target company. However, due diligence can also be used as evidence in a lawsuit. If anyone decides to sue the buyer for negligence in conducting an acquisition, the buyer must be able to prove that it conducted a reasonably thorough investigation of the target. Diligence and negligence are opposites, so the presence of a well-documented due diligence effort suggests the absence of negligence. Thus, not only adequate due diligence, but also the comprehensive documentation of that diligence is an effective defense against lawsuits.

The first level of documentation is to print out all due diligence documentation and store it in an organized manner. Not only does this yield more easily searchable information, but also avoids the risk of loss if electronic files are deleted. For each due diligence binder, label it with the name of the target company, and set up tabs within the binder to identify its contents. Examples of tab headings are:

Overview	Information technology
Accounting	Legal
Competitors	Marketing
Customers	Products
Environmental	Regulations
Facilities	Valuation
Human resources	

The overview section is especially important, because it contains a summary of the reasons for acquiring the target company, the investment thesis behind the acquisition, and the results of the due diligence investigation. Once written, have the buyer's attorneys review the summary document, since it could eventually be used as evidence in a lawsuit.

The documentation contained within the due diligence binder should also be structured. For example, when documenting an interview, write down when and where it occurred, as well as the name and title of the interviewee, any significant information obtained, and the confidentiality of the information provided. Write down the same types of information for every interview, to create consistency between documents. Consider using standard interview forms, so that the document reminds the interviewer of what information to obtain. This same system can be used to collect a variety of information.

The volume of information collected can be immense, requiring substantially more than one binder. If so, use a master index to organize the information across many binders, and appropriately label each binder to make them easily searchable. In addition, if the information is also being stored in an electronic format, download the information into a long-term storage medium, such as a DVD or compact disc, and store it with the binders in a protective cover.

The steps outlined here will clearly require a significant effort. However, having easily searchable and well organized documents is extremely useful. Not only do they represent an excellent defense against negligence, but they are also the best way to answer questions regarding an acquisition that may arise for years afterwards.

SUMMARY

The purpose of due diligence is to give the buyer some degree of exposure to the target company's operations, and to thereby gain an understanding of the risks to which it will be exposed. Based on this information, the buyer will also likely adjust the proposed purchase price based on any excessive risks it may find, or at least attempt to shift some risks to the buyer. Further, the buyer may uncover possible synergies that it was not previously aware of, and which may increase its enthusiasm for the deal. For these reasons, due diligence is an absolutely mandatory part of the acquisition process. Though there is usually a tight timeline within which due diligence is conducted, the buyer should be willing to expand that timeline to ensure that all required review activities are completed to the satisfaction of the due diligence team. Only after the buyer has thoroughly investigated all key areas of concern should it proceed to the next step in the acquisition process, which is the purchase agreement.

The topics addressed in this chapter covered the more important due diligence areas, but were not intended to provide comprehensive coverage of all topics. For a more complete set of due diligence questions, see Appendix A. Even that appendix should not be considered comprehensive, since many additional issues are industry-specific. Thus, it is best to use Appendix A as a foundation for a larger due diligence list that a buyer compiles based on its own experience with acquisitions.

Chapter 6

The Purchase Agreement

The purchase agreement is the legal centerpiece of an acquisition. In it, both parties describe the method of payment and their guarantees to each other, supported by a variety of detailed exhibits. This chapter describes the main elements of a purchase agreement, along with example text.

Please note that the discussion of various components of the purchase agreement in this chapter cannot be combined into a single, fully operational purchase agreement. The discussion merely centers on key segments of the agrement, and also does not include a variety of legal terminology that would detract from the reader's understanding of the agreement.

COMPONENTS OF A PURCHASE AGREEMENT

In some cases, purchase agreements are heavily modified to meet the particular needs of the participants. However, a basic group of sections can be found in most purchase agreements, which are as follows:

- *The merger section.* Also known as the "business combination" section, it describes the basic structure of the transaction and the form of payment to be made.
- *The letter of transmittal section.* Describes the contents of the letter sent to all of the seller's shareholders, explaining the purchase

terms and their right to submit their shares for payment, conversion, or to obtain appraisal rights.

- *The representations and warranties section.* Describes a number of conditions to which both parties state they are in compliance. Though it applies to both parties, the real impact is on the seller, who warrants that its actual operations and financial results are as represented to the buyer.

- *The conduct of business section.* Requires the seller to conduct its business prior to the closing date in the best interests of the buyer.

- *The additional agreements section.* Includes miscellaneous provisions, such as mutual agreements to news releases and covenants to assist in all steps necessary to complete the transaction.

- *The closing section.* States when and where the closing will take place.

- *The termination prior to closing section.* Notes the conditions under which the parties can terminate the transaction prior to the closing.

- *The supporting documents section.* Itemizes the documents that each party must receive before the transaction can be completed.

- *Exhibits and schedules.* Includes a broad array of attachments, such as the seller's articles of incorporation, fixed assets list, shareholder list, and liability and contract itemizations.

The two sections of the purchase agreement over which the most negotiation occurs are the merger section and the representations and warranties section. The first involves the price paid, while the second contains the seller's assurances that the business being sold is as represented to the buyer (and thereby represents a significant liability to the seller).

THE MERGER SECTION

The core of the purchase agreement is the merger section, in which the acquisition and form of payment are described. It begins with a statement of the merger, and the time when it will take effect. The form of merger as described in this section can vary significantly, as described later in the Types of Acquisitions chapter. An example follows, where the selling entity is being merged into the buying entity:

Merger: Subject to the terms and conditions of this Agreement, the Seller shall be merged with and into the Buyer. At the Effective Time (as hereinafter defined), the separate legal existence of Seller shall cease, and the Buyer shall be the surviving corporation in the merger and shall continue its corporate existence under the laws of the State of _____ under the name _____ , Inc.

Effective Time: The merger shall become effective upon the filing of the certificate of merger with the Secretary of State of the State of _____. The time at which the merger shall become effective is referred to as the "Effective Time."

The merger section also includes a statement that the buyer takes on all of the assets and liabilities of the seller. This language can vary considerably if the buyer is only acquiring the assets of the seller, in which case the language is much more restrictive. An example follows:

Assets and Liabilities: At the Effective Time, the Buyer shall possess all the rights, and be subject to all the restrictions of the Seller; and all property and every other interest shall be thereafter the property of the Buyer, and the title to any real estate vested in the Seller shall not be in any way impaired by the merger; but all rights of creditors and all liens upon any property of the Seller shall be preserved unimpaired, and all debts and liabilities of the Seller shall thenceforth attach to the Buyer, and may be enforced against it to the same extent as if said debts and liabilities had been incurred or contracted by the Seller.

If the buyer intends to only acquire selected assets and liabilities of the seller, rather than the seller's entire legal entity, then the description of assets and liabilities is more restrictive. An example follows:

Assets and Liabilities: At the Effective Time, the Buyer shall purchase all of the assets noted in Exhibit A and assume those liabilities noted in Exhibit B. The Buyer shall not acquire any other assets or assume any other liabilities other than those noted in Exhibits A and B.

If the seller thinks that there is significant upside potential for earnings growth and the buyer is skeptical about this assertion, then the parties may agree to an earnout clause. Under this arrangement, the buyer is only obligated to pay an additional amount to the seller if the seller increases its earnings during a clearly defined subsequent period. If the earnout period is extremely long, then index the earnout threshold to the rate of inflation; otherwise, it becomes increasingly easy to attain the earnout over time. An example follows:

Earnout Payment: The Seller may earn an additional payment of $5 cash for every $1 of incremental gain in EBITDA (earnings before interest, taxes, depreciation and amortization) that it earns during the year following the merger over its audited EBITDA during the year prior to the merger. During the measurement period, the Buyer will leave the Seller's management team in full control of the Seller's operations, and shall not impose any corporate overhead charges on the business during that time.

Earnout agreements are exceedingly troublesome, because the buyer and seller may be in continual disagreement about how revenues and expenses are calculated. The level of disagreement generally increases with the complexity of the earnout calculation. For example, if there is a sliding payment scale, the parties will be more likely to dispute the payments if the calculations leave the seller just short of a scheduled payment boost.

Another problem is that the seller may increase its reported profits by selling to customers with doubtful credit during the earnout period. This allows the seller's shareholders to achieve a maximum earnout, but saddles the buyer with an excessive amount of bad debt. This problem can be avoided by including in the earnout clause a provision that the incremental gain in profit shall be reduced by the incremental gain in outstanding receivables more than 90 days old.

An earnout is most effective if the buyer cordons off the acquired entity from the rest of the company during the earnout period, and leaves its existing management in place. However, this means that the buyer has no opportunity to achieve synergies by merging the entities together. A variation that still allows integration of the businesses is to commit to the expenditure of certain sums for sales, marketing, and research, thereby yielding some assurance that the business will continue to be profitable during the measurement period.

The lengthy treatment of this topic should make it clear to the reader that earnout provisions are not usually advisable, unless a deal cannot be reached in any other way. If the buyer agrees to such a provision, it should be fully prepared to pay out the maximum amount of the earnout, if only to avoid costly litigation.

The next step is for the buyer to pay the seller. If the payment is in the buyer's stock, then the text can vary widely. An example that assumes the existence of both common and preferred stock within the selling company follows:

> **Stock Payment:** At the Effective Time, each share of common stock of the Seller shall be converted into one share of common stock of the Buyer. The Seller's stock shall be cancelled and extinguished. At the Effective Time, each share of preferred stock of the Seller shall be converted into two shares of common stock of the Buyer. The shares of the Seller's preferred stock shall be cancelled and extinguished. All shares of common and preferred stock held in the treasury of the Seller shall be cancelled and cease to exist. Upon surrender of a certificate representing shares of the Seller's stock, or an affidavit and indemnification in form reasonably acceptable to counsel for the Buyer stating that such stockholder has lost its certificate, the Buyer shall issue to each stockholder a certificate representing the number of shares of Buyer stock that the stockholder is entitled to receive.

The reference above to an affidavit and indemnification form is an extremely common one in acquisitions. Shareholders frequently lose their stock certificates, and must represent to the buyer that the certificates are lost or destroyed. This representation essentially absolves the buyer from any liability to issue additional shares if the certificates reappear in the future.

The buyer may also pay in cash. If so, it is not customary to pay by check. Instead, the buyer usually pays with certified funds or transmits the cash by wire transfer on the closing date. An example follows:

> **Cash Payment:** At the Effective Time, the Buyer shall pay to the Seller the sum of $___ in certified funds, by wire transfer, or in other form satisfactory to the Seller.

The buyer may also pay the seller with a promissory note for some portion or all of the purchase price. If so, the clause references an exhibit in which the entire loan agreement is listed, and then summarizes its key terms and provisions within the clause. An example follows:

> **Promissory Note:** The Buyer shall pay the Seller $_____ by delivery of the promissory note attached hereto as Exhibit A. The promissory note provides for the payment of the above amount with interest at the rate of 7.5% per annum in equal quarterly installments over a term of six years. As security for payment of the promissory note, the Buyer shall execute the security agreement attached hereto as Exhibit B, which provides the Seller with a senior security interest in all of the assets purchased hereunder. For until such time as the promissory note is paid in full, the Buyer shall send copies of its annual financial statements to the Seller's principal shareholders.

If the seller has options or warrants outstanding, then their holders could potentially convert them into the buyer's stock. To avoid this additional share issuance, the seller should agree to a clause stating that no options or warrants will be outstanding as of the acquisition date. An example follows:

> **Options; Warrants; Other Rights:** All options, warrants, and other rights to purchase Seller stock outstanding as of the Effective Date will be exercised or terminated prior to the Effective Time, and the Buyer shall not have any obligation with respect to such options or rights.

If the buyer has publicly traded stock, then the seller may want a "true-up" provision, under which it receives additional shares of the buyer's stock if the price of those shares subsequently drops. This provision protects the seller from suffering a drop in the value of its shares. The buyer does not want a true-up provision at all, and will at least try to restrict it to a single true-up event in the near future, so that it is not constantly issuing new shares to the seller in the event of a significant, long-term decline in its stock price. An example follows:

> **Additional Shares:** As of six months following the Effective Time, the Buyer will compute the average daily closing price for its common stock for the following 60 trading days. If the average closing price for this period is less than the price at which shares were originally issued to the Seller's shareholders, then the Buyer will promptly issue additional shares, such that the total dollar value of the Buyer's common stock equals the original purchase price, using the subsequent average closing price.

Several optional clauses related to the merger section are described later in the Special Clauses section of this chapter.

THE LETTER OF TRANSMITTAL SECTION

While the preceding merger section discussed the form of payment to be made to the seller's shareholders, the letter of transmittal section describes the mechanics of how this payment is to be achieved. This is boilerplate text that attorneys rarely alter, stating that the buyer will send documents to the seller's shareholders, informing them of their rights under the purchase agreement, and including forms that they must complete in order to convert their shares into the form of payment. A considerably shortened example follows:

> **Letter of Transmittal:** Promptly after the Effective Time, the Buyer shall mail to each holder of record of Seller stock that was converted into the right to receive Buyer common stock a letter of transmittal, which

shall contain additional representations of such stockholder, including that (i) such stockholder has full right to deliver such seller stock and letter of transmittal, (ii) the delivery of such Seller stock will not violate any loan agreement, security agreement or other agreement to which such stockholder is bound, and (iii) such stockholder has good title to all shares of Seller stock indicated in such letter of transmittal. Delivery of Buyer stock shall be effected only upon delivery to the Buyer of _____ certificates evidencing ownership thereof and the letter of transmittal.

Under some state laws, minority shareholders can claim appraisal rights and receive cash payments for their shares. If so, this section should state that appraisal rights will be noted in the letter of transmittal, so that shareholders are fully aware of their rights.

THE REPRESENTATIONS AND WARRANTIES SECTION—SELLER

A crucial section of the purchase agreement is the representations and warranties section, in which each party states that it is in compliance with a number of issues, except as provided in a related exhibit. For example, the seller can represent that there are no outstanding lawsuits, other than those noted in Exhibit A. If subsequent events reveal that this is not actually the case, then the party making the representation or warranty is subsequently liable to the other party. This section deals with *seller* representations and warranties, while the next section covers similar topics for the buyer.

The representations and warranties section works together with the disclosure schedule to present the buyer with a complete set of information about the seller. Either the details about specific transactions, contracts, or conditions are listed in the disclosure schedule, or the seller states within the representations and warranties section that there are no other material issues. Thus, the buyer wants to see a comprehensive representations and warranties section, and will generally get it. Otherwise, there is a potentially excessive risk of unreported liabilities that the buyer must bear.

If the seller insists on providing no representations to the buyer, then the buyer should strongly consider either walking away from the deal, or offering a substantially reduced price that reflects the increased risk that it is assuming. Conversely, the more assurances the seller is willing to give, the lower is the risk to the buyer that there will be an unexpected economic loss, which allows the buyer to offer a higher price.

The seller must warrant that it is a corporation in good standing, and is empowered to enter into the purchase agreement. An example follows:

> **Organization, Standing, Subsidiaries:** The Seller is a corporation duly organized and existing in good standing under the laws of the State of ____, and has all requisite power and authority (corporate and other) to carry on its business, to own or lease its properties and assets, to enter into this Agreement and to carry out its terms. Copies of the Certificate of Incorporation and Bylaws of the Company that have been delivered to Buyer prior to the execution of this Agreement are true and complete and have not since been amended or repealed. The Seller has no subsidiaries or direct or indirect interest (by way of stock ownership or otherwise) in any corporation, limited liability company, or partnership.

The seller should state the number of its authorized and outstanding shares of all types of stock, as well as the presence of any instruments that convert into stock, such as convertible debt, options, or warrants. The seller also provides a complete list of its shareholders, which are included in a separate disclosure schedule. An example follows:

> **Capitalization:** The authorized capital stock of the Seller consists of ____ shares of Common Stock and ____ shares of preferred stock. The Seller has no authority to issue any other capital stock. There are ____ shares of Common Stock issued and outstanding, and such shares are duly authorized, validly issued, fully paid and nonassessable. There are ____ shares of preferred stock issued and outstanding, and such shares are duly authorized, validly issued, fully paid, and nonassessable.

Except as disclosed in the Seller Disclosure Schedule, the Seller has no outstanding warrants, stock options, rights, or commitments to issue Common Stock, Preferred Stock, or other Equity Securities of the Seller, and there are no outstanding securities convertible or exercisable into or exchangeable for Seller Common Stock, Seller Preferred Stock, or other Equity Securities of the Seller. The Seller Disclosure Schedule contains a true and complete list of the names of the record owners of all of the outstanding shares of Seller Stock and other Equity Securities of the Seller, together with the number of securities held. To the knowledge of the Seller, except as described in the Seller Disclosure Schedule, there is no voting trust, agreement or arrangement among any of the beneficial holders of Seller Common Stock affecting the exercise of the voting rights of Seller Stock.

The purchase agreement is usually signed by the seller's chief executive officer. However, this person is doing so on behalf of the seller's board of directors, which normally has sole authority to approve the transaction. A brief authorization statement represents that the seller's board has actually approved the transaction. An example follows:

Corporate Acts and Proceedings: The execution, delivery, and performance of this Agreement have been duly authorized by the Board of Directors of the Seller.

The seller must also attest that the purchase transaction will not require additional approval from third parties, violate government regulations, or affect contracts currently outstanding with its business partners. This is a common problem when loan agreements contain a clause stating that the contracts are voided in the event of a change in control. An example follows:

Compliance with Laws and Instruments: The Seller's operations have been and are being conducted in compliance with all applicable laws, rules, and regulations. The Agreement: (a) will not require any authorization, consent, or registration with, any court or governmental agency, (b) will not cause the Seller to violate (i) any provision of law,

(ii) any government rule or regulation, (iii) any court order, judgment, or decree, or (iv) any provision of the Certificate of Incorporation or Bylaws of the Seller, (c) will not violate or be in conflict with, a default under any loan or credit agreement to which the Seller is a party, and (d) will not result in the creation or imposition of any material lien upon any asset of the Seller.

The buyer does not want to find out that it unexpectedly owes a broker's commission to any third party as a result of the purchase transaction. A representation should state that only the broker fees noted in the seller disclosure schedule are outstanding. An example follows:

Broker's and Finder's Fees: No person has, or as a result of the transactions contemplated herein will have, any claim against the Buyer or Seller for any commission or other compensation as a finder or broker, except as set forth in the Seller Disclosure Schedule.

An extremely important item is the seller representation that it has issued accurate financial statements to the buyer. The buyer is presumably basing a considerable proportion of its purchase price on these documents, so the representation is mandatory. An example follows:

Financial Statements: The Seller has delivered to the Buyer the Seller's audited Balance Sheet, Statement of Operations, Statement of Changes in Shareholders' Equity, and Statement of Cash Flows as of and for the years ended December 31, ___, and December 31, ___. Such financial statements (a) are in accordance with the books and records of the Seller, (b) present fairly in all material respects the financial condition of the Seller at the dates and for the periods therein specified, and (c) have been prepared in accordance with generally accepted accounting principles applied on a basis consistent with prior accounting periods.

If the buyer is only acquiring certain assets, it may insist on a representation that those assets are fully and accurately valued. If it is an asset where an offsetting reserve is normally created, as would be the case for receivables or inventory, then the seller can represent that the asset is fully reserved against. An example follows:

> **Receivables and Inventory:** The Seller has established and disclosed reserves against any declines in value of its uncollected accounts receivable and inventories. These reserves are sufficient for any bad debts or obsolete inventory that may arise from the current balances.

The seller must also warrant that its tax returns have been accurately prepared and filed in a timely manner, and that all taxes have been paid. In addition, it should state that there are currently no tax audits or related claims. An example follows:

> **Tax Returns and Audits:** All required federal, state, local, and foreign tax returns of the Seller have been accurately prepared in all material respects and timely filed and paid in full. The Seller is not and has not been delinquent in the payment of any tax. The reserves for taxes reflected on the most recent balance sheet are sufficient for the payment of all unpaid taxes payable by the Seller with respect to the period ended on the balance sheet date. There are no federal, state, local, or foreign audits or claims relating to any tax returns of the Seller now pending, and the Seller has not received any notice of proposed audits or claims relating to any tax returns.

The seller should state that it has no undisclosed liabilities. If the seller is unwilling to make this representation, then the buyer should strongly consider walking away from the deal. An example follows:

> **Absence of Undisclosed Liabilities:** The Seller has no material obligation or liability arising out of any transaction entered into at or prior to the closing, except (a) as disclosed in the Seller Disclosure Schedule, (b) to the extent reserved against in the Balance Sheet, (c) current liabilities incurred and obligations under agreements entered into in the ordinary course of business since the Balance Sheet date, and (d) by the specific terms of any written agreement, document, or arrangement identified in the Seller Disclosure Schedule.

Since the date when the seller issued financial statements and related supporting documents to the buyer, there will likely have been some changes to the seller's operations in a multitude of areas, including debts, property damage, labor union issues, dividend payments, and so on. It should be represented that these changes were not material, except for those items noted later in the seller disclosure schedule. An example follows:

> **Changes:** Since the Balance Sheet Date, as of the date hereof and except as disclosed in the Seller Disclosure Schedule, the Seller has not, other than in the ordinary course of business, (a) incurred any liabilities, (b) discharged any liens, (c) mortgaged or pledged any assets, (d) sold or leased any assets, (e) suffered any physical damage which could have a material adverse effect on its condition, (f) encountered any labor union difficulties, (g) granted any wage increase or increased any profit-sharing, bonus, or deferred compensation arrangement, (h) issued or sold any shares of capital stock, options, or warrants, (i) declared or paid any dividends, (j) suffered or experienced any change in its financial condition which could have a material adverse effect on its condition, (k) made any change in the accounting principles or practices followed by it, (l) made or permitted any amendment or termination of any material contract to which it is a party, or (m) entered into any agreement, or otherwise obligated itself to do any of the foregoing, none of which could reasonably be expected to have a material adverse effect on the condition of the Seller.

The typical enterprise is party to numerous contracts, of which the most material should be summarized in the disclosure schedule. The seller should represent that there are no other contracts outstanding that have a material impact on its operations, and that complete copies of all enumerated contracts have been provided to the buyer. An example follows:

> **Contracts:** Except as disclosed in the Seller Disclosure Schedule, the Seller (a) is not a party to any agreement that is material to the Seller; (b) does not own any property; and (c) is not a party to any (i) agreement

with a labor union, (ii) agreement for the purchase of fixed assets or materials in excess of normal operating requirements, (iii) agreement for the employment of any officer, other employee, or consultant, (iv) bonus, pension, profit-sharing, retirement, stock purchase, stock option, medical, or similar plan, (v) loan agreement or guarantee of indebtedness, (vi) lease when acting in the role of lessor or lessee, (vii) agreement obligating it to pay any royalty or similar charge, (viii) covenant not to compete or other restriction on its ability to engage in any activity, or (ix) agreement to register securities under the Securities Act. The Seller has furnished complete copies of all agreements disclosed in the Seller Disclosure Schedule.

The seller should represent that it has valid title to all assets used to conduct its business, or current leases on such assets. Otherwise, the buyer may find itself scrambling to replace assets that are actually owned by a third party. This is a particular problem when the seller is spinning off a division to the buyer, and may be retaining some assets for its own purposes. An example follows:

Title to Property and Encumbrances: Except as disclosed in the Seller Disclosure Schedule, the Seller has good title to all assets used in the conduct of its business (except for property held under valid leases which are not in default), except for property disposed of in the ordinary course of business since the balance sheet date.

The seller must represent that there is no undisclosed litigation. As was the case with undisclosed liabilities, if the seller refuses to make this representation, then the buyer should not continue with the transaction. An example follows:

Litigation: Except as disclosed in the Seller Disclosure Schedule, there is no legal action, arbitration, or governmental proceeding pending or threatened against or affecting the Seller. The Seller is not aware of any incident or transaction that might reasonably be expected to result in any such action, arbitration, or governmental proceeding. The Seller is not in default with respect to any order or injunction of any court, arbitration authority, or governmental agency.

Buyers face enormous potential expenses if they acquire an entity's environmental liabilities. Thus, it is increasingly common to see a clause in which the seller represents the absence of such liabilities. An example follows:

> **Environmental Compliance:** The seller is in full compliance with all government laws and regulations relating to the disposal of waste products and environmental regulation, and does not lease or own a facility on any land subject to environmental remediation.

The buyer may be basing a large proportion of its purchase price on the seller's ownership of specific patents or trademarks, or relying on the existence of valid licenses for such intellectual property. If so, it should insist on the seller's warranty that these ownership or licensing rights are valid. An example follows:

> **Patents, Trademarks, Etc.:** Except as disclosed in the Seller Disclosure Schedule, (a) the Seller owns or possesses licenses to use all patent and trademark rights; and (b) the conduct of its business does not conflict with any valid patents, trademarks, or copyrights of others in any way which could reasonably be expected to have a material adverse effect on the business or financial condition of the Seller.

The buyer should insist on a seller representation that it has not made such unlawful payments as bribes or kickbacks. This allows the buyer to hold the seller liable for any government fines subsequently imposed if such payments are later discovered. An example follows:

> **Questionable Payments:** The Seller has not, nor to the knowledge of the Seller, has any director, officer, agent, employee, or other person acting on behalf of the Seller, used corporate funds for (a) unlawful contributions or payments relating to political activity; (b) direct or indirect unlawful payments to government officials or employees; or (c) bribes, rebates, payoffs, kickbacks, or other unlawful payments.

The representations and warranties section generally ends with a "catch-all" statement in which the seller represents that there are no other undisclosed material events that negatively affect the seller's business. An example follows:

> **Disclosure:** There is no fact relating to the Seller that the Seller has not disclosed to the Buyer in writing that materially and adversely affects the condition, assets, liabilities, operations, financial results, or prospects of the Seller.

Throughout the seller's representations and warranties, the seller will want to make representations "to the best of its knowledge." By doing so, it shifts to the buyer all risks of which it is not currently aware. For the same reason, the buyer will attempt to remove this clause from the section.

Though a great deal of attention is generally lavished on the representations and warranties section, there is considerably less need for it when the seller is already a publicly held company. The reason is that there is no one to sue for a misrepresentation or breach of warranty; ownership is diffused over thousands of shareholders, which makes it extremely expensive to litigate.

THE REPRESENTATIONS AND WARRANTIES SECTION—BUYER

The following section of the purchase agreement contains the representations and warranties of the buyer. Its contents generally duplicate that of the seller's representations and warranties, and will not be shown again here. In general, the seller wants assurances that the buyer is properly organized, with sufficient shares authorized and available, and with authorization from its board of directors to complete the transaction. In addition, if the buyer intends to complete the acquisition with some variation on a reverse acquisition with a shell company (see the Types of Acquisitions chapter), the seller wants to know that the shell company has been specially created and intended for the acquisition. An example follows:

Acquisition Corporation: The acquisition corporation is a wholly-owned subsidiary of the Buyer that was formed specifically for the merger and has not conducted any business or acquired any property, except in connection with the transactions contemplated by this agreement.

The seller wants to know that the purchase agreement is binding upon the buyer. Though this is obvious, and the seller can enforce the agreement through the legal system if necessary, the following text may be of use to the seller:

Binding Obligations: The merger documents constitute the legal, valid, and binding obligations of the Buyer, and are enforceable against the Buyer, except as such enforcement is limited by bankruptcy, insolvency, and similar laws.

As a matter of fairness, the buyer should be willing to include the same representations and warranties in the purchase agreement as those for the seller. The seller will not be overly concerned about most of these items if it is receiving cash, since it will be free and clear of the buyer once the agreement has been completed. However, if the seller is accepting stock as full or partial payment, then the value of that stock will be closely tied to the subsequent performance of the buyer. In the latter case, the seller should insist on a full set of buyer representations and warranties.

THE SURVIVAL OF REPRESENTATIONS AND WARRANTIES SECTION

The preceding representations and warranties sections described a variety of issues that both parties claim to be true. If those claims are not true, then either party may be required to make compensatory payments. In this section, the buyer and seller note the duration of the representations and warrants, the maximum amount of any payments, and the form of payment allowed. All three issues are likely to be intensively negotiated by each side. The buyer will want to be protected from undisclosed problems for a fairly lengthy period of time. The buyer will also want a large maximum cap on possible payments to it by the seller, while the seller will want the option of making any payments in the buyer's stock that it receives as part of the original payment from the buyer (helpful if the stock cannot be easily traded). The duration and maximum cap numbers are both heavily negotiated. Expect to see a duration of up to two years, and a maximum cap of roughly 10 percent of the total deal value. The buyer will want a minimum duration extending to at least the receipt of audited financial statements for a full fiscal year of operations following the acquisition. If there are significant risks or uncertainties, the buyer may insist on a longer duration and higher cap. An example follows:

Seller Representations and Indemnification: The representations and warranties of the Seller shall survive for one year beyond the Effective Time. The aggregate amount of damages that may be recovered by the Buyer arising out of or in connection with the breach of any of these representations and warranties shall not exceed $_____. In the event of a breach for which indemnity is available, the Seller shall be entitled to compensate the Buyer either with cash or by returning shares of Buyer common stock, which shares shall be valued at the current market price.

Buyer Representations and Indemnification: The representations and warranties of the Buyer shall survive for one year beyond the Effective Date. The aggregate amount of damages that may be recovered by the Seller arising out of or in connection with the breach of any of these representations and warranties shall not exceed $_____.

Though a section is included for buyer representations and indemnification whose terms match those applicable to the seller, this section is really for the benefit of the buyer against the seller. The seller rarely has a claim against the buyer under this section.

THE CONDUCT OF BUSINESS SECTION

The purchase agreement may be signed before its effective date. During the interval between the signing date and effective date, there is a chance that the seller's management may take actions that are adverse to the best interests of the buyer. To avoid this issue, the agreement should contain a section limiting the seller to transactions that only arise in the ordinary course of business. An example follows:

> **Conduct of Business by the Seller Pending the Merger:** Prior to the effective date, the business of the Seller shall be conducted only in the ordinary course of business. The Seller shall not redeem its capital stock, issue capital stock, issue options or warrants, amend its articles of incorporation or bylaws, split or combine any class of its outstanding stock, or declare or pay dividends. The Seller shall not acquire or dispose of fixed assets, incur additional indebtedness or liabilities other than in the ordinary course of business. The Seller will not enter into any new employment agreements or grant compensation or benefit increases greater than would be consistent with its past practice. The Seller shall preserve intact its organization, including the retention of key officers and employees, and its relationships with key business partners. The Seller will not engage in any negotiations to be acquired by another entity than the Buyer, and will immediately cease any discussions in which it is currently engaged.

This section is a significant one, since there have been numerous instances of selling entities granting significant last-minute payments and stock to their employees, and shifting assets to other entities.

THE ADDITIONAL AGREEMENTS SECTION

A variety of miscellaneous issues can be addressed in the Additional Agreements section. This section is not mandatory; it merely contains clauses that do not logically fall into any other parts of the purchase agreement. Several clauses commonly found here are noted below.

Both parties should have mutual control over the issuance of press releases regarding the acquisition, until such time as the buyer has full control over both entities. This provision is needed so that the buyer and seller will have sufficient time to properly prepare their business partners and employees for the announcement. An example follows:

> **Publicity:** No party shall issue any press release or public announcement pertaining to the merger that has not been agreed upon in advance by the Buyer and Seller.

If there appears to be some danger that the shareholders of the seller could start up or acquire a business that competes against the buyer, the buyer may require a non-compete clause. This clause usually restricts the selling shareholders from competing within a certain time period, and may be limited to a geographic region. The clause is especially useful in service industries, where clients can most easily shift their business elsewhere. There may be a special payment in consideration of this clause, or the payment may be inherent in the entire purchase price. An example follows:

> **Non-competition:** The Seller's shareholders shall enter into the non-competition agreement listed in Appendix C, whereby they agree not to compete with the purchased business for a period of three years following the closing date. This restriction only applies to a geographic range of 100 miles from Seller's present headquarters location.

A court will throw out a non-compete agreement if it is too long or indefinite with respect to the specific activities being restricted. Conversely, the agreement will be valid if it has a reasonable duration and scope, is not harmful to the general public, and is not unreasonably burdensome to the shareholder signing it.

There may be a blanket provision in which both parties agree to use their best efforts to complete all actions necessary to complete the acquisition. This clause is generally intended as a prod for the buyer to use against the seller, who may not be sufficiently active in assisting with the transaction. An example follows:

> **Additional Covenants:** Each of the parties agrees to use its commercially reasonable efforts to take all action and to do all things necessary to consummate and make effective the transactions contemplated by this agreement, including using commercially reasonable efforts to obtain all necessary waivers, and government or regulatory approvals, and to lift any injunction or other legal bar to the merger.

If the purchase consideration includes some of the buyer's stock, then the seller will want registration rights. Under a registration rights agreement, each stockholder of the seller who has received shares in the buyer as part of the purchase transaction has the right to have those shares included in the buyer's next registration statement. A registration statement is a lengthy document describing the company and the specific shares to be registered for trading. If the statement is declared effective by the Securities and Exchange Commission (SEC), selling shareholders will have the right to immediately sell their shares.

If the buyer intends to issue a registration statement, then including the stock of the seller's shareholders in the statement is a minor matter, so the buyer should have no problem with allowing registration rights.

THE CLOSING SECTION

The agreement must contain a brief section that describes the closing process, which is typically held several days or weeks subsequent to the signing of the purchase agreement. At this meeting, all remaining certificates and agreements are delivered by the various parties. An example follows:

> The closing of the merger (the "Closing") shall occur immediately following the fulfillment of the closing conditions. The Closing shall occur at the offices of _____. All of the remaining documents, certificates, and agreements will be executed and delivered at the Closing.

Though not mentioned in the example, the certificates and agreements normally delivered at the closing include such items as a bill of sale, assignment of trademarks, non-compete agreement (if any), and corporation authorizations of the transaction.

THE TERMINATION PRIOR TO CLOSING SECTION

Between the signing of the purchase agreement and the closing, it is still possible for the parties to mutually agree to terminate the transaction, though the conditions under which this is possible should be clearly defined and limited. An example follows:

Termination of Agreement. This Agreement may be terminated at any time prior to the Closing:

a. by the mutual written consent of the Buyer and Seller;

b. by the Buyer, if the Seller (i) fails to perform in any material respect any of its agreements contained herein prior to the closing date, (ii) materially breaches any of its representations, warranties, or covenants contained herein, which failure or breach is not cured within 30 days after the Buyer has notified the Seller of its intent to terminate this agreement;

c. by the Seller, if the Buyer (i) fails to perform in any material respect any of its agreements contained herein required to be performed by it on or prior to the closing date, (ii) materially breaches any of its representations, warranties, or covenants contained herein, which failure or breach is not cured within 30 days after the Seller has notified the Buyer of its intent to terminate this agreement;

d. by either the Seller or the Buyer if there shall be any order or injunction of any court or governmental agency binding on the Buyer or Seller, which prohibits or materially restrains either of them from consummating the transaction;

e. by either the Buyer or the Seller, if the closing has not occurred by [date], for any reason other than delay or nonperformance of the party seeking such termination.

THE SUPPORTING DOCUMENTS SECTION

In order to complete the acquisition transaction, the buyer must receive a variety of legal documents, which can be voluminous. A selection of the items more commonly requested by the buyer from the seller is noted in the following example:

Supporting Documents: At closing, the Buyer shall have received from the Seller the following:

a. Copies of resolutions of the Board of Directors and the stockholders of the Seller, certified by the secretary of the Seller, authorizing and approving the execution of all documents to be delivered pursuant hereto.

b. A certificate of incumbency executed by the secretary of the Seller certifying the names, titles, and signatures of the officers authorized to execute any documents referred to in this agreement and further certifying that the certificate of incorporation and bylaws of the Seller delivered to the Buyer at the time of the execution of this agreement have been validly adopted and have not been amended or modified.

c. A certificate, executed by the Seller's secretary, certifying that (i) all consents and filings with any court or governmental body that are required for the execution of this agreement shall have been obtained, and all material consents by third parties that are required for the merger have been obtained; and (ii) no action or proceeding before any court or governmental body has been threatened or asserted to restrain this agreement.

d. Evidence of the good standing of the Seller issued by the Secretary of State of the State of _____ and evidence that the Seller is qualified to transact business as a foreign corporation in each other state of the United States where the nature of its activities makes such qualification necessary.

Nearly identical verbiage also requires the buyer to provide approximately the same items to the seller at closing.

EXHIBITS

A variety of documents are normally attached as exhibits to the purchase agreement. Anything to be sent to the buyer's shareholders regarding the sale of their shares would fall into this category, and includes the letter of transmittal, any lockup agreements, and the registration rights agreement. Other exhibits include the key organizational documents of the seller, which are its certificate of incorporation and bylaws, as well as any promissory notes and non-compete agreements. If some portion of the purchase price is to be paid with a promissory note, then that note and any related security agreement should also be included. Finally, a certificate of merger should be included (depending on the form of acquisition used). This is a legal document from the secretary of state in the state where the buyer is incorporated, stating which entity is surviving and which is disappearing. The exact form of this certificate will vary by state.

THE SELLER DISCLOSURE SCHEDULE

The seller disclosure schedule is larger than the rest of the purchase agreement because it contains the details of many items referenced earlier in the agreement. It is essentially a large appendix to the representations and warranties section. Here are some of the items usually found in the schedule:

- Bank accounts and account signatories
- Broker fee agreements
- Employee benefit plans
- Encumbered assets
- Equity instruments list, showing the detail for all options and warrants outstanding
- Fixed assets list
- Government permits and licenses held

- Insurance policies
- Key contracts
- Outstanding liabilities
- Patents, trademarks, domain names, and copyrights
- Pending litigation and claims
- Shareholder list, showing the detail for shares held by each person or entity
- Significant changes since the date of the last reported financial statements

THE CLOSING MEMORANDUM

The purchase agreement is a collection of terms and conditions. It does not provide a narrative description of the deal, which can be useful after the deal has closed, in case the parties argue over the intent behind certain aspects of the transaction. To avoid this problem, write a closing memorandum immediately after the purchase agreement has been finalized, and include it in the front of the purchase agreement binder. The closing memorandum should describe the background and substance of the transaction, and any unusual issues that arose. This is written by the buyer's attorneys, and so views the transaction from the buyer's perspective. A synopsis of a closing memorandum follows:

> This memorandum summarizes information relating to the closing of the acquisition of Seller by Buyer.
>
> 1. **Background:** An earlier version of this transaction was planned for closing on [date]. However, the majority holder of the Seller's convertible preferred stock, Mr. Smith, objected to the proposed conversion ratio for his stock into that of the Buyer's common stock. The parties later negotiated a revised conversion ratio, resulting in a term sheet dated _____, which provided a basis for an agreement with the Buyer. The term sheet is an attachment to this memorandum,

although it was not technically a closing document. Given the difficulty of dealing with Mr. Smith, the term sheet may provide a useful point of reference in the event of future problems.

2. **Timing of Closing:** The final closing documents were executed on March __, ____ while the articles of merger were actually recorded a day later. Under our closing provisions, we will take the position that all of the merger transactions occurred simultaneously. Documents were exchanged by fax and overnight delivery service.

3. **Structure:** The transaction was structured as a reverse triangular merger in order to achieve tax deferred status for the Seller. Accordingly, 100 percent of the payment to the Seller was in the form of the Buyer's stock. This was accompanied by a one-year lockup agreement. The parties agreed that a registration rights agreement was not needed, since the seller's shareholders could register their stock under the SEC's Rule 144. The conversion ratio of Seller stock to Buyer stock was set at 0.5532941. Given the high level of the Buyer's stock price fluctuation at the time of the transaction, the parties also agreed to a true-up transaction, whereby the Buyer would issue additional shares to the Seller's shareholders after six months, if the Buyer's stock price had declined by more than 10 percent.

4. **Options:** A complicating factor was the existence of a large number of Seller options. The parties agreed to convert the Seller options into an equivalent number of buyer options, using a conversion ratio of 2:1 (Seller options to Buyer options). Thus, one Buyer option was issued in exchange for the cancellation of two Seller options. The exercise price for each converted option was set at the current fair market value of the Buyer's stock, which was $4.50. Because the new options were issued at fair market value, they should qualify as incentive stock options.

5. **Due Diligence:** The Buyer's due diligence team reviewed the Seller's materials on site during [date range]. One problem area was the need for a bank consent on the Buyer's line of credit, which was paid off following the transaction.

6. **Employment Arrangements:** All Seller employees were required to sign an offer letter from the Buyer. Principal employees of the

Seller were required to enter a non-competition and confidentiality agreement with the Buyer, while other Seller employees only signed a confidentiality agreement.

7. **Indemnification:** The indemnification provisions in the agreement are somewhat weak and were the subject of extended negotiations on both sides. There were arguments about escrowing some of the stock, which were rejected. All Seller stockholders indemnified the Buyer for fraud.

SPECIAL CLAUSES

The foregoing sections have addressed those sections found in most purchase agreements. In addition, the parties may negotiate a variety of special clauses, which are usually located in either the merger or representations and warranties sections of the agreement, but which may also be completed separately, before the purchase agreement.

The *material adverse change clause* (MAC) allows a potential buyer to escape from a purchase transaction if the financial or operating condition of the seller significantly declines prior to consummation of the transaction. Invoking a MAC usually hurts the seller much more than the buyer, so the seller has a strong incentive to completely eliminate the MAC clause, or at least restrict the situations under which it can be invoked. Typical restrictions are for acts of war or terrorism, or changes in the general economy, government regulations, or accounting regulations that negatively impact the seller.

If the buyer invokes the MAC clause, it should be prepared for considerable litigation by the seller, who can claim that any downturn in its business was not sufficient to trigger the MAC clause. Another reason for litigation is that the buyer has just completed due diligence on the seller, and should therefore be fully aware of any risks or imminent problems that might cause a material adverse change to arise.

If there is a MAC clause and an event arises that might be construed as a material adverse change, the buyer can use the mere presence of the clause to negotiate a lower purchase price.

The form of a MAC clause can vary considerably, depending upon the types of risks to which the seller is subjected. Thus, it should be custom-crafted for each acquisition. The due diligence manager should be involved in writing the clause, since he is in the best position to know what types of problems are most likely to arise within the seller's business. A sample MAC clause, using a very broad range of sample exclusions, follows:

> **No Material Adverse Change:** There shall have been no material adverse change in the business, condition, assets, liabilities, operations, or results of operations of the seller since [date]. For purposes of this condition, none of the following shall constitute such a material adverse change: (a) the seller's lack of success in retaining or hiring new employees; (b) the seller's failure to meet any published analyst estimates of revenue or earnings; (c) a change resulting from conditions affecting the national economy; (d) a delay in customer orders arising from the announcement of this purchase agreement; or (e) the completion of any environmental assessment indicating the presence of a liability.

The *lockup arrangement* is normally used to prevent shareholders from tendering their shares for a certain period of time. It can also be used in a purchase transaction to prevent other parties than a single buyer from having a realistic chance of successfully bidding on the seller. For example, in an *asset lockup* agreement, the seller grants to a prospective buyer the right to purchase a key asset, without which the seller's business cannot operate, or will have a significantly reduced value. This is also known as a *crown jewel lockup*. By reserving a key asset for a single prospective buyer, the arrangement effectively eliminates other bidders.

Another variation on the lockup is the *stock lockup*, where the seller grants to a prospective buyer an option to purchase authorized but unissued shares. The buyer can then exercise its option, buy the shares, and vote them in favor of its proposed purchase of the seller. If a second bidder acquires control of the seller, then the first bidder can still exercise its option and sell the acquired shares at a profit (depending upon the exercise price). A variation on the stock lockup is a *reverse lockup*, where selected seller stockholders agree not to tender their shares to a rival bidder. Any type of stock lockup tends to discourage competitive bidding, so a rival bidder may bring suit over the legality of such an arrangement, on the grounds that the seller's board of directors has breached its duty of loyalty to the seller's shareholders. Lock-up agreements are completed earlier in the acquisition process, and so are not found in the purchase agreement.

Another special clause addresses the *bust-up fee*, which is also described as a termination fee. Under a bust-up fee, one party agrees to pay to the other a certain amount if the acquisition does not take place. This is usually paid by the seller to a potential buyer, in compensation for the buyer's expenses incurred. The potential buyer may insist on an extremely large bust-up fee, which discourages the seller from accepting the bids of other potential buyers (which is essentially a lockup arrangement). For that reason, the seller should avoid any demand for an exorbitant bust-up fee. On the other hand, a smaller fee may be entirely reasonable and prudent if it is necessary to attract a bidder or keep it interested in the face of competing bids. It is better for the seller to grant a moderate bust-up fee rather than a no shop provision, since it will then be able to continue soliciting offers from other interested parties.

The bust-up fee is normally agreed to before the purchase agreement, possibly in a letter of intent. The purchase agreement may contain a clause in the representations and warranties section, stating that there are no bust-up fee arrangements. An example follows:

> **Bust-up Arrangements:** No claim exists against the Seller for payment of any bust-up fee or similar compensation arrangement as a result of the transactions contemplated hereby.

The buyer may insist on *setoff rights*, where it has the right to set off any damages it suffers for breach of the contract against payments it owes to the seller. For example, if the purchase price is paid in installments, and the buyer finds that some receivables are not collectible, it can unilaterally reduce an upcoming payment by the amount of the bad debt. A seller will typically resist this clause, since it places total control over payments in the hands of the buyer.

A *basket* is frequently added to the indemnification provision. This is the dollar amount that the buyer must first absorb before it can recover damages under the indemnity provisions. For example, if the basket is set at $30,000 and the buyer suffers indemnifiable losses of $31,000, it can recover $1,000, as well as any additional amounts that may subsequently arise. The basket is a good idea from an efficiency perspective, since it keeps the buyer from pursuing the seller for negligible amounts.

The buyer will argue for a lower basket and the seller for a higher one, with the parties usually settling for a basket in the range of one to two percent of the purchase price. The buyer may also argue for a voided basket if a loss occurs that results from a willful breach of representations and warranties by the seller. This argument rarely succeeds, since it is difficult to determine the seller's intent that caused a loss.

Another possibility is *walk-away rights*, which are used in a stock-for-stock transaction, and which give the seller the option to terminate the purchase agreement if the average price of the buyer's stock falls below a predetermined level. While the trigger point could be a fixed stock price, a better method is to use a percentage decline below a baseline of the stock prices of a group of comparable companies. By using this method, the walk-away clause will not be triggered if there is an industry-wide decline; instead, it will only be triggered by changes specific to the buyer. The clause may also include an option, known as *top-up rights*, under which the buyer can increase the stock exchange ratio or pay more cash, rather than triggering the walk-away right. Though walk-away rights are favored by sellers, they are rarely exercised in practice. Instead, the buyer may still be the best suitor for the seller, so the two parties work out a new purchase price, rather than abandoning the deal.

Instead of walk-away rights, the parties may agree to *collars*. Under a collar arrangement, which always involves a stock-for-stock transaction, the exchange ratio is fixed over a limited range of the buyer's stock price. However, if the buyer's stock price increases beyond that predetermined range prior to the closing, then the exchange ratio decreases to maintain the same total value. Conversely, if the buyer's stock price decreases to a point outside of the low-end collar, then the exchange ratio increases to maintain the same total value. Collars increase the seller's certainty that it will receive its full negotiated value, and so can be a significant inducement to close a deal. Given the increased level of price certainty for the seller, the collar makes a stock deal more similar to a cash deal, while preserving the capital gain deferral aspects of an all-stock payment.

Given that a collar resets the price paid to the seller in the event of a sudden change in the buyer's stock price, this makes it less likely that the two parties will have any need to renegotiate the price. Instead, under any reasonable range of stock prices, the collar arrangement should automatically adjust the purchase price.

POST-CLOSING ACTIVITIES

Once the closing has been completed, the attorneys for both parties will continue to work for some time to complete a variety of related activities. Examples of these activities are:

- Compute post-closing adjustments for such areas as doubtful accounts receivable, earnouts, and inventory write-downs
- File change of registered agent to reflect the new owner
- File notices with the Internal Revenue Service for name changes, entity terminations, or retirement plan amendments
- Pay any sales taxes arising from the transaction
- Receive the signed letter of transmittal from all seller shareholders and issue payment to them
- Record all security documents
- Record transfers of title on assets
- Release seller's shareholders from any personal loan guarantees made on behalf of the seller

- Transfer owner for real estate parcels, along with mortgages and related security interests
- Transfer title to patents, copyrights, and domain names

It is best to create a post-closing checklist of all remaining activities, with assigned responsibilities and expected due dates. There will usually be multiple closing checklists, since each party may have confidential tasks, such as side letters that it wishes to keep confidential. Consequently, there should be a master list for the more generic items and a smaller, more specific list for each party. The attorneys from both sides should manage the checklist like any other project—with status meetings and checklist revisions to ensure that all tasks are completed.

NEGOTIATING THE PURCHASE AGREEMENT

Clearly, the purchase agreement contains many components. This represents a very broad area of discussion for the buyer and seller, which can slow negotiations to a crawl if the parties are determined to dicker over every possible point. To avoid negotiation delays, it is better to create in advance a summary list of the key points of negotiation, and determine which ones are critical. As long as the buyer and seller each restrict themselves to this short list of points, the breadth of negotiations will be substantially reduced.

From the buyer's perspective, protracted negotiations also bring up the possibility of a third party entering the fray and making a competing offer. Also, it reduces any goodwill created through previous contacts with the seller, so that the integration team faces a more resistant management team when it eventually begins its integration work after the purchase agreement is signed.

If the seller resists a broad representations and warranties section, then the buyer should hold out for broad-based representations regarding the seller's financial statements, litigation, undisclosed liabilities, and tax remittances. The other representations involve less risk, so the buyer can give them away during bargaining in exchange for full representations of the key areas just noted.

An assumed point of negotiation, though a critical one, is that the buyer controls the drafting of the purchase agreement. This means that the buyer presents to the seller the initial version of the agreement, the seller recommends changes, and the buyer makes any mutually agreed-upon changes. By using this approach, the buyer can include a broad array of representations and warranties that the seller must then fight to exclude, whereas an initial draft by the seller might exclude this section entirely. Also, the buyer can control the pace of document updates, in case it wishes to accelerate or slow down the acquisition time line.

If the buyer is engaged in an auction with other potential bidders, then the broker representing the seller is usually in charge of the purchase agreement. The broker sends a standard contract to all qualified bidders, who then propose modifications. Under this approach, the broker's agreement only contains limited representations and warranties, so bidders must fight for more adequate risk coverage.

A variety of documents should be received and conditions satisfied prior to the closing, such as a certificate of good standing from the secretary of state where the seller is incorporated. If any such items are not received by the time of closing, the buyer has the option of waiving it or delaying the close. In some cases, it may be possible to issue a waiver, but only in exchange for some concession.

Once the parties have agreed to final terms, it is best to close as quickly as possible. Otherwise, either party may elect to back out at the last minute, or unforeseen occurrences could arise, such as a material adverse condition, that makes the acquisition less palatable.

MECHANICS OF THE CLOSE

The closing only proceeds smoothly if a great deal of document management has occurred in advance. This includes a final review of all documents by both parties, dating of any undated documents to the closing date, document recordation, and wiring of funds to the seller's shareholders. If there is third-party financing, lenders will not release funds until they have confirmation that merger certificates have been filed, and security and title documents have been properly recorded. The key point is that the attorneys of both the buyer and seller must work together closely to ensure that all closing steps have been planned for and completed in an orderly manner. In particular, if the buyer is subjected to a disorderly close, then for its next acquisition, it should consider shifting to a different legal firm that has more experience in closing management.

The purchase agreement is an exceedingly complex document, and there are myriad ways in which some aspect of it cannot be completed on closing day. Thus, both parties should always assume that the close may require several days. To avoid having the legal teams working through a weekend or holiday, it is better to schedule the close to *not* be on a Friday, and preferably early in a week. Also, since funds cannot be transferred to the seller during a weekend or holiday, this also delays the close for enough additional days to increase the odds of a blow-up that will scuttle the deal.

SUMMARY

The purchase agreement describes the transfer of property from the seller to the buyer. This is a complex transaction requiring a number of interlocking legal issues that are embodied in the purchase agreement. While the bulk of the key sections used in a purchase agreement have been described in this chapter, the reader should not use these sections as part of an actual purchase agreement. The legal text shown here has been stripped down to improve readability, which reduces its legal effectiveness. Instead, use the purchase agreement provided by a qualified attorney, and only use this chapter as a checklist to ensure that key sections are included in that agreement.

Chapter 7

The Acquisition Integration Process

Once a buyer purchases a target company (now the "acquiree"), it faces the difficult task of integrating its operations into those of the rest of the company. If it does so effectively, it can realize substantial synergies that more than offset the cost of the purchase. If not, then the buyer will soon realize that it has spent an inordinate amount of money and time on a "boat anchor" acquiree. Thus, the effectiveness of the acquisition integration process is absolutely crucial. In this chapter, we address numerous integration topics, including the integration team, the planning process, and how to integrate an acquiree's employees, processes, and specific functions.

INTEGRATION TIMING

The integration of an acquiree into the buying entity can be slow and painful, or fast and painful. There is simply no way to avoid a significant amount of dislocation within the acquiree, especially if the buyer wants to achieve major synergies. Consequently, the best thing a company can do is to move as rapidly as possible to complete all integration tasks, thereby reducing the period of dislocation through which the acquiree will undoubtedly suffer.

A good target period over which to complete the bulk of all integration activities is one year, even for a very large acquiree. Due to their complexity, some efforts will linger on for multiple years after the purchase, but at least 80 percent of the integration activities should be completed within one year. This is in opposition to many acquisitions, where large-scale integration projects are still in process as much as five years later.

It is even possible to begin integration work before a purchase transaction has closed, though this is mostly limited to preparatory work. To do so, any of the buyer's employees who are involved in the integration effort must work under the assumption that the deal could still collapse. This means that the buyer's team must track the receipt and disposition of all documents received from the potential acquiree, and catalog them for destruction or return, if the companies do not combine. Further, the buyer should not dictate business decisions to the potential acquiree at this time.

The key point with integration timing is to not delay—there are few activities in a corporation where haste is of more importance. However, the speed of integration must go hand-in-hand with a detailed project plan.

INTEGRATION PLANNING

The integration of an acquiree's operations into the buyer requires a considerable amount of planning. The planning process should begin with an implementation charter that sets forth the statement of overall objectives, synergy targets, and the resources available to the team. The team then uses this information to create an integration plan that itemizes the tasks to be completed in achieving the objectives noted in the charter, as well as measurement systems to ensure that targets have been achieved. A serial acquirer usually constructs a standard list of acquisition tasks, such as those shown below, around which it tailors a comprehensive plan that matches its intentions for a specific acquiree.

Accounting

- Arrange for forwarding of supplier invoices to central payables
- Convert new staff to corporate payroll system
- Create new bank account in corporate sweep account system
- Create subsidiary financial statement formats within central system
- Distribute corporate accounting policies to acquiree accounting staff
- Enter acquiree fixed assets into central register
- Forward cash from old accounts and close the accounts
- Hire valuation firm to create acquiree valuation report
- Load acquiree receivables and payables into central accounting system
- Notify tax accountants of the acquisition
- Pay off and cancel lines of credit
- Set up expense report direct deposit
- Verify prepaid assets and accrued liabilities

Legal

- Apply for trademarks on acquired business name and products
- Load acquiree contracts into corporate contract management system

Marketing

- Add key staff to corporate Web site
- Add new products/services to corporate Web site
- Describe acquisition on corporate Web site
- Issue new business cards

- Issue press release
- Upgrade acquiree Web site

Human Resources

- Add new employees to company-wide contact list
- Add new employees to e-mail list
- Distribute ethics documents to new managers
- Roll forward accrued vacation time into vacation tracking system
- Shift benefits to parent company plan
- Shift garnishments and tax levies to central payment system
- Shift new employees to corporate timekeeping system
- Upgrade employee files to corporate standards

Risk Management

- Merge insurance policies
- Notify D&O insurance provider of acquisition

SEC Reporting

- Issue initial 8-K report (within four days)
- Issue financial results 8-K report (within 75 days)

Portions of the integration plan can be written during the due diligence process, to include any issues arising at that time. The due diligence teams will be too busy with their own work to volunteer this information to the integration manager, so the manager should meet frequently with the teams to elicit this information. At a minimum, a first draft of the plan should be completed as soon after the purchase transaction as possible.

The plan should identify all key personnel resources and the time period during which they are available. Examples of this group are the integration manager and all function-specific experts, such as process analysts and outside consultants. Since the integration requires the active participation of a key group of experts, this part of the plan is crucial.

If the buyer is acquiring a company that is being spun off by another entity, the integration team should determine if any services were being provided by the selling entity. If so, it needs to immediately locate the source of replacement services, as well as their cost, and which local managers shall be responsible for them. Unless these services are still to be provided for some period of time under the purchase agreement, they will have been removed when the agreement was signed. If the latter is the case, and the services are significant, then the acquiree stands in immediate need of help, for which considerable short-term planning is needed.

The basic timing of the plan is that most of the key decisions should be finalized within the first 100 days. This should certainly include all staff and organizational structure decisions (which, if possible, should be completed within the first week). All key customers should have been contacted multiple times during this period to increase the odds of their retention, as noted later in the Sales Integration section. Also, the most obvious "quick hit" synergies should have been identified and addressed. The team should also have a good idea of how the processes of both organizations compare to each other, and what steps should be taken to integrate them. In addition, the plan should have been fleshed out with a full set of budgets, timelines, and allocation of responsibilities. In short, 100 days is sufficient time to uncover the easier synergies, restructure human resources, and give the team a detailed view of what tasks must still be completed.

The integration plan must also go through an approval process, since many of the proposed synergies may be difficult or expensive to achieve, require special resources, or have risky side-effects. This calls for a review by an expert, typically the line managers who are responsible for taking over various sections of the acquiree. Since these people have a long-term incentive to ensure that the integration goes well, they will be most inclined to heavily critique the plan.

The plan should also be reviewed by the analysis team that originally proposed the purchase price for the acquiree. This group will have made certain assumptions about the types of synergies to be obtained in order to justify the purchase price, and so will have an interest in the amount of savings that the integration team feels it can achieve.

Once the integration process begins, the integration plan will be tweaked constantly, as the integration team goes on-site and finds that conditions do not match its initial expectations. Thus, a staff person should constantly assess progress against the plan and recommend adjustment steps to the integration manager. By the time integration has been completed, the integration plan will look substantially different than the first version that was initially compiled.

The internal audit department is scheduled last in the integration planning process. After all other integration work is completed, the internal auditors review the various synergies and process integrations that have been completed. They compare these results to the initial plan, as well as the buyer's expectations at the time of the acquisition, and issue a report that evaluates the impact of the acquisition on the buyer. Beyond the usual cost-benefit analysis, this report itemizes what the buyer did well, and those areas in which it could do a better job when it integrates other acquisitions.

SYNERGY REALIZATION

The most important part of the integration plan centers around the realization of synergies, since this is where the buyer justifies the price paid for the acquiree. A financial buyer may be content to simply wait for appreciation in the value of the acquiree. However, a strategic buyer has usually paid a higher price, because it feels it can achieve cash flow improvements through a variety of synergies where the combined entities can be more profitable than if they operated separately. These synergies fall into the general categories of cost savings, revenue increases, capital spending, financial engineering, and tax benefits.

Of these synergy types, the most reliable ones to achieve are cost savings, since they are entirely within the control of the buyer. The areas most commonly targeted for cost reductions are:

- *Administrative expenses.* There are strong possibilities for cost reduction by centralizing a variety of administrative positions. Several accounting areas may be integrated, with the most common being accounts payable, payroll, and treasury, while billing and collections tend to be more localized.

- *Duplicate management.* One of the most common cost-saving areas is the elimination of duplicate management teams. Since the acquired company's management may have just sold its shares or been paid significant severance packages, this can involve a downright cheerful set of employee departures.

- *Duplicate research and development.* In industries where product development is a key determinant of success, there is a possibility for staff reductions, especially when the R&D staffs of both companies are working on the same product. However, this area is also fraught with political maneuvering, because senior managers may support their "pet projects," while outside analysts may question why there are R&D cuts going on that may negatively impact future sales. The usual result is a modest cutback in expenses that is less than initial expectations.

- *Duplicate sales staff.* If the intent is for the sales staff to sell the products of the combined companies, then there is a strong likelihood of overlapping or overstaffed sales territories. While this may involve the departure of a number of salespeople, it more commonly is preceded by a significant shuffling of sales territories, so that the best sales people (a precious commodity) can be retained, while the worst performers are pushed out.

- *Field service consolidation.* If both companies operate similar field service staffs, it may be possible to eventually integrate them, thereby reducing the combined headcount to some extent. However, it takes time to achieve this synergy, since the surviving staff must be cross-trained in the servicing of new products. Also, since servicing volumes are likely to remain consistent from before the acquisition, the same staff totals will still probably be needed. Also, if there are aggressive plans to boost sales, the entire existing field service staff may still be needed to service the increased sales base.

- *Marketing consolidation.* The two companies may have been conducting similar advertising campaigns, attending the same trade shows, and so on. These duplicate costs can be consolidated, though the savings will only be significant if the two entities operate in the same market, and sell very similar products. Even if marketing activities cannot be consolidated, there is a possibility that greater purchasing volumes can result in somewhat reduced costs.

- *Pension plans.* If the acquiree has a defined-benefit plan, the buyer can shut it down and shift employees over to a defined-contribution plan, which is much less expensive. While this conversion is certainly hazardous to employee relations, the cost savings can be substantial. If the acquiree has a union, its collective bargaining agreement may require continuation of the defined-benefit plan, leaving no possibility of a cost reduction in this area.

There are a multitude of issues involved with merging any kind of pension plan. One way to avoid them is to require the selling entity to terminate its plan prior to the acquisition date. Once the acquisition takes place, the acquiree's employees can then rollover their plan benefits into the buyer's plan, with much less risk of any further problems arising.

If the buyer has a defined-benefit plan and intends to shift the acquiree's employees into it, then a significant cost issue is whether to credit their years of service prior to the acquisition. This issue should be settled as part of the purchase negotiations, since it can greatly increase the overall cost to the buyer.

- *Process improvements.* Either the buyer or the acquiree may have unusually efficient processes that are the result of a gradual build-up of best practices over time. If so, an enlightened integration effort will not just impose the buyer's processes on the acquiree, but instead will compare all systems and select the best from either side. While this can result in significant long-term cost reductions, the mutual enhancement of processes is a lengthy endeavor.

- *Product overlap.* If the companies support similar products, the buyer may elect to phase some out. This is not a simple decision, since there may be long-term warranties or field service operations that require ongoing support for a number of years. Thus, cost reductions in this area tend to be of a more long-term nature.

- *Purchasing power.* When companies combine, there is always a prospect for greater purchasing power, due to greater buying volume. This can result in a gain of several percent in net profits. However, it also requires a great deal of coordination in purchasing activities, and may not be possible at all if the acquiree is outside of the area occupied by the buyer's supplier distribution regions.

Cost savings can be especially great when the buyer acquires a company within the same industry and in the same geographical region in which it already operates. By doing so, there is a high probability of function duplication, which can be eliminated. Likely targets for cost reduction will be duplicate sales forces, production facilities, and administrative staff.

Though the simplest way to immediately achieve gains is through cost reductions, one must also consider the costs associated with achieving them. For example, if the buyer plans for massive layoffs, it must factor in the cost of severance and plant closures, which may also be affected by firing restrictions in some foreign countries. In addition, if it plans to retain some employees for knowledge transfer purposes and then let them go, then there is the cost of retention bonuses to consider. Consequently, when modeling potential synergies, these new costs must be offset against the planned cost reductions.

Depending on the circumstances, the net effect of cost reductions and new costs may not yield any significant cost reductions until more than a year has passed.

Sales synergies are much more difficult to achieve than cost savings, because the newly-combined companies must now rely on third parties (customers) to boost sales. The usual assumptions for a revenue increase are that:

• The combined entities have gained sufficient critical mass that they can now attract revenue that neither company could have realized alone, or

• The combined entities can offer enhanced products or services

Another variation on revenue synergies is for the buyer to acquire a strong brand, and then shift its own, lesser-known products under that brand. The intended result is to increase consumer approval of the added products by association. However, the acquiree's brand awareness may have been built up over many years through a continuing quality and customer support program; if the buyer's products are not of a sufficient quality level, then adding them to the acquired brand may have an overall impact of reducing the perceived quality of the brand, with no net increase in sales (if not the reverse). Consequently, a buyer should only attempt to expand an acquiree's brand with the greatest care.

Though these revenue synergies may be valid, they also take a considerable amount of time to realize; and the size of any possible gains may be impossible to predict. Also, some customers may not want to concentrate an excessive proportion of their purchases with a single supplier, which places an upper cap on sales growth. In addition, competitors may lower their prices to avoid losing sales to the newly merged entity. For all of these reasons, many valuations do not include *any* revenue-related benefits. Instead, the emphasis is on concrete gains from cost reductions that are entirely within the control of the buyer.

An area in which few companies consider the possibility of synergies is in the avoidance of capital expenditures. If either party to an acquisition has already made a significant expenditure, then it is entirely possible that the other party can avoid a similar payment by using the excess capacity generated by the preceding investment. Consequently, part of the integration process should be a comparison of planned capital expenditures by both companies to see if any can be combined.

There may also be some savings to be gleaned in the area of financial engineering. Combined entities can pool their foreign currency positions for receivables and payables, resulting in fewer foreign exchange transactions. Also, the buyer may be able to refinance the acquiree's debt at a more favorable interest rate, if the buyer has a significantly higher credit rating. Further, the buyer can sweep the acquiree's cash balances into a centralized bank account, where it can take advantage of overnight investments, and also handle the acquiree's short-term borrowing needs from its own cash pool. These improvements are not overwhelmingly large by themselves, but can add a noticeable amount to the total synergies achieved.

It is also possible to develop tax synergies. This can be achieved by acquiring an entity within a low-tax region, and then transferring brands and other intellectual property to it. Alternatively, if the buyer acquires a company in a high-tax region, it can push debt down into that subsidiary in order to create interest expenses and reduce its reported level of income. However, it is unwise to base acquisition synergies entirely upon their tax ramifications, since tax rates are under the control of governments that may change rates at any time. Instead, acquire for other synergies, and then take advantage of tax synergies if they happen to exist.

There is also a subtle synergy to be gained in the area of public relations. The company can issue press releases that imply a greater level of corporate stability because it is now a larger entity. This can be used by the sales force to show customers that the newly enlarged company is now a more reliable and long-term supplier, with whom they should place more orders.

When itemizing synergies, it is useful to record the information on a chart that shows the value to the buyer of each item. A sample follows:

Synergy Valuation Chart

Synergy Description	One-Time Profit	Recurring Profit	No Profit Change
Capital expenditure merge	—		$400,000
Centralize bank accounts	—	$5,000	—
Merge company names	—	—	—
Merge facilities & sublease	—	130,000	—
Payroll centralization	—	70,000	—
Product re-branding	—	150,000	—
Shift to defined contribution plan	—	62,000	—
Total synergies	$0	$417,000	$400,000

This table is then used by the integration manager to determine which synergies will yield the most benefit, and so justify the largest amount of attention.

THE INTEGRATION MANAGER

The integration of a newly acquired company into the buyer is an extremely complex affair, and so requires the services of a single talented manager to achieve. This integration manager only serves in the role until the main integration targets have been met, and then moves on to other projects. The integration manager is responsible for the following tasks:

- Supervise integration planning
- Monitor integration progress

- Identify synergies
- Facilitate team reviews
- Interpret and mitigate cultural issues
- Mobilize project teams

While the preceding bullet points appear to indicate a rigid job description, it usually begins as an extremely sketchy one and gradually fills out over time, as the integration manager learns more about the tasks to be completed and the types of problems to be overcome. By keeping his job description relatively fluid, the integration manager can shift his efforts into a variety of areas, as needed.

The integration manager is always an employee of the buyer. This is because he must have direct links to the more powerful people within the buyer's organization who can support the integration effort. In addition, he must have an in-depth knowledge of the buyer's key processes, and who controls each one. This allows him to directly reach those individuals within the buyer's organization who can most readily assist with and support him in achieving integration goals. If he were to come from the acquiree, there would be no such support network, and he would also have no knowledge of the buyer's organization.

Because the integration manager has such strong ties into the buyer organization, he can also assist acquiree employees in locating their counterparts. He can also educate them about how a variety of buyer processes function, such as annual personnel reviews, pay change procedures, and the budgeting cycle. Further, if reports are available that might be of assistance to the acquiree, he can arrange to have them fitted to the acquiree's specific needs, and sent to them on a predefined distribution schedule.

The integration manager's role between the organizations also works in the other direction. He can educate the buyer's management team about the acquiree's culture and any idiosyncrasies that may impact relations between the two companies. Also, whenever he feels there is a need for closer links between the entities, he can arrange for social events where he brings together specific groups of people.

Though this person comes from the buyer, he cannot have a "bull in a china shop" mentality and forcibly impose buyer practices on the acquiree. Instead, he must have a singular ability to appreciate and work with the acquiree's culture (see the Cultural Issues section later in this chapter). This requires extraordinary listening skills, as well as the ability to determine how integration goals can be achieved within the confines of cultural issues.

The integration manager is extremely independent, and must be able to operate with almost no supervision. By working in this manner, he can make snap decisions on site, without having to run them up through the buyer's management structure for approval.

The integration manager should be appointed during the early stages of the due diligence process, as soon as it becomes reasonably likely that a purchase transaction will occur. By doing so at any early stage, the integration manager can fashion an integration plan by modifying the buyer's standard plan to allow for target-specific issues that are uncovered during the due diligence process.

A common problem that the integration manager is responsible for monitoring is the bureaucracy accumulation effect (BAE). Normally, the procedures and related forms of the buyer will be imposed on the acquiree, which results in a large number of information requests arriving on the desks of the acquired employees, right in the middle of what may be a difficult integration process. Though each request may not require much time, the sudden onslaught of requests from multiple buyer systems can appear overwhelming. The result is usually a righteous sense of indignation by the acquiree's employees that they are being nagged with insignificant trivia, while also being asked to achieve multiple difficult goals. The integration manager cannot entirely eliminate BAE, but is in an ideal position to monitor the amount of information requests being made upon the acquiree staff, and can work with the originators to delay or entirely eliminate these irritants.

Finally, being an integration manager involves that person's physical presence at the acquiree location. The designated person cannot manage the integration process long-distance, from his office at corporate headquarters. Given the extraordinary amount of time needed in face-to-face meetings with acquiree employees, the integration manager must spend nearly all of his time on-site. This requires a commitment to live near the acquiree for the duration of the integration process. Further, because some issues will require the participation of the buyer's management team, he should be prepared to make numerous trips back to corporate headquarters to consult with senior management.

In brief, the integration manager occupies the central role in an acquisition. The individual must have sufficient heft within the buyer's organization (as defined by experience, skill, and leadership ability) to coordinate all aspects of the integration effort. This is an extremely involving role, requiring more than a normal working day, dealing with a broad range of conflicts, and necessitating living away from home for long periods of time. Consequently, a high-grade integration manager should be treated as a prized asset.

THE INTEGRATION TEAM

The integration manager is only one member of a large integration team. This group is responsible for completing dozens or even hundreds of integration activities. The team's skill sets will be extremely broad, covering every functional area of the acquiree. There may even be sub-teams of specialists who are responsible for very specific activities (such as merging pension plans). Among the more common sub-teams will be ones responsible for human resources, manufacturing, legal, environmental, research and development, purchasing, finance, information technology, sales and marketing, and culture. For buyers who do not make a regular practice of acquiring companies, there may also be a consultant who dispenses advice, as well as assistance with management of the integration effort and ongoing maintenance of the project plan.

Specialization within the integration team is an excellent idea, because it focuses efforts on tightly defined projects that yield fast results. Where possible, try to include acquiree employees in the sub-teams, since they can be of great assistance in bridging cultural gaps between the companies. This approach is most useful when a high level of acquiree cooperation is needed to achieve a goal, and less so when the project involves a technical issue (such as consolidating legal entities).

A key member of the integration team is the assistant to the implementation manager. This person should come from the acquiree. His role is to represent the acquiree on the team at a senior level. This means he should collect feedback from employees regarding a number of implementation initiatives, and advise the implementation manager regarding how targets can be achieved while disturbing the acquiree to the minimum extent possible. This person should have considerable seniority with the acquiree, and be well-known and trusted within that organization.

The integration team should have a strong incentive to not only meet its management-imposed integration targets, but to exceed them. Since team members are already deeply involved in the operations of both companies, they are in the best position to spot additional synergies that might have been missed during the initial creation of the integration plan. Thus, the integration manager should be given control over several types of bonuses, such as spot bonuses to be paid out for minor improvements and major bonuses for exceeding the initial cost reduction target.

While the integration team is extremely useful, especially for larger integration projects, it is not intended to be a permanent fixture. Instead, the integration plan should include a milestone (typically one year) after which the team is disbanded. At that point, any remaining integration activities become the responsibility of the business unit managers who are now running the integrated businesses.

INTEGRATION COMMUNICATIONS—INTERNAL

Once the integration process is under way, an integration team of any size will find that it loses touch with the progress of other team members. This is a particular problem when they are operating in multiple locations. Given the extremely tight timelines normally associated with an integration effort, it is not usually possible to bring the team together for periodic status meetings. The usual result is a weekly conference call involving all sub-team managers, which uses an agenda, structured reporting, and a follow-up report that itemizes who is responsible for the issues discussed during the call.

In addition to a conference call, consider introducing a more personal touch by authorizing a periodic team newsletter. This can be used to document integration "wins," as well as progress scorecards and recognition of those teams completing major milestone projects.

The integration team must also maintain an issues log. This is an itemization of unresolved problems that are interfering with the completion of various tasks in the implementation plan. The log is intended to be a summary of remaining issues, who is responsible for each item's resolution, and the date by which it should be completed. A sample issues log is noted below.

Issues Log

Issue	Responsibility	Action	Due Date
Select sales personnel for layoff	M. Sarnoff	Facilitate selection meeting with sales managers	Jan. 15
Legal entity not shut down	A. Weatherby	Re-write landlord contract for new entity	Jan. 21
ABC facility not sub-leased	T. Arnold	Meet with leasing agent to determine market rate for sublease	Jan. 27

The communication systems outlined here are especially important for large teams, where it would otherwise be impossible for participants to remain knowledgeable about overall activities.

INTEGRATION COMMUNICATIONS—EXTERNAL

Communicating with the acquiree's employees is a large part of the integration staff's job. Employees will be ultra-sensitive about any changes to the content of their jobs, their compensation, and their reporting relationships, and will interpret every contact, question, and request for information with suspicion. The integration team can fully expect that their most inconsequential comment will be magnified far out of proportion and misinterpreted, sometimes to an extraordinary degree.

Due to the sensitivity of the acquiree's staff, there should be a system for regular communication. This system can involve a combination of methods, such as a Web site, newsletter, voice mails, video conferences, and so on. Whatever methods are used, the integration team must be careful to present a consistent message about the acquisition, what the team intends to do, and when it plans to complete its work. These messages cannot prevaricate in any way, since acquiree employees are poring over them in detail to see if the buyer is doing what it says. Further, communications should not react to events, but rather be issued as soon as the integration team becomes aware of anything that may impact employees. That being said, some communications will be reactive, since events will arise that were not planned.

Communication frequency is also important. There should be at least weekly updates on progress. If information is not released at these intervals, then employees will make up their own news about the integration, which may vary wildly (and inaccurately) from the real situation. There should be some communication, even if there are no concrete accomplishments to report. Merely stating that there is some progress toward a milestone is better than a period of prolonged silence.

One person should be responsible for all information dissemination. This individual ensures that the same message is consistently stated across all forms of communication, and that communications are made as soon as new information becomes available to the integration team. Do not consider this position to be secondary—the cooperation of acquiree employees is essential, so they must be treated as partners by keeping them informed through a first-class communications system.

Some buyers may think that they are already handling the communications process, because the top-level managers from each entity are actively engaged in conversations with each other, every day. However, these people forget to inform those lower-level managers working for them, who in turn have no information to pass along to the non-management staff. Further, even if the top-level managers were diligent in imparting information, they would be doing so individually—which abrogates the principle of having a consistent message across all forms of communication. Thus, it is not sufficient to assign responsibility for communications to a group of people; only a single communications manager will do.

ANGER MANAGEMENT

An inevitable part of any integration effort is that some employees will be angered by the loss of jobs, status, range of authority, perceived bureaucratic bungling, or other issues. The integration manager is at the forefront of dealing with these issues.

Employees must be allowed to vent their frustrations, since the alternative is pent-up anger that can result in employee departures or lack of support. Consequently, the integration team should immediately create several formal communication channels that are specifically for the use of anyone impacted by an integration project. One example is a hotline, through which employees can informally relay concerns. For smaller projects, this can simply be the integration manager's direct phone line; however, there may be a flood of calls during larger integration efforts, so it is better to impose an intermediary who can summarize calls.

Another option is an electronic bulletin board, which the project team monitors closely to detect patterns of concerns that require immediate action.

Whatever communications methods are used, the integration team must respond rapidly, or else employee comments through the formal channels will dwindle rapidly. Obviously, the best form of response is to take clearly discernible actions that offset the stated problem. However, in many cases, the integration team cannot accede to employee demands. For example, an employee may present a strong case for not closing down a facility, but the integration team must do so in order to meet its cost saving target. If so, someone from the team must respond to the comment, stating the countervailing reasons. Thus, even if employees may not be happy with responses to their comments, they will at least know that some consideration is being given to their point of view.

PROGRESS REPORTING—EXTERNAL

If the buyer is a publicly held company, then the integration manager should work with the investor relations officer (IRO) to construct the best methodology for revealing integration progress to the investment community. This information is generally revealed in the company's quarterly filings with the Securities and Exchange Commission, as well as through its quarterly conference calls.

The basic approach is for the integration manager to forward target results to the IRO at the start of the integration process, and to then report on progress against those goals over the course of the integration period. The investment community wants to see the same metrics being used over time to measure progress, so the integration manager should be certain at the start of the integration that the correct metrics are being used. If a company is a serial acquirer, then there should be a standard reporting methodology already in place from which he can draw.

The IRO is responsible for forwarding progress information to the investment community. Under no circumstances should the integration manager be drawn into any discussions with investors or analysts, since the IRO is far more cognizant of what information should be disclosed to the public.

CULTURAL ISSUES

The remainder of this chapter itemizes a considerable number of specific integration issues, including employees, processes, technology, and so on. In order to achieve any degree of success in these areas, the integration team must first be aware of the acquiree's culture. Making changes that do not interfere with an existing culture will be far more likely to succeed than those that do not. Culture involves a number of issues, including the following:

- *Awards and ceremonies*. This is the recognition of employees for their performance, and the manner in which they are recognized. Examples are sales awards at an annual banquet, or an employee of the month award.

- *Bureaucracy*. This is the extent to which formal policies and procedures drive company activities. For example, there may be rigid policies and procedures in place, with strict attention to risk management. Alternatively, employees may be given a great deal of "wiggle room" within a broad set of policy guidelines, and are encouraged to innovate and take risks. The level of bureaucracy tends to increase in older firms.

- *Customary events*. This is repeating events that have been ongoing for some time, and to which employees are accustomed. For example, there may be a Friday afternoon beer bash, or an informal off-site gathering at a local pub, or a monthly bowling tournament during lunch.

- *Customer service*. This is an organization's level of focus on customer needs. For example, a company may have an engineering mindset, where it develops interesting products and pushes them into the marketplace in hopes of making a few sales, or it may have a customer feedback loop for new product development that extends into customer service metrics and goals.

- *Decision making*. This is the degree to which the decision- making process is pushed down within an organization. For example, decisions can be made in an autocratic manner at the top of the organization, or they can be arrived at using a high degree of consensus building.

- *Dress code.* While seemingly trivial, a company's dress code provides significant clues regarding the general tenor of management. If the dress code is highly formal, then there is a good chance that the management structure is more autocratic, with a significant amount of bureaucracy. The reverse is more indicative of a distributed decision-making structure.

- *Feedback.* This is the degree to which management informs employees about their performance and objectives. Examples are formal, structured annual reviews, informal "hallway" meetings, regularly scheduled meetings, or a policy of "open access" to all managers.

- *Goal linking.* This is the extent to which the acquiree focuses on the achievement of goals. Examples are the specific linking of annual goals with employee bonus plans, follow-up meetings to emphasize goals, and promotions based on the achievement of goals.

- *Information dissemination.* This involves the amount and type of information issued within the company. For example, who receives financial statements, and how much information is included in the financials package? When there are meetings, is it customary to issue meeting notes to participants? What information is routinely withheld from employees? Are there employee meetings, and what is discussed at those meetings?

- *Leadership style.* This is the type of behavior exhibited by the management team as a group. For example, they may use an autocratic, military style, or they may coach their employees in making their own decisions.

- *Physical environment.* This is the working environment inhabited by employees. For example, a company may always use secondhand furniture in order to give the impression of having a cost-conscious environment, or its facilities may be custom-designed, with a focus on high-end employee productivity. There may also be significant differences between the furnishings enjoyed by senior managers and other employees.

- *Speed.* This is the sense of urgency imposed on a company by its leaders. For example, the management group may use an organized system of imposing meeting agendas and durations, while assigning specific responsibility for task completion within a short period of time. Alternatively, it may ignore these techniques and adopt a more relaxed approach to achieving goals.

- *Training.* This is the type and frequency of training provided to employees. For example, they may be accustomed to an annual trip to an off-site seminar, or the reimbursement of college classes, or in-house training programs.

Gathering information about culture can be a tedious process, and does not necessarily follow the usual path of formally interviewing people with the assistance of a questionnaire. Though that method will certainly compile a useful amount of data, in-depth information gathering requires a more relaxed and informal approach. The interviewer needs to delve for stories and anecdotes that reveal the acquiree's culture. This information may be most readily available through lower-level staff people who have been with the company for a long time, and not the usual crop of managers who are more likely to be interviewed.

The integration team should keep all of these issues in mind when deciding upon the proper way to implement changes. By doing so in accordance with the existing culture (especially by matching multiple cultural issues), the team will vastly increase the level of acceptance of its changes. Conversely, the team can roil the organization by ignoring its culture. In particular, implementation teams have a tendency to impose multiple decisions on the acquiree within a short period of time. If the employees subjected to this treatment are accustomed to a collaborative culture, their reaction will not be pleasant. However, if the acquiree's employees have been accustomed to a top-down, autocratic culture, the imposed changes may not meet with much resistance.

Since the integration team's mission is all about making a variety of changes, it is reasonable to expect that it will negatively impact the acquiree's culture at some point. If the level of culture modification becomes too extreme, the team will eventually meet with a higher level of resistance that impedes its progress. To monitor culture slippage, the team can periodically administer a culture survey to determine the areas in which some correction is needed. By using exactly the same survey every time, the team can achieve a considerable degree of consistency in creating a timeline that shows its impact on cultural issues.

But if the integration team must complete its tasks in order to make the acquisition cost-effective for the buyer, doesn't it have to ram through changes, irrespective of how those changes impact the acquiree's culture? Yes and no. Integration targets should be considered guidelines rather than concrete requirements, within which the team has the leeway to find the best ways to achieve synergies. For example, the buyer's integration plan may call for a layoff of five salespeople, due to overlapping sales territories of the buyer and acquiree. Knowing that the acquiree has a team-building approach to decision making, the integration manager brings the five-layoff target to the attention of the acquiree sales manager, who works with his team to figure out which salespeople will be let go. While the layoff goal certainly will not be met with cheering, the method taken for implementing it fits nicely into the acquiree's culture for decision making.

It is entirely possible that the acquiree's culture is so incompatible with that of the buyer that the integration team has no chance of successfully completing its task. This is not their fault, but rather that of the due diligence team. An investigation of acquiree culture is one of the most important due diligence items, but is the area most frequently ignored, because it involves "soft" information that is more difficult to collect.

In short, cultural issues form the underlying fabric around which a company is built. Though time-consuming, the integration team must spend time learning about cultural issues in order to find the path of least resistance in achieving its goals. Anyone ignoring an acquiree's culture will likely meet with a prolonged and less successful integration effort.

EMPLOYEE INTEGRATION—QUALIFICATION ASSESSMENT

Once the legal aspects of a purchase transaction have been completed, the most pressing issue for the buyer is to assess the qualifications of the acquiree's employees. Those functions that are handled strictly by the acquiree are normally left in the hands of the existing employees, using their in-place reporting structure. However, the integration team must determine whether functions *to be combined* shall be run by the personnel of the acquiree or the buyer. This calls for a rigidly defined and time-compressed evaluation process.

The integration team must use a standard evaluation form when reviewing acquiree employees, so that each person is evaluated using the same criteria. While a very compressed process may call for a single interview of each person, it is better to obtain a more rounded view by conducting multiple interviews, preferably by interviewers having different skill sets. Their numerical scores for each person can then be summarized in a grid and averaged to arrive at scores across various skill categories. While the following scoring grid can be used, it is designed to evaluate lower-level managers, and should be altered to match the requirements of each job position. The integration team should also compile all ancillary comments into a single comment sheet that accompanies the scoring grid. By using this rigid approach, it is much simpler to arrive at a quantitative score, as well as qualitative opinions and comments.

Employee Evaluation Scoring Grid

	Change Management	Communi-cations	Leader-ship	Problem Solving	Task Planning	Technical Skills
Reviewer 1	3	2	1	4	4	5
Reviewer 2	4	1	1	5	3	4
Reviewer 3	3	3	3	4	4	5
Reviewer 4	5	2	2	4	5	4
Averages	3.8	2.0	1.8	4.3	4.0	4.5

Note: scores are 1 to 5, with 5 being the best.

The sample scoring matrix shows results for an individual who obviously has considerable technical skills, but poor people skills. The scores relating to each of these attributes would be more difficult to discern if the scores for all columns were summarized into a single overall score. Thus, it is best not to arrive at a single numerical score, but rather to present a set of scores addressing a broad range of categories, thereby giving decision-makers a better view of an employee's entire set of attributes.

When using the scoring system to decide who will be given certain jobs, it is extremely helpful to conduct a transparent and unbiased review that results in the retention of the most qualified candidates. By demonstrating to the acquiree's personnel that the system is fair, they will be more inclined to stay with the company. The best way to immediately show how the system works is to deliberately review several highly qualified people at the start of the evaluation process, so that they can be placed in high-profile positions at once.

EMPLOYEE INTEGRATION—JOB POSITIONING

During a normal eight-hour working day, studies have shown that employees are effective for about six hours. However, this number drops to just one hour when there is a change in control, and will continue at that level until such time as all control issues are resolved. For example, if a 100-person company were to experience just one hour of reduced productivity per day, this would extrapolate into roughly 26,000 hours of wasted time per year. Thus, consider the enormous cost of lost productivity if employees are not properly integrated into the buying company. This is a sterling incentive for the integration team to move rapidly to establish employee roles and reporting relationships.

Many employees will fear for their jobs, and will likely be conducting job searches, if only to keep their employment options open. While it is inevitable that some will leave, one can reduce the losses by emphasizing rapid integration of employee roles. By doing so, there is a shortened period of uncertainty, which should effectively stop a number of informal job searches.

The integration team assists in determining who reports to whom. They are not responsible for making these decisions, but can facilitate the process of doing so. By rapidly clarifying reporting relationships, the responsibility for job positioning now passes to the line managers who are taking over groups of employees. By swiftly settling this issue, employees will shift their focus away from internal matters, and back to the customer-centric focus that builds profitability. This also eliminates wasted time among the respective management teams, who would otherwise jockey for position to take over the combined operations.

The reporting relationship decision is so important that the integration manager should essentially put the responsible decision-makers in one room and not let them out until all decisions have been made. Further, they should establish secondary choices for each key position, since some acquiree employees can be expected to leave despite any incentives to the contrary. Once all decisions are made, immediately notify all affected staff. If a decision involves a change to a new location, then give people additional time to decide if they will accept (see the following Employee Integration—Relocations section).

Any employees who do leave the acquiree represent a unique opportunity for the buyer. First, there should be an exit interview with key departing employees, to determine what specific actions by the buyer caused the departure. The implementation manager can use this information to alter the integration process to reduce any further employee losses. Also, the company should continue to recruit any employees who leave, because bringing them back can be trumpeted as an indicator that the acquiree is still a good place to work. Returning employees can be a powerful motivator for other staff who are contemplating a job switch.

EMPLOYEE INTEGRATION—RELOCATIONS

A major fear for employees is being required to move to a different company location. This impacts their perceived quality of life, since they are being uprooted from neighborhoods and school systems to which they may have strong ties. While the retention rate for employees being moved is normally low, there are some techniques for increasing the odds of success. First, involve employee families in the decision. This means flying entire families (or at least spouses) to the new location for visits to local communities. Second, remove all economic issues from the decision by paying for 100 percent of the moving costs, altering their compensation if they are moving to a higher-cost area, and even offering to buy out their homes if they cannot sell them. Third, do everything possible to welcome them into the new location by assigning a manager to introduce them to employees and sponsor informal off-site gatherings. All of these techniques will improve the odds of success, but many employees simply will not move, no matter what inducements are offered.

Conversely, some employees will be *very* interested in a relocation. They may feel that, because their company is now a subsidiary, the best job opportunities have shifted to corporate headquarters. They then perceive a reduced level of job growth, reduced autonomy, and perhaps even a worsening work environment—all of which contribute to more employee turnover. In these cases, the company should actively advocate relocating employees, if this is the best option for retaining them.

EMPLOYEE INTEGRATION—KEY EMPLOYEES

In any acquisition, the acquiree will have a key cluster of employees who are subject matter experts or rain makers who are responsible for the bulk of all sales. These employees are likely at the core of the acquiree's central value proposition, and so are extremely valuable. In addition, they may be the key drivers behind the acquiree's overall level of productivity and quality of work. The problem for the integration manager is that these people, because of their skills, are most likely to have held shares in the acquired entity, and may now have sufficient wealth to walk away from the company. If they leave, there may be a devastating decline in organizational knowledge and morale, along with a very high replacement cost.

To retain this core group, the first task is to create a retention matrix, showing the impact of losing each key employee, what issues might cause them to leave, what tactics shall be used to retain them, and who is responsible for implementation. The integration manager uses this matrix to select the most appropriate retention tactics, and to assign responsibility for follow-up with the targeted employees.

Retention tactics can cover a considerable range of options, and can only be narrowed down to the most effective alternatives by talking to each key employee individually to determine their concerns. Here are some options:

- *Altered benefits.* An employee may have a special need, such as short-term disability coverage, that is not addressed by the standard company benefits package. In many cases, these additional requirements are not overly expensive, and can have a profound impact on their decision to stay with the company.

- *Autonomy.* This is one of the most cherished prerogatives of an independent-minded manager, but only allow it if the employee is still linked to highly quantitative goals.

- *Change reporting relationship.* An employee may have conflicts with an oppressive manager, so switching to a different manager may not only improve retention, but also increase the effectiveness of the employee.

- *Culture*. Employees may identify strongly with their company's culture, and will leave if it changes. Culture issues may include a relaxed dress code, working from home, periodic beer bashes, and so on. The integration team should be very careful about altering any cultural issues that might alienate key employees.

- *Importance*. Some employees are used to being crucial to an enterprise's success, because of some unique skill. If so, retention may simply require the buyer to periodically reassure an individual that he is needed, and important to the company—and then prove it through whatever methods are needed to provide assurances to the targeted person.

- *Increased pay*. An increase in pay will certainly gain the attention of an employee, but keep in mind that pay changes can be matched by a competing firm, and may also shift an employee into a pay level that is well outside of the normal range for his position.

- *Job content*. Simply making a job more interesting can retain employees. This may require a process change, so that more tasks within a process are concentrated on one person.

- *Learning opportunities*. An employee may want to obtain a technical skill or an entire college degree, so offer to either pay the entire cost or to share it with the employee. However, this situation sometimes results in the prompt departure of the individual once he has obtained the extra education, so require a payback agreement if he leaves the company within a certain period of time following completion of the training.

- *New location*. Moving an employee against his wishes to a new company location is a prime method for losing him to a competitor. On the other hand, if there is another company facility where he might *prefer* to work, then allow the change and pay for a housing move, too—but only if the employee can be effective in the new location.

- *New title.* While a new title is the ultimate in inexpensive perks, it is also easily matched by a competing company, and so does not help much to retain an employee.

- *Promotion.* Promoting an employee to a higher-grade position with more responsibility is a strong inducement to remain, though there is a risk of promptly losing anyone who becomes uncomfortable in the new role.

- *Work from home.* With the pervasive use of mobile communications, working from home, at least to a limited extent, is an excellent option, especially for those employees with long commutes or medical care issues.

Key employee desires may require some items entirely outside of the preceding list, so be open to other options that they may bring up.

Another solution is to give them enough additional shares to gain their attention, but only if there is a sufficiently long vesting period associated with the shares to retain them for a number of years. The most common approach is proportional vesting (e.g., 20 percent vesting in each of five years), but as key employees gradually gain vested shares, they have less inclination to stay with the company. As a result, some firms prefer to vest a larger proportion of stock near the end of a vesting period, as an incentive to keep key personnel for as long as possible. Also, there is a risk that employees will wait out their retention periods without adding any value to the company. To avoid this problem, consider tying any retention payments to a specific performance metric or deliverable.

While the discussion thus far has been about the retention of key employees, it is equally important to obtain their backing of the acquisition. These people are opinion leaders, so obtaining their "stamp of approval" for the transaction means that they in turn will sway the opinions of a number of other employees. While some key employees will make their decisions about the transaction right away (either negatively or positively), a few will be undecided for some time.

Dealing with key employees is similar to the political stratagems used by a candidate for political office—one must determine what promises are needed to create a majority of backers. However, and as is the case with a politician, it is not necessary, nor always desirable, to issue a vast number of assurances to obtain the support of *all* key employees. Some employees will be so disaffected or demanding that it is not economical or prudent to accede to their demands. Instead, the integration manager seeks to work with as many key personnel as possible, and to mitigate the negative opinions of a select minority.

There will be cases where the opinions of key personnel cannot be swayed in favor of the buyer. This is most common in hostile takeovers, where vigorous defenses are raised against an acquisition attempt, and public statements may extend to smear campaigns against opposing managers. In these cases, the buyer may have no other choice than to replace a large proportion of the acquiree's staff with new employees who do not hold prior allegiances within the organization, or who have been brought in from other buyer locations.

The discussion in this section has been about how to retain and sway the opinions of key acquiree employees. However, when the success of an acquisition is contingent upon the retention of a *single* individual, then there are much greater odds of failure. This is a simple case of probabilities—circumstances may easily arise that lead to the departure of that one person, and which may be totally outside of the control of the buyer (such as a death in the family). Thus, it is better to acquire companies having multiple key people, on the grounds that a buyer would be hard put to it indeed to alienate an entire group of employees.

EMPLOYEE INTEGRATION—FOUNDERS

Company founders present a special problem (and opportunity) for integration. While many founders are simply cashing out of their businesses and retiring, others are still young enough and may be sufficiently interested in a continuing role at the buying entity.

However, the typical entrepreneur prefers to be his own boss, and so does not operate well as a small cog within a larger corporate environment. A possible solution is to tap the founder's entrepreneurial proclivities by creating a special R&D unit that he can run, unimpeded by corporate bureaucracy. Another alternative is to fund a portion of the founder's next start-up company, with an option to buy a controlling interest in it at some point in the future.

At a minimum, the buyer should consider retaining the founder as an employee emeritus, with a stipend, in order to obtain advice or contacts within the industry. These options allow the buyer to tap the enormous expertise of the founder, while still allowing enough room for him to operate successfully within a larger entity.

The worst possible scenario is to have conflicts with the founder, who then leaves in a cloud of acrimony. When this happens, he is likely to sow disaffection among the remaining employees, who may be intensely loyal to him. If the founder does not have a non-compete agreement with the buyer, then he may very well start or buy a competing firm, and gradually siphon away some of the acquiree's best talent.

In short, it is better to carve out a role for the founder, however small it may be, in order to maintain access to expertise that may prove invaluable.

EMPLOYEE INTEGRATION—UNIONS

If a buyer acquires the legal entity of an acquiree, then it inherits any labor unions formerly recognized by it. If the buyer only acquires the assets of the acquiree, then it may still be required to recognize any unions that formerly represented the acquiree's employees. This situation arises when the buyer hires a "substantial and representative complement" of the acquiree's union workforce, even if the acquiree had been shut down for some time prior to the acquisition. The following five factors are considered by the courts when determining the existence of a "substantial and representative complement" of employees:

- Whether the job classifications of the acquiree are substantially filled
- Whether the acquiree is at essentially normal production levels
- The number of employees needed when the acquiree is running at normal production levels
- The time period before a substantially larger workforce is needed
- The likelihood of expansion to a significantly larger workforce

In short, a buyer should assume that, if a potential acquiree has recognized one or more unions, then it must do so as well, irrespective of the type of purchase transaction, unless it plans to lay off the bulk of the acquiree's employees.

LAYOFFS

Part of the integration plan may include the layoffs of some acquiree employees. The integration team should pay special attention to the mechanics of the layoff process, because it can have a major impact on the attitudes of the remaining staff. For example, if layoffs are made abruptly, with minimal severance pay, and with little respect for the people being let go, this sends a strong message to the remaining employees regarding the type of company that they are now working for. Conversely, if departing employees are given reasonable severance packages, job search support, and the use of company facilities, then employees will realize that they may now have an excellent employer.

The integration team must also pay particular attention to the very real possibility of litigation by those employees being let go. Many states have "right to work" laws that allow for layoffs without a significant amount of proof by the employer. Nonetheless, employees can claim that they were discriminated against as minorities. There are so many groups of minorities, such as veterans, women, or those over 40 years old or with disabilities, that employers may sometimes wonder which staff are *not* minorities. In fact, about 10 percent of all litigation involving companies is for wrongful termination, with minority status being the core reason for the lawsuits. Thus, it is wisest to establish a logical and defensible layoff ranking system, such as by seniority, but to also review this list for minority concentrations. When in doubt, employ a labor attorney to review prospective layoffs and ascertain where there may be some risk of litigation.

Also, disseminate a clear statement of termination benefits to all employees being laid off, so there is no confusion about payments to be made. Where possible, pay termination benefits at once, which tends to reduce resentment.

If acquiree employees are part of a union, then the layoff process is more involved. Their union contract may state that they must be given a certain amount of notice prior to either a layoff or a plant closing. Not only does this create a significant and potentially costly delay, but it also gives the union more time in which to devise various legal barriers to throw in the way of the layoff, or to bargain over the effects of the change. The integration team should use the services of a labor attorney to determine the likelihood of union-related problems, and what mitigation steps can be taken.

If a company has at least 100 employees, then it must be in compliance with the Worker Adjustment and Retraining Notification Act (WARN). In essence, the Act requires that a company provide 60 days written notice to workers of impending plant closings and mass layoffs. This only applies if there will be a plant closing resulting in employment loss for 50 or more workers within a 30-day period, or a mass layoff which does not result from a plant closing, but which will yield an employment loss for 500 or more employees, or for 50–499 employees if they make up at least one-third of the active workforce.

COMPENSATION INTEGRATION

Unless subsidiaries are to be kept totally separate, the buyer must at some point address the problem of pay disparities between the employees of the buyer and the acquiree. While it is certainly possible to use pay cuts to achieve post-acquisition equality, there are few actions more likely to bring about a significant number of employee departures. Instead, the buyer should consider enacting a small number of pay raises among key employees to achieve pay equality, without making significant pay rate increases elsewhere. By doing so, key staff members are less likely to leave, while the company as a whole does not incur a significant increase in payroll expenses.

However, companies may have pay plans so radically different that there is no way to achieve a reasonable degree of payroll integration. For example, a mature business is more likely to pay employees within rigid pay ranges, and pay smaller bonuses. Conversely, a company in a high-growth field may have a compensation system structured to pay out much larger bonuses, possibly in stock, though with reduced base pay. Any attempt to integrate these plans will be more likely to cause serious disruption among the staff. If so, the only reasonable alternative may be to leave the compensation systems entirely separate in the short term. Over the long term, the operating environments of the companies will gradually change, which eventually makes it possible to incrementally alter the pay systems to bring them into greater alignment.

Even if pay systems cannot be integrated, there are still excellent opportunities for integrating benefit plans. If the buyer acquires companies on a regular basis, it can be quite expensive to maintain and administer a multitude of benefit plans. Instead, there are significant opportunities for cost savings by combining all benefits into a single, centrally-administered plan. While this will likely call for some changes to the benefit plans of every acquired company, the scale of change is not normally so significant as to cause undue employee dissatisfaction.

The bonus plans of both companies may also be substantially different. If so, a common practice is to allow employees to complete the current fiscal year under their existing plans. This is especially common if a number of employees are close to completing their targeted goals, and only need a few more months to meet targets. If the buyer were to eliminate these plans just prior to award dates, disaffection among the acquiree's employees could be high. However, if the fiscal year has just begun, it is not especially difficult to replace existing bonus plans with those of the buyer. Another alternative is to buy out existing bonus plans, based on the proportion of the year that has been completed under the plan, and the degree of success thus far achieved in completing goals. This last option allows the buyer to immediately alter bonus targets so that they support integration goals.

SALES INTEGRATION

The success of any company begins with its customers, and this is precisely where an acquiree tends to suffer directly after an acquisition. Some customers will be concerned about changes in service, product, or pricing, and will take their business elsewhere. In addition, competitors will view an acquisition as an opportunity to poach customers, and will actively solicit them as soon as the deal is announced.

To avoid these problems, it is essential that the sales departments of the two companies meet immediately after the purchase transaction for a comprehensive briefing on the acquiree's key customers, as well as its products, pricing, and sales strategy. The key result of this meeting should be a plan for how to deal with all key customers. In addition, the meeting should yield a general direction for the treatment of products and pricing, so that the sales force can give a general idea of the situation to those customers who inquire about what will happen next.

To keep from losing customers, senior managers should travel to the major customers several times, to hear their concerns and to discuss issues related to the integration. For smaller customers, the acquirer can use other forms of communication, such as memos, e-mails, newsletters, or even the services of a public relations firm. The mindset at this point should not be to pressure customers for more sales, but simply to ensure that they do not take their business elsewhere.

As the combined companies gradually determine how they will integrate their products together and establish pricing, they should communicate this information back to the customers, preferably through personal visits. By transmitting this information face-to-face, managers can immediately ascertain customer reactions, and adjust their plans if those reactions are excessively negative.

Another way to avoid a short-term decline in sales is to counteract it with a short-term sales incentive plan. This can include bonuses for the acquiree sales team for simply matching or slightly exceeding their normal sales volumes. The marketing department can also run additional repetitions of its normal advertising campaigns. The intent is to avoid the initial drop in sales that might otherwise trigger a continuing decline in sales.

A common practice is to have the sales staffs of both companies represent each other's products and services before the combined customer base. The theory is that combining sales forces will increase the total dollar value of each sales call. However, if the products being sold are not similar, it will take more time for the sales staffs to learn about the products, and will also require longer sales calls. Thus, even though the total dollar value of each sales call may indeed increase, there may be fewer sales calls made, with offsetting results.

Also, it is difficult to combine sales forces if the underlying products have substantially different sales strategies. For example, if a product has a very high price point, then it likely involves different buyers and permission levels, and therefore a much longer sales cycle. In this case, a sales team with a long-term compensation arrangement will probably be more successful than an individual salesperson whose compensation is based on short-term sales. Thus, the type of sale may mandate entirely different sales forces, even if the buyer and acquiree share exactly the same customers.

In brief, the integration team should initially be less concerned with ramping up sales, and more involved with the retention of existing customers. In many cases, hoped-for sales gains through merging the sales forces will be structurally difficult to achieve. Thus, sales integration carries with it a significant risk of loss, rather than the gains to which many buyers aspire.

PROCESS INTEGRATION

There are few areas causing more resentment than when a buyer unilaterally imposes its own processes on the acquiree, especially if the acquiree feels that it has the better process.

The most critical point is not to immediately impose the buyer's processes on the acquiree without some initial discussion. Ideally, this should include a side-by-side analysis of the processes used by each entity, with acquiree representatives participating in the analysis. A likely offshoot of this review will be comparative matrices showing the strengths and weaknesses of each process, and which ones require more or fewer steps. This review may result in a blended process that incorporates the best features of both systems.

A company that engages in frequent acquisitions does not have time to engage in the aforementioned comparative process analysis. Instead, it has already adopted a core system, and must impose it on every acquiree in order to maintain its pace of acquisitions. When this scenario arises, the implementation team should make the acquiree's staff thoroughly aware of why the process changeover must be made, without any changes to accommodate their local needs or preferences.

An alternative that stands midway between the preceding alternatives is to compare the process metrics of the acquiree and buyer; if the buyer's metrics are clearly better, then the integration team immediately imposes the buyer's process on the acquiree with minimal further investigation. However, if the acquiree can quantitatively prove that it has a better process, then the integration team can take a deeper look at the acquiree's process.

A significant amount of history has probably built up around each process, including periodic process training, improvement rewards, and the simple inertia of many people growing accustomed to a fixed methodology over time. The integration team can knock some supporting struts from beneath these process edifices by eliminating anything that perpetuates them. This includes the elimination of training classes and any rewards geared to the ongoing use of the process. Also, most processes are strongly supported by long-term employees who have used them for many years, and who may have originated them. If so, it may be necessary to re-assign these people, possibly into another facility entirely, so that they will be unable to interfere with any process integration activities.

Because of their significant impact on day-to-day work, process revisions can be exceedingly disruptive, so be sure to use a considerable amount of change management while doing so.

TECHNOLOGY INTEGRATION

Among the most difficult integration chores is that of consolidating disparate information technology platforms. It is exceedingly common for the two parties to an acquisition to use heavily-modified legacy software solutions, which makes it extremely difficult to achieve a reasonable degree of integration. However, without integration, the combined company must maintain separate support staffs, as well as diverging hardware and software maintenance agreements and upgrade paths.

The best solution for the acquirer is to first purge all of its own legacy systems, in favor of the most reliable and scalable commercial solutions on the market. By doing so, the acquirer will have a much easier time shifting acquiree systems over to its own systems. Despite this level of preparation, the buyer will likely find that several years will be needed to fully integrate the systems of both companies.

It is also possible that the buyer has *only* bought the acquiree for its technology. If so, the integration process may involve the complete elimination of all other parts of the acquiree, with the integration team spending nearly all of its time creating a comfortable environment for the development and support staff surrounding the acquiree's technology.

CONTROLS INTEGRATION

The buyer must create an adequate system of internal controls at the acquiree, or else there will be a significant risk of financial loss.

It is easier to create an adequate system of internal controls when the acquiree is significantly smaller than the buyer. This is because the buyer is more likely to already have the more comprehensive set of controls, and so can impose the bulk of its own systems directly onto the acquiree. Conversely, if the purchase involves two entities of essentially the same size, it is far more likely that two will squabble over whose controls will be adopted. In the later case, it is not uncommon for control problems to persist for several years.

Controls integration is of great concern when the acquiree is run by one or more autocratic managers. These individuals are used to having absolute control over their company's systems, and so are extremely uncomfortable in acceding to controls changes imposed by the buyer. Because of their natures, it is more likely that these people will have either intentionally or inadvertently caused control breaches within their organizations. Thus, the integration team can expect significant trouble in creating adequate control systems in such environments, unless the autocrats are removed.

If the buyer is a public company, it must also be concerned with conducting a Sarbanes-Oxley Section 404 controls assessment of the acquiree, to see if there are any control weaknesses. Because this involves sending in controls auditors to test a broad range of systems, it can interfere with the completion of other integration activities. However, it is acceptable to waive the controls assessment for a period of up to one year from the date of the acquisition. If so, the exclusion must be noted in a public filing.

Entirely new systems of internal control may be needed when a small acquiree becomes part of a much larger buyer. This issue arises when the smaller company was formerly able to avoid regulatory requirements under a small business waiver, but must now be in compliance with tougher large-company standards. For example, large government contractors must have robust cost accounting systems, from which reports are run that support the amounts billed to the government. A small acquiree would find itself out of compliance with these requirements, and would need to adopt new costing systems at once. Compliance systems can be expensive and difficult to install, so the integration team should budget for the funds and personnel needed to do so.

Given the more urgent need to locate and realize synergies in the short term, many integration teams will accept the risk of financial loss and delay any work on controls until some time has passed. This is not usually a problem, except where regulatory compliance is an issue.

BOARD INTEGRATION

In nearly all cases, one entity is buying another, and there is no merger of equals. Nonetheless, in those rare cases where two entities truly intend to merge, the boards of directors of both entities may want to be retained in the surviving company. Depending on the size of the original boards, this may result in an unwieldy group that is simply too large to effectively make decisions. Since most company by-laws specify a one-year term for board members, it is usually a simple matter to vote a smaller group into director positions in the following year. If the by-laws mandate staggered terms, then this process will require a few additional years. If the acquiree insists on ongoing board membership in the surviving entity, then there should be some discussion about how to accommodate this request without creating a board too large to make decisions in an effective manner.

INTEGRATION METRICS

The success of an acquisition is ultimately measured by the increase in value of the combined firms over their values just prior to the purchase transaction. For a publicly held firm that acquires another public company, this result can be approximately measured by determining their average market capitalizations over a few weeks just prior to the announcement of the transaction. For private companies or mixed public-private transactions, the best approach is to measure discounted cash flows before and after the transaction, including the payout to the selling company's shareholders.

In order to achieve these before-and-after valuation metrics, the integration team must use a multitude of additional metrics. Many are based on the simple achievement of milestones, such as the variety of intermediate steps needed to eventually arrive at a single payroll system for the entire company, or the combination of multiple company locations into one. In these cases, individual steps will not increase profitability by themselves, but are still necessary for proving the ultimate value of the transaction. Thus, the integration team may deal with dozens of transient metrics which all roll together into the planned level of cash flow needed to justify the acquisition.

Metrics can span an extraordinary range of activities. For example, from a cultural integration perspective, an appropriate metric might be the weekly dissemination of a newsletter to the acquiree's employees. If treasury activities are to be combined, then another metric could be the number of acquiree bank accounts still open. If a computer system is to be replaced with one used by the buyer, then metrics would include a series of milestones, such as converting acquiree databases, completing system training for new users, and shutting down software licenses for the system being discontinued. Thus, the metrics used will vary based on the exact types of integration contemplated.

Metrics should also track signs that an acquisition is not working. If an acquiree's staff is not happy, then this may appear through a higher total number of customer service calls, or the loss of key customers or employees. These examples are quantitative, and can easily be tracked. Other indicators of failure are more qualitative, such as the persistence of a "them versus us" mentality, or difficulty in transferring the buyer's core values to the acquiree's management team. In these later cases, a periodic survey can uncover the extent of attitudinal problems. Of course, the overriding indicator of a problematic integration effort is when the integration team remains on-site past the planned date, and is not available to work on other acquisitions.

INTEGRATION PACING

The buyer may have a strong interest in conducting a rapid series of acquisitions. This desire may be triggered by opportunities in an industry that is suffering an economic downturn, or because the buyer wants to roll up a significant portion of an industry. While a rapid pace of acquisitions may be exciting for the chief executive officer, it is a logistical nightmare for the integration team.

Smaller companies do not have enough employees to appropriately staff a multitude of integration teams, and even larger companies may feel the strain if there are several large integrations going on at once. This results in an integration bottleneck, where some acquirees may not see an integration team for months, or integrations are only perfunctory, and do not attempt to achieve any synergies. Thus, companies who go on buying sprees without proper integration planning will find themselves at high risk of not meeting their performance goals.

The best solution to this quandary is to use a proper level of acquisition pacing. By spreading out acquisitions, the integration team will have sufficient time to address all issues at the last acquiree before moving on to the next one. While acquisitions are by their nature "lumpy" (i.e, acquisition dates cannot be predicted with precision), a company can adopt a policy of restricting itself to a certain amount of acquired sales volume per year, which will generally allow integration efforts to be completed at a reasonable pace.

If the buyer has multiple divisions, then it can achieve a faster pace by shifting acquisitions around the various divisions in rotation. This spreads out the integration efforts among different line-management people in the divisions, without placing an undue burden on any single group.

SUMMARY

If the buyer treats an acquisition as a financial transaction where the acquiree is a stand-alone operation, there is a good chance that only the most minimal integration activities will be needed. However, if the buyer treats it as a strategic transaction, where it plans for full integration with the rest of the company, then it must deal with a complex series of activities that will be difficult to coordinate and which will be at considerable risk of failure.

The key factors in the integration of a strategic acquisition are to have a dedicated integration team, and to act at once. When a decisive manager announces all major changes within a few days of a purchase transaction, it keeps the acquiree's personnel from squandering time worrying about their circumstances. Conversely, a creeping integration that spans several years causes ongoing uncertainty, and drains value from the combined companies.

Chapter 8

Accounting for Acquisitions[1]

Accounting for an acquisition involves the assignment of the purchase price to all acquiree assets, which requires the identification of a variety of intangible assets that the acquiree did not record on its books at all. A key result of this step is the creation of a *goodwill asset*, which the buyer must periodically test for impairment, and write off if necessary. This chapter deals with both issues, as well as the specifics of how to initially record an acquisition on the buyer's books.

PURCHASE PRICE ALLOCATION

When a buyer acquires another company, a major consideration is how to allocate the purchase price to the various assets and liabilities that it has acquired. Where the legal form of combination is a merger or consolidation, the buyer records all the acquired assets and assumed liabilities at their fair values (not the acquired entity's book values). If the actual cost exceeds the fair values of the assets acquired, this

[1] Adapted with permission from pp. 554-613 of *Wiley GAAP 2008*, with permission.

excess is recorded as an intangible asset (goodwill). Many acquisitions will involve the recognition of considerable amounts of goodwill.

There are also situations where the buyer pays an exceedingly low price, which is less than the fair value of the net assets acquired. In this case, the deficiency of cost under fair value is first allocated as a pro rata reduction of the amounts that otherwise would be assigned to the acquired assets other than cash and cash equivalents, trade receivables, inventory, financial instruments that are required to be carried on the balance sheet at fair value, assets to be disposed of by sale, and deferred income tax assets. If the initially recorded amounts of these acquired assets are entirely eliminated, the excess, called *negative goodwill*, is generally recognized immediately as an extraordinary gain.

FAIR VALUE DETERMINATION

The buyer must make a determination of the fair value of each of the acquiree's identifiable tangible and intangible assets and of each of its liabilities, as of the date of combination. The list below indicates how this is to be accomplished for various assets and liabilities:

1. *Marketable securities.* Fair values, which, for trading and available for sale securities, are already reflected in the acquiree's balance sheet

2. *Receivables.* Present values of amounts to be received determined by using current interest rates, less allowances for uncollectible accounts and collection costs, if applicable

3. Inventories

   a. Finished goods and merchandise inventories—Estimated selling prices less the sum of the costs of disposal and a normal profit

   b. Work in process inventories—Estimated selling prices less the sum of the costs of completion, costs of disposal, and a normal profit

   c. Raw material inventories—Current replacement cost

4. Property, plant, and equipment

    a. If expected to be used in operations—Current replacement costs for similar capacity unless the expected future use of the assets indicates a lower value to the acquirer

    b. If expected to be sold—Fair value less cost to sell

5. Identifiable intangible assets and other assets (such as land, natural resources, and nonmarketable securities). Appraised (fair) value

6. Liabilities (such as notes and accounts payable, long-term debt, warranties, claims payable). Present value of amounts to be paid determined at appropriate current interest rates

7. *Single-employer defined-benefit pension plans.* Liabilities for a projected benefit obligation (PBO) in excess of the fair value of plan assets (or, conversely, assets representing the fair value of plant assets in excess of PBO) are to be determined pursuant to FAS 87, *Employers' Accounting for Pensions*

8. *Single-employer defined-benefit postretirement plans.* Liabilities for accumulated postretirement benefit obligations (APBO) in excess of the fair value of plan assets (or, conversely, assets representing the fair value of plan assets in excess of APBO) are to be determined pursuant to FAS 106, *Employers' Accounting for Postretirement Benefits other than Pensions*

FASB Statement 157, *Fair Value Measurements*, offers detailed guidance on the criteria to be employed in determining fair values in a variety of applications, including purchase business combinations. A key provision of the standard is the elimination of any entity-specific valuations (e.g., unique value in use to the acquiring entity), in favor of objectively determinable valuations (e.g., relying upon market-based values).

INTANGIBLES IDENTIFICATION

The buyer must identify an intangible asset associated with the acquired entity separately from goodwill. The identified intangibles can be generally grouped into permits, intellectual property, technology tools, procurement rights, competitor arrangements, and customer arrangements. Among the permits are:

1. Broadcast rights, defined as being a license to transmit over certain bandwidths in the radio frequency spectrum, granted by the operation of communication laws
2. Certification marks, or the right to be able to assert that a product or service meets certain standards of quality or origin, such as "ISO 9000 Certified"
3. Collective marks, or rights to signify membership in an association
4. Construction permits, which are rights to build a specified structure at a specified location
5. Franchise rights, or permits to engage in a trade-named business, to sell a trademarked good, or to sell a service-marked service in a particular geographic area
6. Internet domain names
7. Operating rights, permits to operate in a certain manner, such as that granted to a carrier to transport specified commodities, and
8. Use rights, which are permits to use specified land, property, or air space in a particular manner, such as the right to cut timber, expel emissions, or land airplanes

Intellectual property includes items such as:

1. Copyrights, or the rights to reproduce, distribute, etc. an original work of literature, music, art, photography, or film
2. Newspaper mastheads, the rights to use the information that is displayed on the top of the first pages of newspapers
3. Patents, which are rights to make, use, or sell an invention for a specified period
4. Service marks, rights to use the name or symbol that distinguishes a service

5. Trade dress, defined as access to the overall appearance and image (unique color, shape, or package design) of a product; trademarks, which are rights to use the word, logo, or symbol that distinguishes a product; trade names, or the right to use the name or symbol that distinguishes a business; trade secrets, which consist of information, such as a formula, process, or recipe, that is kept confidential; and unpatented technology, or access to the knowledge about the manner of accomplishing a task

Technology tools may consist of computer software, including programs, procedures, and documentation associated with computer hardware, as well as databases, which are collections of a particular type of information, such as scientific data or credit information.

Procurement rights include:

1. Construction contracts, which are rights to acquire the subject of the contract in exchange for taking over the remaining obligations (including any payments)

2. Employment contracts, or rights to take the seller's place as the employer under the contract and thus obtain the employee's services in exchange for fulfilling the employer's remaining duties, such as payment of salaries and benefits, under the contract

3. Lease agreements, which, when they are assignable, are rights to step into the shoes of the lessee and thus obtain the rights to use assets that are the subject of the agreement, in exchange for making the remaining lease payments

4. License agreements, rights to access or use properties that are the subjects of licenses in exchange for making any remaining license payments and adhering to other responsibilities as licensee

5. Royalty agreements, which are rights to take the place of payors and thus assume the payors' remaining rights and duties under the agreements

6. Service or supply contracts, or rights to become the customer of particular contracts and thus purchase the specified products or services for the prices specified in those contracts

Competitor arrangements may include non-compete agreements, which are rights to assurances that companies or individuals will refrain from conducting similar businesses or selling to specific customers for an agreed-upon period; and standstill agreements, which convey rights to assurances that companies or individuals will refrain from engaging in certain activities for specified periods.

Finally, customer arrangements are items such as:

1. Customer lists, defined as information about companies' customers, including names, contact information, and order histories that a third party, such as a competitor or a telemarketing firm would want to use in its own business

2. Customer relationships, or relationships between entities and their customers for which

   a. The entities have information about the customers and have regular contacts with the customers, and

   b. The customers have the ability to make direct contact with the entity

3. Contracts and related customer relationships which arise through contracts and are of value to buyers who can "step into the shoes" of the sellers and assume their remaining rights and duties under the contracts, and which hold the promise that the customers will place future orders with the entity

4. Noncontractual customer relationships, arising through means such as regular contacts by sales or service representatives, the value of which are derived from the prospect of the customers placing future orders with the entities

5. Order or production backlogs, providing buyers rights to step into the shoes of sellers on unfilled sales orders for services and for

goods in amounts that exceed the quantity of finished goods and work-in-process on hand for filling the orders

The buyer may have a difficult time assigning the purchase price of an acquisition to any of the above intangible assets, simply because of inexperience with valuation techniques. If so, consider hiring a professional valuation firm, which has developed methodologies for doing so.

DUPLICATIVE ASSETS AND ASSETS TARGETED FOR DISPOSITION

Acquiree assets having no value are to be assigned no allocated cost. A typical example arises when facilities of the acquired entity duplicate those of the buyer and accordingly are to be disposed of. The cost allocated to these facilities is equal to the estimated net salvage value, zero if no salvage value is expected, or a negative amount equal to the estimated costs of disposal, if warranted. On the other hand, if facilities of the acquired entity duplicate and are superior to facilities of the purchaser, with the intention that the latter will be disposed of, fair value must be allocated to the former. Eventual disposition of the redundant facilities of the acquirer may later result in a recognized gain or loss. This would fall into the general category of indirect costs of acquisition, which are not capitalizable or allocable to assets acquired in the acquisition.

EXAMPLE OF THE ACCOUNTING FOR AN ACQUISITION (WITH GOODWILL)

Jorie Corp. acquired all of the common stock of Balkin Boiler Manufacturing Co. at a cost of $32 million, consisting of $15 million in cash and the balance represented by a long-term note to former Balkin stockholders. Immediately prior to the transaction, Balkin's balance sheet is as follows, with both book and fair values indicated ($000 omitted):

	Book Value	Fair Value		Book Value	Fair Value
Cash	$1,000	$1,000	Current liabilities	$26,200	$26,200
Accounts receivable, net	12,200	12,000	Long-term debt	46,000	41,500
Inventory	8,500	9,750	Guarantee of debt	—	75
Other current assets	500	500			
Property, plant, and equipment, net	38,500	52,400			
Customer list	—	1,400			
Patents	2,400	3,900			
In-process research and development	—	8,600	Stockholders' equity (deficit)	(9,100)	21,775
Totals	$63,100	$89,550		$63,100	$89,550

The fair value of inventory exceeded the corresponding book value because Balkin had been using LIFO (last in, first out) for many years to cost its inventory, and actual replacement cost was therefore somewhat higher than carrying value at the date of the acquisition. The long-term debt's fair value was slightly lower than carrying value (cost) because the debt carries a fixed interest rate and the market rates have risen since the debt was incurred. Consequently, Balkin benefits economically by having future debt service requirements that are less than they would be if it were to borrow at current rates. Conversely, of course, the fair value of the lender's note receivable has declined since it now represents a loan payable at less than market rates. Finally, the fair value of Balkin's receivables have also declined from their carrying amount, due to both the higher market rates of interest and to the greater risk of uncollectibility because of the change in ownership. The higher interest rates affect the valuation in two ways: (1) when computing the discounted present value of the amounts to be received, the higher interest rate reduces the computed present value, and (2) the higher interest rates may serve as an incentive for customers to delay payments to Balkin rather than borrow the money to repay the receivables, with that delay resulting in cash flows being received later than anticipated, thus causing the present value to decline.

Balkin's customer list has been appraised at $1.4 million and is a major reason for the company's acquisition by Jorie. Having been internally developed over many years, the customer list is not recorded as an asset by Balkin, however. The patents have been amortized down to $2.4 million in Balkin's accounting records, but an appraisal finds that on a fair value basis the value is somewhat higher.

Similarly, property, plant, and equipment has been depreciated down to a book value of $38.5 million, but has been appraised at a value of $52.4 million.

A key asset being acquired by Jorie, albeit one not formally recognized by Balkin, is the in-process research and development (IPR&D), which pertains to activities undertaken over a period of several years aimed at making significant process and product improvements which would enhance Balkin's market position and will be captured by the new combined operations. It has been determined that duplicating the benefits of this ongoing R&D work would cost Jorie $8.6 million. The strong motivation to make this acquisition, and to pay a substantial premium over book value, is based on Balkin's customer list and its IPR&D.

Balkin had guaranteed a $1.5 million bank debt of a former affiliated entity, but this was an "off the books" event since guarantees issued between corporations under common control are exempt from recognition. The actual contingent obligation has been appraised as having a fair value (considering both the amount and likelihood of having to honor the commitment) of $75,000.

Thus, although Balkin's balance sheet reflects a stockholders' deficit (including the par value of common stock issued and outstanding, additional paid-in capital, and accumulated deficit) of $9.1 million, the value of the acquisition, including the IPR&D, is much higher. The preliminary computation of goodwill is as follows:

Purchase price		$32,000,000
Net working capital	$(2,950,000)	
Property, plant, and equipment	52,400,000	
Customer list	1,400,000	
Patents	3,900,000	
In-process research and development	8,600,000	
Guarantee of indebtedness of others	(75,000)	
Long-term debt	(41,500,000)	21,775,000
Goodwill (excess of price over fair value)		$10,225,000

All assets and liabilities are recorded by Jorie at the allocated fair values, with the excess purchase price being assigned to goodwill. The entry to record the purchase (for preparation of consolidated financial statements, for example) is as follows:

Cash	1,000,000	
Accounts receivable, net	12,000,000	
Inventory	9,750,000	
Other current assets	500,000	
Property, plant, and equipment	52,400,000	
Customer list	1,400,000	
Patents	3,900,000	
Goodwill	10,225,000	
Research and development expense	8,600,000	
Current liabilities		26,200,000
Guarantee of indebtedness of others		75,000
Long-term debt		41,500,000
Notes payable to former stockholders		17,000,000
Cash		15,000,000

Note that, while the foregoing example is for a stock acquisition, an asset and liability acquisition would be accounted for in the exact same manner. Also, since the debt is recorded at fair value, which will often differ from face (maturity) value, the resulting differential (premium or discount) must be amortized using the effective yield method from acquisition date to the maturity date of the debt, and thus there will be differences between actual payments of interest and the amounts recognized in the income statements as interest expense. Finally, note that property, plant, and equipment is recorded "net"—that is, the allocated fair value becomes the "cost" of these assets; accumulated depreciation previously recorded in the accounting records of the acquired entity does not carry forward to the post-acquisition financial statements of the consolidated entity.

EXAMPLE OF THE ACCOUNTING FOR AN ACQUISITION (WITH NO GOODWILL)

Haglund Corp. acquires all the capital stock of Foster Co. for $800,000 in cash. A formerly successful enterprise, Foster had recently suffered from declining sales and demands for repayment of its outstanding bank debt, which were threatening its continued existence. Haglund management perceived an opportunity to make a favorable purchase of a company operating in a related line of business, and accordingly made this modest offer, which was accepted by the stockholders of Foster, the acquiree. Foster's balance sheet at the date of acquisition is as follows, with both book and fair values indicated ($000 omitted):

	Book Value	Fair Value		Book Value	Fair Value
Cash	$800	$800	Current liabilities	$2,875	$2,875
Accounts receivable, net	3,600	3,400	Long-term debt	11,155	11,155
Inventory	1,850	1,800			
Property, plant, and equipment	6,800	7,200	Stockholders' equity (deficit)	(980)	1,570
Net operating loss carryforwards	—	2,400			
Totals	$13,050	$15,600		$13,050	$15,600

Foster had provided a valuation allowance for the deferred income tax asset attributable to the net operating loss carryforward benefit, since recurring and increasing losses made it more likely than not that these benefits would not be realized. Haglund Corp., which is highly profitable, is in the same line of business, and intends to continue Foster's operations, expects to be able to realize these benefits, and therefore will have no valuation allowance against this asset.

Thus, although Foster's balance sheet reflects a stockholders' deficit (including outstanding common stock, additional paid-in capital and accumulated deficit) of $980,000, the value of the acquisition is much higher, and furthermore the acquirer is able to negotiate a bargain purchase. The preliminary computation of negative goodwill is as follows:

Net working capital	$3,125,000	
Property, plant, and equipment	7,200,000	
Net operating loss carry-forward	2,400,000	
Long-term debt	(11,155,000)	1,570,000
Purchase price		800,000
Negative goodwill (excess of fair value over cost)		$770,000

The negative goodwill is first used to offset all acquired assets other than cash and cash equivalents, trade receivables, inventory, financial instruments that are required to be carried on the balance sheet at fair value, assets to be disposed of by sale, and deferred income tax assets, on a pro rata basis. In the present instance, only the property, plant, and equipment are available for this offsetting. The entry to record the purchase before allocating negative goodwill is therefore as follows:

Cash	800,000	
Accounts receivable, net	3,400,000	
Inventory	1,800,000	
Property, plant, and equipment	7,200,000	
Deferred income tax asset	2,400,000	
Current liabilities		2,875,000
Long-term debt		11,155,000
Cash		800,000
Negative goodwill		770,000

The entry to record the offsetting of the negative goodwill is as follows:

Negative goodwill	770,000	
Property, plant, and equipment, net		770,000

Since the negative goodwill is fully absorbed by the property, plant, and equipment, there will be no residual to recognize in earnings.

INITIAL GOODWILL IMPAIRMENT TESTING

After completing the purchase price allocation, any residual of cost over fair value of the net identifiable assets and liabilities is assigned to the unidentifiable asset, goodwill. Impairment testing must be applied periodically, and any computed impairment will be presented as a separate line item in that period's income statement, as a component of income from continuing operations (unless associated with discontinued operations, in which case, the impairment would, net of income tax effects, be combined with the remaining effects of the discontinued operations). It is necessary to ensure that the amount presented in the financial statements does not exceed the goodwill's estimated fair value at any point in time.

Goodwill impairment testing is a two-step process. In the first step, the possibility of impairment is assessed by comparing the fair value of the "reporting unit" taken as a whole to its carrying (book) value. If the fair value of the reporting unit exceeds its book value, there is no need for further analysis, since no impairment will be found to have occurred.

If, however, the carrying value exceeds fair value, a second step must be performed to indicate whether goodwill is impaired and, it if is impaired, by how much. In the second step, the recorded goodwill is compared to its implied fair value, computed in the same manner as when completing a business combination's "purchase price allocation." Thus, the fair value of the reporting unit is allocated to all the unit's assets and liabilities (including any unrecognized intangibles), including, as a residual, goodwill. If the amount thus assigned to goodwill (its implied fair value) is less than its carrying value, the excess book value must be written off as an impairment expense. No other adjustments are to be made to the carrying values of any of the reporting unit's other assets or liabilities.

In order to facilitate periodic assessments of possible impairment, it is necessary that a *benchmark assessment* be made. This benchmark assessment is performed in conjunction with most significant acquisitions, regardless of how much goodwill arises from that acquisition. Similarly, a benchmark assessment is performed in conjunction with a reorganization of an entity's reporting structure.

The benchmark assessment involves identifying the valuation model to be used, documenting key assumptions, and measuring the fair value of the reporting unit. The most common valuation model is the *expected present value technique*, which uses the sum of probability-weighted present values in a range of estimated cash flows adjusted for risk, all discounted using the same interest rate convention.

In determining how goodwill is to be assigned to "reporting units," a reasonable and supportable approach must be adopted. In general, goodwill is assigned consistent with previous recognition of goodwill and with the reporting units to which the acquired assets and liabilities had been assigned. Goodwill assigned to a reporting unit is measured by the difference between the fair value of the entire reporting unit and the collective sum of the fair values of the reporting unit's assets, net of its liabilities.

While it may be costly to accomplish, this benchmark assessment is necessary to ensure that the entity has identified and documented all key assumptions and tested the outputs of the selected valuation model for reasonableness prior to actually testing goodwill for impairment. Furthermore, measuring the fair value of the reporting unit as part of the benchmark assessment will provide management with a "reality check" on whether the amount of goodwill assigned to the reporting unit is reasonable, by comparing the fair value of the reporting unit with its carrying (book) value. If the fair value of the reporting unit is found to be less than its carrying amount, the goodwill allocation methodology should be reassessed, and the selected valuation model and the assumptions underpinning the initial valuation critically reexamined. In those cases where the indicated fair value of the reporting unit is still less than its carrying amount, goodwill would be tested for impairment.

ONGOING GOODWILL IMPAIRMENT TESTING

There is a requirement for annual impairment testing, although interim testing also remains necessary when an event or circumstance occurs between annual tests suggests that the fair value of a reporting unit might have declined below its carrying value. Examples of such occurrences include an adverse change in the business climate or market, a legal factor, an action by regulators, the introduction of new competition, or a loss of key personnel. Goodwill is also required to be tested for impairment on an interim basis when it is deemed "more likely than not" that a reporting unit or a significant portion of a reporting unit will be sold or otherwise disposed of Annual testing, however, is not triggered by such circumstances, but rather, is required in all cases.

The Securities and Exchange Commission has indicated that it will likely raise concerns if a registrant is found to have frequently changed the date of its annual goodwill impairment test, especially if it appears that the change in testing dates has been made with the intent of accelerating or delaying an impairment charge.

The two-step testing regime requires as the first step that a threshold test be applied: Is the fair value of the reporting unit greater than, or less than, its carrying value? If the fair value is lower than the carrying value, impairment is suggested. The impairment, however, is not validly measured by the shortfall computed in step one, because to do so would effectively be to adjust the carrying value of the entire reporting unit to the lower of cost or market.

Impairment is the condition that exists when the carrying amount of goodwill exceeds its implied fair value. Implied fair value, in turn, is the excess of the fair value of a reporting unit as a whole over the individual fair values assigned to its assets and liabilities. Once the fair value of a reporting unit is determined, the fair value of the goodwill component of that unit's net assets must be computed; this is then compared to the carrying value of that goodwill, to ascertain if any impairment loss is to be recognized. For the purpose of making this determination, fair value of a reporting unit is the amount at which the unit as a whole could be bought or sold in a current transaction between willing parties.

The second step of the process is as follows:

1. Allocate the fair value of the reporting unit to all assets and liabilities, and to any unrecognized intangibles, as if the unit had been acquired at the measurement date. Any excess of fair value over amounts assigned to net assets (including the unrecognized assets such as in-process research and development) is the implied fair value of goodwill.

2. Compare the implied fair value of goodwill to its carrying amount (book value). If the carrying amount of the goodwill is greater than its implied fair value, a write-down of the carrying amount is required. Once written down, goodwill cannot later be written back up, even if later tests show that the fair value has recovered and exceeds carrying value.

EXAMPLE OF GOODWILL IMPAIRMENT TESTING

Armand Heavy Industries is a holding company that has two reporting units that were acquired as wholly owned subsidiaries. Armand's relevant reporting units are Bardige Diesel Engines and Ciarcia Transmissions. Upon acquisition of the two businesses (which are operated as subsidiaries), Armand recorded the assets and liabilities at fair values and recognized the excess of the purchase prices over these assigned fair values as goodwill. On the testing date, the carrying values of the assets and liabilities are as follows

	(Amounts in millions)	
	Bardige Diesel	Ciarcia Transmissions
Cash	$20	$10
Accounts receivable	100	20
Inventories	10	700
Land, buildings, and equipment	1,400	1,800
Identifiable intangibles	300	0
Goodwill	400	200
Accounts payable	(80)	(300)
Long-term debt	(300)	(400)
Totals	$1,850	$2,030

Summary income statement information for the two companies is as follows:

	(Amounts in millions)	
	Bardige Diesel	Ciarcia Transmissions
Revenues	$1,000	$800
Pre-tax income	$ 200	$120
Net income	$ 120	$ 30

It is Armand's policy to perform its annual goodwill impairment testing for both reporting units as of the end of the calendar year.

The following data is available, at reasonable cost, to management of Armand:

BARDIGE DIESEL

There are no comparable publicly held companies that have similar economic characteristics to this operation. However, management is able to develop reasonably supportable estimates of expected future cash flows associated with the group of assets. That computation yielded a fair value for Bardige Diesel of $1,700.

CIARCIA TRANSMISSIONS

A competitor of Ciarcia Transmissions, the Gaffen Gearbox Co., is publicly held and traded on the NASDAQ. Its stock has consistently sold at a multiple of 3 times revenues. Management of Armand Heavy Industries believes that the stock price is fairly representative of the fair value of Gaffen Gearbox, and accordingly that using the multiple in assessing the value of Ciarcia will result in a fair estimate.

	(Amounts in millions)	
	Bardige Diesel	Ciarcia Transmissions
Fair value of reporting unit	$1,700	$2,400
Carrying amount of reporting unit including goodwill	1,850	2,030
Fair value over (under) carrying value	$(150)	$370

1. Step 1—Test for potential impairment. Compare fair value of the reporting unit to its carrying amount, including goodwill.

   a. In the case of Bardige Diesel, the carrying amount exceeds the fair value of the reporting unit, and thus the goodwill of this reporting unit must be tested further to determine whether it is impaired.

   b. In the case of Ciarcia Transmissions, the fair value of the reporting unit exceeds the carrying value, and thus the goodwill of this reporting unit is not impaired and no further testing is required.

2. Step 2—Measure the amount of the impairment loss. For Bardige Diesel, management used the guidance in FAS 141 on business combinations and computed the implied value of goodwill and resulting impairment loss as follows:

	(Amounts in millions)	
	Carrying value	Fair value
Cash	$20	$20
Accounts receivable	100	90
Inventories	10	8
Land, buildings, and equipment	1,400	1,200

In-process research and development	—	100
Identifiable intangibles	300	350
Customer lists	—	100
Goodwill	400	NA
Accounts payable	(80)	(80)
Long-term debt	(300)	(280)
Total (net) carrying value	$1,850	
Total (net) fair value assigned to assets and liabilities		1,508
Fair value of reporting unit		1,700
Implied fair value of goodwill		192
Carrying value of goodwill		400
Impairment loss		$208

As indicated above, Ciarcia Transmissions does not have to proceed to Step 2 because its goodwill was found in Step 1 not to be impaired.

TIMING OF ANNUAL GOODWILL IMPAIRMENT TESTING

The annual impairment tests need not be performed at fiscal year-ends. Instead, the fair value measurement for each reporting unit could be performed any time during the fiscal year, as long as that measurement date is used consistently from year to year. Different measurement dates can be used for different reporting units. Once elected, however, a reporting unit's annual impairment measurement date is not permitted to be changed.

PUSH-DOWN ACCOUNTING

Under push-down accounting, the amounts allocated to various assets and liabilities can be adjusted to reflect the arm's-length valuation reflected in a significant transaction, such as the sale of a majority interest in the entity. For example, the sale of 90 percent of the shares of a company by one shareholder to a new investor, which under the entity concept would not alter the accounting by the company itself, would, under new basis accounting, be "pushed down" to the entity. The logic is that, as under purchase method accounting for an acquisition, the most objective gauge of "cost" is that arising from a recent arm's-length transaction.

Traditionally, GAAP has not permitted new basis accounting, in part because of the practical difficulty of demonstrating that the reference transaction was indeed arm's-length in nature. (The risk is that a series of sham transactions could be used to grossly distort the "cost" and hence carrying values of the entity's assets, resulting in fraudulent financial reporting.) Also heavily debated has been where the threshold should be set (a 50 percent change in ownership, an 80 percent change, etc.) to denote when a significant event had occurred that would provide valid information on the valuation of the entity's assets and liabilities for financial reporting purposes.

In its deliberations on this subject, the FASB has agreed that a transfer of control over assets from one entity to a joint venture is an event that should result in gain recognition in the financial statements of the transferor, and that a new basis of accountability would be established for those assets. This is a marked departure from past practice, under which a transfer of appreciated assets to a joint venture or partnership was to be accounted for at book value.

Many of the more general issues of push-down accounting (those applicable to traditional business acquisitions) have yet to be dealt with. For example, proponents of push-down accounting point out that in an acquisition a new basis of accounting is established, and that this new basis should be pushed down to the acquired entity and should be used when presenting that entity's own, separate financial statements. However, practical problems remain: for example, while push-down makes some sense in the case where a major block of the investee's shares is acquired in a single free-market transaction, if new basis accounting were to be used in the context of a series of step transactions, continual adjustment of the investee's carrying values for assets and liabilities would be necessary. Furthermore, the price paid for a fractional share of ownership of an investee may not always be meaningfully extrapolated to a value for the investee company as a whole.

The SEC's position has been that push-down accounting would be required if 95 percent or more of the shares of the company have been acquired (unless the company has outstanding public debt or preferred stock that may affect the acquirer's ability to control the form of ownership of the company); that it would be permitted, but not mandated, if 80 percent to 95 percent has been acquired; and it would be prohibited if less than 80 percent of the company is acquired.

While there is no requirement under GAAP to apply the push-down concept, the SEC position is substantial authoritative support and can be referenced even for nonpublic company financial reporting. It would be defensible in any instance where there is a change in control and/or a change in ownership of a majority of the common shares, when separate financial statements of the subsidiary are to be presented. Full disclosure is to be made of the circumstances whenever push-down accounting is applied.

For example, assume that Pullup Corp. acquires, in an open market arm's-length transaction, 90 percent of the common stock of Pushdown Co. for $464.61 million. At that time, Pushdown Co.'s net book value was $274.78 million (for the entire company). Book and fair values of selected assets and liabilities of Pushdown Co. as of the transaction date are summarized as follows ($000,000 omitted):

	Book value		Fair value	Excess of
	100% of entity	90% interest	of 90% interest	FV over book
Assets				
Receivables	$24.6	$22.14	$29.75	$7.61
Inventory	21.9	19.71	24.80	5.09
Property, plant & equipment, net	434.2	390.78	488.20	97.42
All others	223.4	201.06	201.06	0.00
Additional goodwill			120.00	120.00
Total assets	$704.1	$633.69	$863.81	$230.12

(Continued)

(Continued)

Liabilities				
Bonds payable	104.9	94.41	88.65	5.76
All other liabilities	325.0	292.50	310.55	18.05
Total liabilities	429.9	386.91	399.20	12.29
Equity				
Preferred stock	40.0	36.00	36.00	0.00
Common stock	87.4	78.66	78.66	0.00
Revaluation surplus*			217.83	217.83
Retained earnings	146.8	132.12	132.12	0.00
Total equity	274.2	246.88	464.61	217.83
Liabilities + Equity	$704.1	$633.69	$863.81	$230.12

*Net premium paid over book value by arm's-length of "almost all" common stock

Assuming that "new basis" accounting is deemed to be acceptable and meaningful, since Pushdown Co. must continue to issue separate financial statements to its creditors and holders of its preferred stock, and also assuming that a revaluation of the share of ownership that did not change hands (i.e., the 10 percent non-controlling interest in this example) should not be revalued based on the majority transaction, the entries by the subsidiary (Pushdown Co.) for purposes only of preparing stand-alone financial statements would be as follows:

Accounts receivable	7,610,000	
Inventory	5,090,000	
Plant, property and equipment (net)	97,420,000	
Goodwill	120,000,000	
Discount on bonds payable	5,760,000	
Other liabilities		18,050,000
Paid-in capital from revaluation		217,830,000

The foregoing entry would only be made for purposes of preparing separate financial statements of Pushdown Co. If consolidated financial statements of Pullup Corp. are also presented, essentially the same result will be obtained. The additional paid-in capital account would be eliminated against the parent's investment account, however, since in the context of the consolidated financial statements this would be a cash transaction rather than a mere accounting revaluation.

SUMMARY

This chapter has primarily focused on accounting for the initial acquisition transaction, where the buyer must allocate the purchase price to the acquiree's assets, and on both the initial and subsequent testing of goodwill for impairment. Impairment testing has become a common activity for nearly all companies that have engaged in an acquisition, and so has been addressed here in some detail. An important subsequent event is consolidating the results of an acquiree into those of the buyer; for an extremely detailed treatment of consolidation, please consult the *Wiley GAAP Guide*.

Chapter 9

Types of Acquisitions

In an acquisition, the overriding issue for the seller is to avoid paying income taxes. In order to do so, the form of reorganization must comply with several key sections of the Internal Revenue Code (IRC), specifically sections 354–358 and 367–368. These sections define the various types of permissible tax-free acquisitions, and the conditions under which they apply. This chapter addresses the various types of acquisitions, and their tax (and other) implications for the participants.

THE TAX IMPLICATIONS OF AN ACQUISITION

When determining the proper structure of an acquisition, the taxability of the transaction to the seller plays a key role. It is possible that the seller may want to pay income taxes immediately, rather than delaying the recognition of a gain. This scenario arises when their tax basis in the acquiree is more than the price being paid for it, resulting in the complete avoidance of taxes. However, it is far more likely that the seller will have a minimal tax basis in the acquiree, and so wishes to avoid the immediate recognition of a gain. To avoid gain recognition, the Internal Revenue Service (IRS) has stipulated that the following requirements be met:

- The transaction must have a bona fide business purpose other than tax avoidance.

- There must be a *continuity of interest*, where the ownership interests of the selling stockholders continue into the acquiring entity. This is achieved by having the buyer pay a substantial portion of the purchase price in its own stock. The IRS considers a "substantial portion" of the purchase price to be at least 50 percent. Some transactions are structured to pay sellers preferred stock rather than common stock, so that they still meet the requirements of the continuity of interest rule, but also give the sellers rights to additional payments, as would be the case with debt.

- There must be a *continuity of business enterprise*, where the buyer must either continue the seller's historic business or use a significant proportion of the acquired assets in a business.

The IRS has incorporated these requirements into four types of legal reorganization, which are commonly described as Type A, B, C, or D reorganizations. The letter designations come from the paragraph letters in the IRC under which they are described. All four types of reorganizations, as well as several variations, are described in greater detail later in this chapter.

In an acquisition, the buyer generally recognizes no gain or loss. Instead, its primary tax concern is the tax basis and holding period of the assets it acquires. Ideally, it wants to restate the assets to their fair market values (FMV), on the assumption that the FMV is higher than the tax basis of the seller. If the FMV is indeed higher, then the buyer can record a larger amount of asset depreciation, which reduces its future tax liability. The buyer can only restate assets to their FMV if it acquires them through an asset acquisition (see next section). Otherwise, it will retain the assets' tax basis and holding period. However, retaining the original tax basis and holding period may be acceptable if the purchase price of the assets is less than their carry-forward basis, since the buyer can recognize more depreciation expense than if it were to restate the assets to their FMV.

There is one scenario where the buyer can complete a non-taxable reorganization and still record the acquired assets at their FMVs. This is possible under Section 338 of the IRC, which allows this treatment if the buyer acquires at least 80 percent of the total voting power and 80 percent of the total value of the seller's stock within a 12-month period. However, Section 338 is laced with a variety of restrictions that reduce its applicability.

In short, the primary driver of the type of acquisition used is the seller's need to defer taxes. The buyer's interests involve a far smaller tax impact than that experienced by the seller, so the seller's wishes generally determine the method used.

THE ASSET ACQUISITION

The only type of acquisition that is *not* addressed by the IRC is the asset acquisition, because this is a taxable transaction.

In an asset acquisition, the buyer acquires either all or a selection of the seller's assets and liabilities. This transaction is most favorable to the buyer, who can record the acquired assets at their FMV (which is usually an increase from the seller's tax basis), thereby yielding more depreciation to use as a tax shield. This also results in a smaller gain if the buyer subsequently sells the assets. However, it must also obtain legal title to each asset it acquires, which can require a considerable amount of paperwork. Also, depending on the circumstances, the seller may have to notify its creditors of the impending transaction. For example, if the buyer intends to acquire a seller's below-market asset lease agreement, the lessor may only agree to the sale if it can increase its lease rate.

An asset sale is not tax-efficient for the seller. Of primary importance is that the seller must pay income taxes on the difference between the consideration received and the seller's basis in the entity. The situation is more dire if the selling entity is a "C" corporation, due to a dual taxation scenario. First, the "C" corporation must pay taxes to the extent that the total consideration received exceeds its adjusted basis in the assets sold. In addition, assuming that the "C" corporation intends to distribute its remaining assets to stockholders and dissolve, the stockholders must pay taxes to the extent that the distributions received exceed their cost basis in the stock.

Also, if the seller had previously claimed an investment tax credit on an asset that it is now selling, the credit may be recaptured, thereby increasing its income taxes.

An asset acquisition can be used to avoid acquiring unknown or contingent liabilities. For example, if the selling entity is the subject of a lawsuit and the buyer wishes to avoid any liability related to the lawsuit, then it can selectively purchase assets, leaving the selling entity with responsibility for any legal settlement. However, some environmental laws stipulate that the liability for future hazardous waste cleanups can attach to assets. Consequently, the buyer of real estate assets should go to considerable lengths to verify the extent of any environmental contamination prior to purchase.

An asset acquisition is also useful for the partial sale of a business that has multiple products or product lines. For example, a buyer may only want to purchase a single product in order to fill out its product line, leaving the seller with most of its original business intact. Though it is also possible to spin off such assets into a separate legal entity, it is often easier to simply conduct an asset sale.

The form of the purchase agreement varies from that used for an entity purchase. Instead, the parties use a general assignment and bill of sale, with an attached schedule that itemizes each asset or liability being transferred.

Depending upon the proportion of assets sold to the buyer, this transaction can require the direct approval of at least a majority of the seller's stockholders. The selling entity remains in existence, and continues to be owned by the same stockholders. However, if most or all of its assets are sold, then the seller's stockholders normally liquidate the entity.

Key features of the asset acquisition are noted in the summary table at the end of this chapter.

THE TYPE "A" REORGANIZATION

A type "A" reorganization is governed by paragraph A of Section 368(a)(1) of the IRC, which simply states that a reorganization is "a statutory merger or consolidation." To expand upon this limited definition, a statutory merger involves the transfer of all seller assets and liabilities to the buyer in exchange for the buyer's stock, while a statutory consolidation involves the transfers of the assets of two companies into a new entity in exchange for the stock of the new entity. In both cases, the selling entities are then liquidated.

An additional requirement of a Type A reorganization is to have a continuity of interest, as explained earlier in the Tax Implications of a Reorganization section. In order to meet this rule, the buyer should issue at least 50 percent of its stock as part of the purchase price. The transaction must also meet the continuity of business enterprise rule.

This transaction allows for tax-deferral by the seller for that portion of the purchase price paid with the buyer's stock. The buyer must assume all of the seller's assets and liabilities.

The boards of both entities must approve the transaction, as well as at least a majority of the stockholders of the selling entity. Since the selling entity's board of directors must approve the transaction, this is not a suitable vehicle for a hostile takeover.

The principal difference between the Type A and B reorganizations is that other consideration besides stock can be paid under a Type A, whereas the price paid under a Type B must be solely for stock. Also, the selling entity is dissolved in a Type A, but can be retained in a Type B reorganization.

The Type A reorganization is not commonly used when valuable contracts are associated with the selling entity, because they may be terminated at the option of the business partners when the selling entity is liquidated at the end of the reorganization.

In summary, the Type A reorganization is primarily of benefit to the seller, who can obtain some cash, debt, or preferred stock as part of the purchase price, while still retaining tax deferred status on the purchase price that is paid with the buyer's stock. It is less useful for the buyer, who runs the risk of losing contracts associated with the selling entity. Key features of the Type A reorganization are noted in the summary table at the end of this chapter.

THE TYPE "B" REORGANIZATION

A type "B" reorganization is governed by paragraph B of Section 368(a)(1) of the IRC. The paragraph is as follows:

> "The acquisition by one corporation, in exchange solely for all or a part of its voting stock (or in exchange solely for all or a part of the voting stock of a corporation which is in control of the acquiring corporation), of stock of another corporation if, immediately after the acquisition, the acquiring corporation has control of such other corporation (whether or not such acquiring corporation had control immediately before the acquisition)."

In essence, the buyer exchanges nothing but its stock for the stock of the seller, resulting in the selling entity becoming a subsidiary of the buyer. The IRS has clarified the basic definition to state that only *voting* stock can be used in the transaction. For example, if the buyer issues any preferred or non-voting stock as part of the deal, then it no longer qualifies as a Type B reorganization. Also, the seller cannot give the selling entity's stockholders the option of being paid with cash instead of stock.

In addition, the buyer must gain immediate control over the seller, which the IRS defines as the buyer receiving at least 80 percent of the stock of the selling entity. However, it is allowable to gain *creeping control* over the seller, where the buyer gains control over a period of no more than 12 months. Creeping control is only allowable if the buyer has a plan for gaining control during this time period.

Finally, this transaction is subject to the IRS' continuity of interest and continuity of business enterprise requirements.

In summary, the Type B reorganization is most useful when the selling entity must be retained, usually because it has valuable contracts that would otherwise be terminated if the entity were to be liquidated. Key features of the Type B reorganization are noted in the summary table at the end of this chapter.

THE TYPE "C" REORGANIZATION

A type "C" reorganization is governed by paragraph C of Section 368(a)(1) of the IRC. The paragraph is as follows:

> "The acquisition by one corporation, in exchange solely for all or a part of its voting stock (or in exchange solely for all or a part of the voting stock of a corporation which is in control of the acquiring corporation), of substantially all of the properties of another corporation, but in determining whether the exchange is solely for stock the assumption by the acquiring corporation of a liability of the other shall be disregarded."

In order to be a non-taxable transaction, paragraph C requires that the seller transfer essentially all of its assets in exchange for the buyer's voting stock. Further, those assets transferred must be critical to the continuation of the business, which is an element of the continuity of interest requirement discussed earlier. Also, the continuity of business enterprise requirement must be fulfilled. Finally, the stock paid for the transaction must be entirely the seller's *voting* stock, and the selling entity must liquidate itself.

To qualify under the asset transfer requirement of the Type C reorganization, the seller must transfer to the buyer at least 90 percent of its net assets, including all of those assets considered critical to the ongoing operations of the business.

It is possible for the buyer to pay some cash as part of this transaction. However, at least 80 percent of the FMV of the assets purchased must be solely for stock, so only the remaining asset value can be paid for with cash. The seller must pay income taxes on any portion of the purchase that is not paid for with the buyer's stock.

Any dissenting shareholders may have the right to have their ownership positions appraised and then paid in cash. The extent of these cash payments will increase the total proportion of non-stock payment made, which can affect the non-taxable nature of the entire transaction. Thus, a significant proportion of dissenting shareholders can prevent the "C" reorganization from being used.

In summary, the Type C reorganization is most useful when the seller is willing to accept mostly stock in payment, while the buyer does not need the selling entity, which is liquidated. The buyer can also record the acquired assets at their FMV, which is generally higher than the tax basis that would otherwise be inherited from the seller. Key features of the Type C reorganization are noted in the summary table at the end of this chapter.

THE TYPE "D" REORGANIZATION

A type "D" reorganization is governed by paragraph D of Section 368(a)(1) of the Internal Revenue Code. The paragraph is as follows:

"A transfer by a corporation of all or a part of its assets to another corporation if immediately after the transfer the transferor, or one or more of its shareholders (including persons who were shareholders immediately before the transfer), or any combination thereof, is in control of the corporation to which the assets are transferred; but only if, in pursuance of the plan, stock or securities of the corporation to which the assets are transferred are distributed in a [qualifying transaction]."

Type D reorganizations can be either *acquisitive* or *divisive*. An *acquisitive* reorganization is when the seller transfers substantially all of its assets to the buyer in exchange for at least 80 percent of the buyer's voting and non-voting stock. This is also known as a reverse merger.

A divisive Type D reorganization is when a single entity separates into two or more separate entities. The division occurs in two steps. First, a company transfers some of its assets to a corporation in exchange for voting control of that entity. It then transfers the acquired control to its own stockholders. There are three types of divisive reorganizations, all of which are tax-free:

- *Spin-off.* Stockholders end up with shares of both the original and new entities.

- *Split-off.* Some stockholders retain their shares in the original entity, while others swap their stock in the original entity for shares of the new entity. This approach is most useful if there is a difference of opinion among the stockholders regarding the future direction of the original entity, since they now have a choice regarding which entity to own.

- *Split-up.* The original entity creates two new entities, transfers its assets to them, and then liquidates. Stockholders end up with shares in the surviving entities. As was the case with a split-off, this approach is also useful for separating internal factions who disagree about how the company is being managed.

All of the variations noted here are also subject to four requirements. First, the original entity must distribute the stock of the new entity to its stockholders, resulting in their control of it. Second, the original entity can only distribute the stock of the new entity to its stockholders. Third, subsequent to the transaction, both entities must be actively engaged in business. Finally, the transaction cannot be intended to avoid tax payments.

A type "D" reorganization is primarily intended to govern the tax-free division of a company into smaller entities, rather than to acquire another entity. As such, the decision points related to its use are not addressed in the summary table at the end of this chapter.

THE TRIANGULAR MERGER

A triangular merger is a reorganization in which a subsidiary owned by the buyer merges with the seller, with the selling entity then liquidating. Being a merger rather than an acquisition, the transaction will eliminate all minority stockholders, since they are legally required to accept the buyer's purchase price. Also, the approval of only the selling entity's board of directors is needed, not the selling stockholders.

For a triangular transaction to be non-taxable, the buyer must have at least 80 percent control over its subsidiary, and must acquire at least 90 percent of the FMV of the buyer's net assets. Also, the transaction between the subsidiary and the selling entity must satisfy the requirements noted earlier for a Type A reorganization, which include the presence of a continuity of interest and a continuity of business enterprise.

THE REVERSE TRIANGULAR MERGER

A reverse triangular merger is a reorganization in which a subsidiary owned by the buyer merges into the seller, with the subsidiary then liquidating. The buying parent company's voting stock is then transferred to the selling stockholders in exchange for their stock in the selling entity. Being a merger rather than an acquisition, the transaction will eliminate all minority shareholders, since they are legally required to accept the buyer's purchase price. Also, the approval of only the selling entity's board of directors is needed, not the selling stockholders.

For a reverse triangular merger to be non-taxable, the selling entity must acquire substantially all of the assets of the buyer's subsidiary, and the buyer must obtain at least 80 percent control of the selling entity. Also, the buyer must acquire at least 90 percent of the FMV of the buyer's net assets.

The reverse triangular merger is most commonly used when the selling entity has valuable contracts that would otherwise be cancelled if the selling entity were not to survive the acquisition transaction. It is also used when the selling entity's stock is too widely held to make a direct stock purchase practicable, or where there may be a significant proportion of dissenting stockholders.

Sellers tend to be less enthralled with a reverse triangular merger, because this type of reorganization severely limits the amount of cash they can receive. Because the selling entity must give up at least 80 percent of its stock for the stock of the buyer's subsidiary, this leaves no more than 20 percent of the total purchase price available for payment in cash. Nonetheless, this is one of the most common types of reorganization in use.

THE ALL-CASH ACQUISITION

What if a seller has no interest in deferring any taxable gains arising from the sale of his business? This is most likely when an owner wishes to "cash out" of a business and retire. If so, the seller is most likely to insist on selling the entire entity and not just its assets, thereby avoiding all potential liabilities. Given this transfer of risk to the buyer, and the difficulty of obtaining sufficient cash for the deal, the buyer is more likely to insist on a lower purchase price.

The result for the seller is an entirely taxable transaction. The seller will pay income tax on the difference between the cash paid and his basis in the entity being sold. Conversely, the buyer will step up the basis of the acquiree's assets to their FMV, thereby gaining more depreciation to offset against future gains.

If the buyer intends to acquire the seller's legal entity, then the approval for an all-cash transaction is generally limited to the seller's board of directors. If the intent is to only acquire selected assets, then the approval process usually extends to the shareholders, too.

Key features of the all-cash acquisition are noted in the summary table at the end of this chapter.

APPRAISAL RIGHTS

If a shareholder of a selling entity does not approve of an acquisition, he can exercise appraisal rights, under which the buyer must offer

alternative consideration (typically cash) for their shares, which is
based on the appraised value of the selling entity. This can be a real
problem in a Type B reorganization, where virtually all of the consideration must be in stock.

Appraisal rights are less of an issue when both entities are publicly
held. For example, if a company is incorporated in Delaware, the
Delaware court does not give appraisal rights to the stockholders of a
public company when the consideration is the stock of another public
company.

SUMMARY

There are many types of reorganizations available for use. The type
selected is subject to many factors, of which the most important is the
taxability of the transaction to the seller. Next in importance is the
buyer's ability to retain valuable contracts controlled by the selling
entity, followed by the buyer being able to record the selling entity's
assets at their fair market values. Also of concern is the potential for a
dissenting stockholder of the selling entity to exercise appraisal rights,
which would eliminate the use of the popular Type B reorganization.
The following table summarizes the key options available under most
of the reorganization methods described in this chapter.

	Asset Sale	Type A	Type B	Type C	Pure Cash
Business enterprise rule	N/A	Yes	Yes	Yes	N/A
Continuity of interest rule	N/A	Yes	Yes	Yes	N/A
Maximum cash payment	N/A	50%	None	20%	100%
Selling entity liquidated?	No	Yes	No	Yes	N/A
Appraisal rights allowed?	No	Yes	Yes	Yes	N/A

Taxable to sellers?	Yes	Only cash portion	No	Only cash portion	Yes
Selling shareholder approval needed?	Yes	Yes	No	Yes	No
Buyer basis in acquired assets?	FMV	Carryover	Carryover	FMV	FMV

The type of reorganization selected is critical to both parties to an acquisition, especially the seller. Thus, the seller should carefully explore the available options with an attorney experienced in such transactions, rather than accepting whatever form of reorganization is initially proposed by the buyer.

Chapter 10

Government Regulation

Government regulation of merger and acquisition activity includes the outright prohibition of such transactions due to anti-trust concerns, and can also include the imposition of heavy fines and cleanup costs for acquired hazardous wastes. This chapter addresses both types of regulation.

ANTI-TRUST REGULATIONS

The general guideline for anti-trust legislation was created in the Clayton Act of 1914, which outlawed any mergers having monopolistic effects. The relevant section of the Act is Section 7, which prohibits a merger "where in any line of commerce or in any activity affecting commerce in any section of the country, the effect of such acquisition may be substantially to lessen competition, or to tend to create a monopoly." Section 15 of the Act gives the government the authority to seek a court order to halt such a merger.

The Hart-Scott-Rodino Antitrust Improvement Act of 1976 (HSR Act) creates procedures to facilitate the government's review of potentially monopolistic transactions. Specifically, it requires an acquiring company to report prospective acquisitions to the Federal Trade

Commission (FTC) and the Department of Justice (DoJ), but only under certain circumstances. If an acquirer is subject to this Act, it cannot complete an acquisition for at least 30 days, thereby giving government regulators sufficient time to review the anti-trust implications of the prospective transaction. If the acquisition appears to pose a threat to competition, then either the FTC or DoJ can issue an additional request for information that extends the waiting period by 20 days. As a result of its examination, the government can file an injunction to halt the acquisition.

The acquirer must describe the proposed transaction on the *Notification and Report Form for Certain Mergers and Acquisitions* (FTC Form C4). The form describes the parties to the transaction, the monetary value of the deal, the percentage of ownership to be acquired, geographic market information, and the industry within which the acquisition is being made. It is extremely important to file this form, since the penalty is up to $11,000 per day for non-compliance. The rules for determining who must file the form are complex, but essentially the following two conditions must be met:

1. One party to the transaction has net sales or total assets of at least $100 million, and the other party has net sales or total assets of at least $10 million, *and*
2. The acquirer will hold more than $15 million of the target's stock and/or assets, or will hold more than 50 percent of the voting securities of a target having at least $25 million in net sales or assets.

Once the government receives the notification form, it reviews the anti-competitive aspects of the proposed transaction, using its Horizontal Merger Guidelines (which can be viewed at www.usdoj.gov). The government is particularly interested in any increase in the concentration of market share, which it describes in Section 1.5 of the Guidelines.

As noted in Section 1.5, when reviewing a proposed transaction for its impact on market concentration, the DoJ uses the Herfindahl-Hirschman Index (HHI). This is an indicator of the amount of competition between companies in a specific industry. The basic calculation is the sum of the squares of the market shares of each firm in an industry. If an industry's HHI is in the range of 0–999, it is considered to be a competitive market with no dominant players. If its HHI is between 1000 and 1800, then it is moderately concentrated, while any score above 1800 indicates a highly concentrated industry. For example, if an industry consists of four firms with market shares of 15 percent, 20 percent, 25 percent, and 40 percent, then its HHI is 2850 ($15^2 + 20^2 + 25^2 + 40^2$).

Any transaction that increases the HHI by more than 100 points in an already concentrated market will raise anti-trust concerns. Thus, it is considerably more difficult for a company with significant market share to acquire another firm in the same industry than it would be for a company with minor market share to acquire the same firm. For example, Company A has five percent market share, which is an HHI of 25 (5^2), and wants to acquire Company B, which also has five percent market share. The post-acquisition HHI of the two companies is 100 (10^2). With a net HHI gain of 50 points, this transaction would likely be acceptable to the DoJ. However, if Company C, with a 10 percent market share, were to acquire Company B, then its HHI would rise from 100 (10^2) to 225 (15^2). This second transaction would increase Company C's score by 125 within that market, while eliminating the 25 score of Company B, resulting in a net HHI increase within the industry of 100 points. This would likely flag the transaction within the DoJ.

The worst-case scenario is for a company having very large market share, since its HHI score essentially bars it from acquiring anyone. For example, a company having 50 percent market share has a score of 2500 (50^2), so even acquiring a company with just one percent market share will increase its score to 2601 (51^2). Thus, the HHI eventually produces a hard limit on a company's ability to increase its size through acquisitions in a single market.

The government may still approve a proposed transaction under the failing company doctrine, even if it results in a significant increase in the HHI. This doctrine is dealt with in Section 5 of the Horizontal Merger Guidelines, which states that:

A merger is not likely to create or enhance market power if the imminent failure of one of the merging firms would cause the assets of that firm to exit the relevant market. In such circumstances, post-merger performance in the relevant market may be no worse than market performance had the merger been blocked and the assets left the market.

A merger is not likely to create or enhance market power if the following circumstances are met: 1) the allegedly failing firm would be unable to meet its financial obligations in the near future; 2) it would not be able to reorganize successfully under Chapter 11 of the Bankruptcy Act; 3) it has made unsuccessful good-faith efforts to elicit reasonable alternative offers of acquisition of the assets of the failing firm that would both keep its tangible and intangible assets in the relevant market and pose a less severe danger to competition than does the proposed merger; and 4) absent the acquisition, the assets of the failing firm would exit the relevant market.

Section 5 also states that the same logic applies to a failing company division. To fall within the failing company doctrine, a selling company's division must have negative cash flow on an operating basis, and the company must plan to "exit its assets from the market" in the near future in the absence of a sale transaction.

In summary, smaller companies falling below the minimum standards of the HSR Act are essentially immune from anti-trust legislation, but larger companies having significant market shares may find that their acquisition activities are seriously constrained.

INTERNATIONAL ANTI-TRUST REGULATIONS

The Department of Justice and the Federal Trade Commission have jointly issued Anti-Trust Enforcement Guidelines for International Operations, which can be viewed at www.usdoj.gov. The Guidelines summarize the effects of a number of earlier Acts, and provide illustrative examples of a variety of potentially anti-competitive situations. While the majority of the Guidelines are concerned with other issues than acquisitions (such as dumping), Section 4.22 addresses the circumstances under which an international acquisition will be exempt under the Hart-Scott-Rodino Act (as discussed in the last section). No reporting is required if a United States person acquires foreign assets, when there are no sales in or into the United States attributable to those assets, or when the acquired assets do not generate more than $25 million in sales. Also, a foreign entity buying a United States entity is exempt from reporting if the target has sales of less than $25 million or has a book value of less than $15 million, or if the target is also foreign-owned and the aggregate annual net sales of the merging firms is less than $110 million and their combined total assets in the United States are less than $110 million. In addition, there is no reporting requirement if the parent of either the buyer or seller is controlled by a foreign state, and the acquisition is of assets located within that foreign state.

ENVIRONMENTAL REGULATIONS

There are a number of strict environmental regulations that can turn an otherwise promising acquisition into a nightmare of litigation and environmental remediation expenditures. These regulations are mostly located within Title 42 of the U.S. Code, which deals in general with public health and welfare. Key environmental laws impacting acquisitions are as follows:

- *Clean Air Act.* Regulates emissions into the air from both fixed (i.e., refineries and utilities) and mobile (i.e., automobiles) sources.
- *Clean Water Act.* Makes it unlawful to discharge any pollutant into navigable waters without a permit. The government can issue a temporary or permanent injunction, and can also impose daily fines of as high as $50,000 and multi-year jail terms.
- *Comprehensive Environmental Response, Compensation, and Liability Act (CERCLA).* Requires that anyone causing waste must clean it up. Specifically, liability encompasses the current owner or

operator of a site, the owner or operator at the time when hazardous disposal occurred, the entity that arranged for disposal, and the entity that transported the substance to the site. The liabilities of companies that generated wastes dumped in a common site are joint and several, so that every contributor is theoretically liable for the entire cleanup. Noncompliance can result in daily fines of as much as $25,000.

- *Resource Conservation and Recovery Act.* Controls the generation, transportation, storage, and disposal of hazardous waste.

- *Toxic Substances Control Act.* Restricts the use of polychlorinated biphenyl (PCB) products, as well as asbestos, indoor radon, and lead-based paint. The government can require cleanup of these substances, and can impose a daily fine of up to $27,500 per violation.

Of the laws just noted, the key one is CERCLA, which is also known as the Superfund Act. The government uses it to cast an extremely wide net in assigning liability for hazardous waste cleanup. CERCLA is especially dangerous, because liability can even extend to the directors and officers of a company.

When acquiring real estate, always have an expert conduct a thorough environmental review. If there is a rush to complete an acquisition before an environmental review can be completed, then it may make more sense to cancel the transaction than to run the risk of incurring a potentially massive environmental liability. Even if the odds of having a liability are low, the incurrence of such a liability can bankrupt the company, so only the chief executive officer should be allowed to make the decision to proceed without an environmental review. Also, if a review *does* reveal the risk of an environmental liability, then only the CEO or Board of Directors should make the decision to proceed with the transaction. The risk is so great that no one else should be burdened with the decision.

When conducting a review of a target's potential environmental liabilities, due diligence questions must be unusually detailed. At a minimum, consider asking about the following issues:

- Were hazardous substances used or generated, and were they shipped off site for disposal?
- Are there settling ponds containing hazardous wastes?
- Are there underground storage tanks?
- Is there asbestos insulation on the premises?
- Was lead-based paint used in the facility?
- Are there unusually high levels of radon gas in the facility?
- Is there insulation made from urea-formaldehyde foam?
- Are there septic systems or wells?
- Is there a discharge permit if waste is discharged into something other than a publicly owned treatment facility?

Also, if the target is publicly owned, review its annual 10-K report to see if it has disclosed any environmental liabilities or risks.

Given the extreme expense associated with environmental liabilities, it would be extremely imprudent of a buyer to not conduct a very detailed environmental review. A number of companies that did not do so have been bankrupted by the resulting liabilities.

SUMMARY

The burden of being a large company with significant market share is that it cannot escape the government's anti-trust regulations, from which smaller firms are exempt. A qualified attorney who is experienced with acquisition activity can provide advice regarding when the buying entity should notify the government of an acquisition that may fall under the anti-trust statutes.

It cannot be emphasized enough that acquiring a company with hazardous waste liabilities will also be hazardous to the financial health of the buyer! Though the risk of environmental liability is generally low in most cases, the resulting cleanup costs and fines are so massive that it behooves the buyer to strictly attend to environmental due diligence.

Due Diligence Checklist

The due diligence analysis of a target company involves the examination of a great many areas. While the Due Diligence chapter touched upon a number of the more important items, it did not address many more, which are listed in this appendix. Please note that even this expanded list should not be considered comprehensive, since there are many more topics that are industry-specific. Thus, the buyer should use this list solely as a foundation for a more comprehensive list that it tailors to its own needs.

Market Overview:

1. What is the size of the market?
2. How is the market segmented?
3. What is the market's projected growth and profitability?
4. What are the factors affecting growth and profitability?
5. What are the trends in the number of competitors and their size, product innovation, distribution, finances, regulation, and product liability?

Corporate Overview:

1. When and where was the company founded, and by whom?
2. What is its history of product development?
3. What is the history of the management team?
4. Has the corporate location changed?
5. Have there been ownership changes?
6. Have there been acquisitions or divestitures?
7. What is its financial history?

Culture:

1. What type of command structure is used? Does it vary by department?
2. Is there a set of standard policies and procedures that govern most processes? How closely do employees adhere to it?
3. What practices does the company use to retain employees?
4. What types of social functions do employees engage in as a group?
5. Does the company generally promote from within, or from the outside?
6. What types of training does the company require of its employees?
7. What types of orientation programs are used for new employees?
8. What types of awards and ceremonies are used to recognize employee achievements?
9. What level of customer service is the company accustomed to provide? Does it support "above and beyond" levels of support, and publicize these efforts?
10. What dress code does it follow? Does this vary by location?
11. What types of feedback mechanisms are used to discuss issues about employee performance?

12. How does the company disseminate information to its employees? Is it a formal method, such as a monthly newsletter, or more informal employee meetings?

13. What is the physical environment? Does the company emphasize low costs with cheap furnishings, or incentivize performance with more expensive surroundings?

14. Is there a sense of urgency in completing tasks, or is the environment more relaxed?

Personnel:

1. Obtain a list of all employees, their current compensation, compensation for the prior year, date of hire, date of birth, race, sex, and job titles.

2. Obtain a list of all inactive employees, stating the reason for their inactive status and the prognosis for their return.

3. Obtain copies of the I-9 forms for all active employees.

4. Obtain copies of any employment agreements.

5. Obtain copies of performance evaluation criteria and bonus plans.

6. Obtain copies of any non-compete, intellectual property, and/or confidentiality agreements. Also obtain copies of non-compete agreements that currently apply to terminated employees.

7. Obtain copies of any salesperson compensation agreements.

8. Obtain copies of any director compensation agreements.

9. Summarize any loan amounts and terms to officers, directors, or employees.

10. Obtain any union labor agreements.

11. Determine the number of states to which payroll taxes must be paid.

12. Obtain a copy of the employee manual.

13. Conduct background investigations on principal employees.

14. Summarize the names, ages, titles, education, experience, and professional biographies of the senior management team.

15. Obtain copies of employee résumés.

16. What has been the employee turnover rate for the past two years?

17. Obtain a list of all involuntary terminations within the past year, stating the reason for termination and the age, sex, race, and disability status of each person terminated.

18. Obtain a copy of the organization chart.

Benefits:

1. Review accrued 401(k) benefits. What is the company contribution percentage? What is the level of employee participation?

2. Obtain copies of all pension plan documents, amendments, and letters of determination.

3. Obtain copies of the pension assets, liabilities, expenses, and audits for the past three years.

4. Determine the funding status of the company pension plan, and the ten-year projected cash expense associated with it.

5. Itemize all fringe benefits, along with current and projected employee eligibility for and participation in each one.

6. Obtain a list of all former employees using COBRA coverage, and the dates on which their access to COBRA coverage expires.

7. Itemize all executive perquisites above the standard benefits package, and the extent of these expenses for the past two years.

Intellectual Property:

1. Review all current patent, trademark, service mark, trade name, and copyright agreements, and note renewal dates.

2. Obtain an itemization of all pending patent applications.

3. Determine annual patent renewal costs.

4. Determine the current patent-related revenue stream.

5. Document the patent application process. Have any potential patents not been applied for?

6. List all trademark and service mark registrations and pending applications for registration. Verify that all affidavits of use and renewal applications have been filed, and prosecution of all pending applications is current.

7. List all unregistered trademarks and service marks used by the organization.

8. Collect and catalog copies of all publications and check for unlisted trademarks and service marks, proper notification.

9. List all copyright registrations.

10. List all registered designs.

11. Does the company have any information that provides a competitive advantage? If so, verify that the information is marked as "confidential."

12. Have all employees executed Invention Assignment and Confidentiality agreements?

13. Obtain copies of all licenses of intellectual property in which the company is the licensor or licensee.

14. List all lawsuits pertaining to intellectual property in which the organization is a party.

Brands:

1. Review any branding strategy documents. Does the company have a long-term plan for brand support?

2. Review budgeted and actual expenditures for customer support, marketing, and quality assurance related to branding.

3. What types of advertising and promotion are used?

4. Ensure that the company has clear title to any branded names.

5. How well is the brand supported on the company Web site?

6. Note the amount and trend of any legal fees needed to stop brand encroachment.

Risk Management:

1. Is there a risk management officer? What is this person's job description?

2. Does the company have an overall risk mitigation plan that it updates regularly?

3. Review all corporate insurance, using a schedule from the company's insurance agency. If there is material pending litigation, determine the extent of insurance coverage and obtain insurance company confirmation. Note whether insurance terms are for "claims made" or "claims incurred," as well as the amounts of deductibles.

4. Have aggregate insurance amounts been penetrated, or is there a history of coming close to the aggregate totals?

5. Have there been substantial premium adjustment in the past?

6. To what extent does the company self-insure its activities? Are there uninsured risks that the company does not appear to be aware of or is ignoring?

Capacity:

1. Determine the facility overhead cost required for minimum, standard, and maximum capacity.

2. Ascertain the amount of capital replacements needed in the near future.

3. Determine the periodic maintenance cost of existing equipment.

4. Determine the maximum sustainable production capacity by production line.

5. Estimate the cost of modifications needed to increase the capacity of each production line or facility.

Assets:

1. Verify bank reconciliations for all bank accounts harboring significant cash balances.

2. Obtain current detail of accounts receivable.

3. Determine the days of receivables outstanding and the probable amount of bad debt. Review the bad debt reserve calculation.

4. Obtain a list of all accounts and notes receivable from employees.

5. Obtain a list of all inventory items, and discuss the obsolescence reserve. Determine the valuation method used.

6. Obtain the current fixed asset listing, as well as depreciation calculations. Audit the largest items to verify their existence.

7. Appraise the value of the most expensive fixed assets.

8. Obtain an itemized list of all assets that are not receivables or fixed assets.

9. Ascertain the existence of any liens against company assets.

10. Obtain any maintenance agreements on company equipment.

11. Is there an upcoming need to replace assets?

12. Discuss whether there are any plans to close, relocate, or expand any facilities.

13. Itemize all capitalized research and development or software development expenses.

14. Determine the value of any net operating loss carryforward assets.

Liabilities:

1. Review the current accounts payable listing.

2. Obtain a list of all accounts payable to employees.

3. Review the terms of any lines of credit.

4. Review the amount and terms of any other debt agreements. Review covenants in the debt agreements, and determine if the company has breached the covenants in the past, or is likely to do so in the near future.

5. Look for unrecorded debt.

6. Verify wage and tax remittances to all government entities, and that there are no unpaid amounts.

7. Review the sufficiency of accruals for wages, vacation time, legal expenses, insurance, property taxes, and commissions.

8. Obtain copies of all unexpired purchasing commitments (purchase orders, etc.).

Equity:

1. Obtain a shareholder list that notes the number of shares held and any special voting rights.

2. Review all Board resolutions authorizing the issuance of stock to ensure that all shares are validly issued.

3. Review all convertible debt agreements to which the company or any subsidiary is a party. Note any restrictions on dividends, on incurring extra debt, and on issuing additional capital stock. Note any unusual consent or default provisions. Note the conversion trigger points.

4. Review any disclosure documents used in the private placement of securities or loan applications during the preceding five years.

5. Review all documents affecting ownership, voting or rights to acquire the company's stock for required disclosure and significance to the purchase transactions, such as warrants, options, security holder agreements, registration rights agreements, shareholder rights, or poison pill plans.

Profitability:

1. Obtain audited financial statements for the last three years.

2. Obtain monthly financial statements for the current year.

3. Obtain copies of federal tax returns for the last three years.

4. Determine profitability by product, customer, and segment.

5. What are the revenues and profits per employee?

6. What is direct materials expense as a percentage of revenue?

7. How have revenues, costs, and profits been trending for the past three years?

8. How many staff members are directly traceable to the servicing of specific customer accounts?

9. Are there any delayed expenses? Has the customer avoided necessary maintenance expenditures or wage increases in order to boost profitability?

10. Has the company capitalized a disproportionate amount of expenses?

11. Obtain the budgets for the past three years. Does the company routinely achieve its budgets, or does it fall short?

Cash Flow:

1. Construct a cash forecast for the next six months. Will the company spin off or absorb cash?

2. Review the trend line of work capital for the past year. How is it changing in relation to total sales?

3. Categorize working capital by segment, product line, and customer. What parts of the business are absorbing the most cash?

4. Determine historical and projected capital expenditure requirements. Does the company have enough cash to pay for its capital investment needs?

Customers:

1. How concentrated are sales among the top customers?

2. What is the distribution of sales among the various products and services?

3. What is the current sales backlog by customer?

4. What is the seasonality of sales? Are sales unusually subject to changes in the business cycle?

5. What is the financial condition of key customers? Does it appear that their businesses are sufficiently robust to continue supporting purchases from the company?

6. How long has the company had sales relationships with its key customers?

7. How profitable is each of the key customer accounts? Do any customers require a disproportionate amount of servicing, or require special terms and conditions?

8. Itemize any customer contracts that are coming up for renewal, and likely changes to the key terms of those agreements.

9. Is there a history of complaints from any customers? How profitable are the customers who appear to be the most dissatisfied?

10. Obtain a list of all customers who have stopped doing business with the company in the last three years.

Sales Activity:

1. Determine the amount of ongoing maintenance revenue from standard products.

2. Obtain copies of all outstanding proposals, bids, and offers pending award.

3. Obtain copies of all existing contracts for products or services, including warranty and guarantee work.

4. What is the sales strategy (e.g., add customers, increase support, increase penetration into existing customer base, pricing, etc.).

5. What is the structure of the sales organization? Are there independent sales representatives?

6. Obtain the sales organization chart.

7. How many sales personnel are in each sales position?

8. What is the sales force's geographic coverage?

9. What is the sales force's compensation, split by base pay and commission?

10. What was the average sales per salesperson for the past year?

11. What was the sales expense per salesperson for the past year?

12. What is the sales projection by product for the next 12 months?

13. Into what category do customers fall—end users, retailers, OEMs, wholesalers, and/or distributors?

14. How many customers are there for each product, industry, and geographic region?

15. What is the average order size?

16. Does the company have an Internet store? Does the site accept on-line payments and orders? What percentage of total sales comes through this medium?

17. What is the structure of the technical support group? How many people are in it, and what is their compensation?

18. Does the company use e-mail for marketing notifications to customers?

19. What are the proportions of sales by distribution channel?

20. How many customers can the company potentially market its products to? What would be the volume by customer?

21. What is the company's market share? What is the trend?

22. Are there new markets in which the products can be sold?

Product Development:

1. Obtain a list of development projects in the product pipeline. What is the estimated remaining time and expense required to launch each one?

2. What attributes make the company's new products unique?

3. Have any products been in the development pipeline for a long time, and have no immediate prospects for product launch?

4. Who are the key development personnel? What is their tenure and educational background?

5. Does the company primarily use incremental product improvements, or engage in major new product development projects?

6. How much money is invested annually in development? As a proportion of sales? How does this spending compare to that of competitors?

7. Does the company have a history of issuing inadequately engineered products that fail? Is this finding supported by warranty claim records?

8. Is there a product development plan? Does it tend to target low-cost products, ones with special features, or some other strategy? How closely does the development team adhere to it?

9. Does the company use target costing to achieve predetermined profitability targets?

10. Does it design products that avoid constrained resources?

Production Process:

1. Does the company have a push or pull manufacturing system?

2. Does the company practice constraint management techniques?

3. Does the company use work cells or continuous assembly lines?

4. Is there an adequate industrial engineering staff? Does it have an ongoing plan for process improvement?

5. What is the production area safety record? What types of problems have caused safety failures in the past?

6. What issues have caused shipping delays in the past?

7. What is the history of product rework, and why have rework problems arisen?

Information Technology:

1. What systems use third-party software, and which ones use custom-built solutions? Are the third-party systems under maintenance contracts, and are the most recent versions installed?

2. To what degree have third-party systems been modified? Have they been so altered that they can no longer be upgraded?

3. Are user computers monitored for unauthorized software installations?

4. Are software copies secured and only released with proper authorization?

5. What is the level of difficulty anticipated to integrate the company's databases into the buyer's systems?

6. Are there adequate backup systems in place with off-site storage, both for the corporate-level databases and for individual computers?

7. What is the level of security required for access to the company's servers?

Internet:

1. Does the company use the Internet for internal use as an interactive part of operations? What functions are used in this manner?

2. Has the company's firewall ever been penetrated, and how sensitive is the information stored on the company network's publicly available segments?

3. Does the company provide technical support information through its Web site?

4. Are Web site usage statistics tracked? If so, how are they used for management decisions?

5. In what way could operational costs decrease if the company's customers interacted with it through the Internet?

Legal Issues:

1. Obtain the articles of incorporation and bylaws. Review for the existence of pre-emptive rights, rights of first refusal, registration rights, or any other rights related to the issuance or registration of securities.

2. Review the bylaws for any unusual provisions affecting shareholder rights or restrictions on ownership, transfer, or voting of shares.

3. Obtain certificates of good standing for the company and all significant subsidiaries.

4. Review the articles of incorporation and bylaws of each significant subsidiary. Determine if there are restrictions on dividends to

the company. For each subsidiary, review the minutes of the Board of Directors for matters requiring disclosure.

5. Obtain a list of all states in which the company is qualified to do business and a list of those states in which it maintains significant operations. Determine if there is any state where the company is not qualified but should be qualified to do business

6. Obtain the minutes from all shareholder meetings for the past five years. Review for proper notice prior to meetings, the existence of a quorum, and proper voting procedures; verify that stock issuances have been authorized; verify that insider transactions have been approved; verify that officers have been properly elected; verify that shares are properly approved and reserved for stock option and purchase plans.

7. Obtain the minutes of the Executive Committee and Audit Committee for the past five years, as well as the minutes of any other special Board committees. Review all documents.

8. Review all contracts that are important to operations. Also review any contracts with shareholders or officers. In particular, look for the following provisions:
   • Default or termination provisions
   • Restrictions on company action
   • Consent requirements
   • Termination provisions in employment contracts
   • Ownership of technology
   • Cancellation provisions in major supply and customer contracts
   • Unusual warranties or the absence of protective provisions

9. Obtain copies of all asset leases, and review for term, early payment, and bargain purchase clauses.

10. Obtain copies of all office space lease agreements, and review for term and renewal provisions.

11. Review all related party transactions for the past three years.

12. Review the terms of any outbound or inbound royalty agreements.

13. Was any company software (either used internally or resold) obtained from another company? If so, what are the terms under which the code is licensed? Are there any associated royalty payments?

14. Review all legal invoices for the past two years.

15. Review all pending and threatened legal proceedings to which the company or any of its subsidiaries is a party. Describe principal parties, allegations, and relief sought. This includes any governmental or environmental proceedings. Obtain copies of existing consent decrees or significant settlement agreements relating to the company or its subsidiaries.

16. If the company is publicly held, obtain all periodic filings for the past five years, including the 10-K, 10-Q, 8-K, and Schedule 13D.

17. Review all annual and quarterly reports to shareholders.

18. Review the auditors' letter to management concerning internal accounting controls and procedures, as well as any management responses.

19. Review any reports of outside consultants or analysts concerning the company.

20. Research any press releases or articles about the company within the past year.

21. Review all related party transactions for the past three years.

22. Review the terms of any outbound or inbound royalty agreements.

23. Was any company software (either used internally or resold) obtained from another company? If so, what are the terms under which the code is licensed? Are there any associated royalty payments?

24. Review title insurance for any significant land parcels owned by the company.

Regulatory Compliance:

1. Review the company's correspondence with the Securities and Exchange Commission, any national exchange, or state securities commission, other than routine transmittals, for the past five years.

Determine if there are or were any enforcement or disciplinary actions or any ongoing investigations or suggestions of violations by any of these entities.

2. Review any correspondence during the past five years with the Environmental Protection Agency, Federal Trade Commission, Occupational Safety and Health Administration, Equal Employment Opportunity Commission, or Internal Revenue Service. Determine if there are any ongoing investigations or suggestions of violations by any of these agencies.

3. Review any required regulatory compliance and verify that necessary licenses and permits have been maintained, as well as ongoing filings and reports.

4. If there is a General Service Administration schedule, when does it come up for renewal?

5. Obtain copies of the most recently filed EEO-1 and VETS-100 forms.

6. Obtain copies of any affirmative action plans.

7. Obtain copies of any open charges of discrimination, complaints, or related litigation, or any such cases that have been closed within the past five years.

Policies and Procedures:

1. Obtain the accounting policies and procedures manual.

2. Review all key accounting policies to ensure that they comply with generally accepted accounting principles.

3. Obtain the standard offer letter format, the standard termination letter format, and the employment application form.

4. Obtain the human resources policies relating to sexual harassment, background investigations, and drug testing.

The Purchase Transaction:

1. If the transaction involves the issuance of stock, are there sufficient authorized shares for the offering, including any conversion rights,

taking into account any shares reserved for issuance pursuant to outstanding options, warrants, convertible securities and employee benefit plans?

Red Flag Events:

1. Has an auditor resigned within the past three years?
2. Is there evidence of continual changes in accounting methods?
3. Are there unusually complex business arrangements that do not appear to have a business purpose?
4. Is the company continually exceeding its loan covenant targets by very small amounts?
5. Do any of the principals have criminal records?
6. Have there recently been significant insider stock sales?
7. Is the internal audit team subjected to significant scope restrictions?
8. Are a large proportion of monthly sales completed during the last few days of each month?
9. Has the company tried to sell itself in the past and failed?
10. Has the company received major warnings from regulatory agencies?
11. Does the company appear to manipulate reserve accounts in order to smooth or enhance its reported earnings?

Index